Palgrave Gothic

Series Editor
Clive Bloom
Middlesex University
London, United Kingdom

This series of gothic books is the first to treat the genre in its many inter-related, global and 'extended' cultural aspects to show how the taste for the medieval and the sublime gave rise to a perverse taste for terror and horror and how that taste became not only international (with a huge fan base in places such as South Korea and Japan) but also the sensibility of the modern age, changing our attitudes to such diverse areas as the nature of the artist, the meaning of drug abuse and the concept of the self. The series is accessible but scholarly, with referencing kept to a minimum and theory contextualised where possible. All the books are readable by an intelligent student or a knowledgeable general reader interested in the subject.

Editorial Advisory Board
Dr Ian Conrich, University of South Australia
Barry Forshaw, author/journalist, UK
Professor Gregg Kucich, University of Notre Dame, USA
Professor Gina Wisker, University of Brighton, UK
Dr Catherine Wynne, University of Hull, UK
Dr Alison Peirse, University of Yorkshire, UK
Dr Sorcha Ní Fhlainn, Manchester Metropolitan University, UK
Professor William Hughes, Bath Spa University, UK

More information about this series at
http://www.springer.com/series/14698

Paulina Palmer

Queering Contemporary Gothic Narrative 1970–2012

Paulina Palmer
University of Warwick and Birkbeck College
London, United Kingdom

Palgrave Gothic
ISBN 978-1-349-67170-0   ISBN 978-1-137-30355-4 (eBook)
DOI 10.1057/978-1-137-30355-4

© The Editor(s) (if applicable) and The Author(s) 2016
The author(s) has/have asserted their right(s) to be identified as the author(s) of this work in accordance with the Copyright, Designs and Patents Act 1988.
This work is subject to copyright. All rights are solely and exclusively licensed by the Publisher, whether the whole or part of the material is concerned, specifically the rights of translation, reprinting, reuse of illustrations, recitation, broadcasting, reproduction on microfilms or in any other physical way, and transmission or information storage and retrieval, electronic adaptation, computer software, or by similar or dissimilar methodology now known or hereafter developed.
The use of general descriptive names, registered names, trademarks, service marks, etc. in this publication does not imply, even in the absence of a specific statement, that such names are exempt from the relevant protective laws and regulations and therefore free for general use.
The publisher, the authors and the editors are safe to assume that the advice and information in this book are believed to be true and accurate at the date of publication. Neither the publisher nor the authors or the editors give a warranty, express or implied, with respect to the material contained herein or for any errors or omissions that may have been made.

Cover image © Stuart Aylmer / Alamy Stock Photo

Printed on acid-free paper

This Palgrave Macmillan imprint is published by Springer Nature
The registered company is Macmillan Publishers Ltd.
The registered company address is: The Campus, 4 Crinan Street, London, N1 9XW, United Kingdom

for the queer community in Cambridge

Preface

This book develops my interest in the intersection between Gothic and different queer sexualities and genders in contemporary fiction that I first explored in my earlier publication *Lesbian Gothic: Transgressive Fictions* (1999). Having noticed the popularity that motifs with Gothic associations, such as spectrality, the vampire and the witch, were enjoying in contemporary lesbian feminist novels and story collections and that, rather than being employed in a misogynistic or lesbophobic way as had occurred in earlier periods, they were utilised affirmatively, in the manner of a form of counter-discourse, to represent and explore lesbian sexuality, I started researching the roles they play in these texts. My research was assisted by the stimulating intellectual environment furnished by the English Department at the University of Warwick, where I taught for a number of years. I was also fortunate, while writing the book, to enjoy access to several feminist and LGBT bookshops such as Sister Write, Silver Moon and Gay's the Word in London, Libertas in York and Out in Brighton that, on account of the exorbitant increase in rents in city centres and other reasons, have now sadly folded.

On retiring from Warwick University, I taught for several years as a sessional lecturer for the MA in Gender and Sexuality at Birkbeck College, University of London. It was while I was teaching there that I became aware of the important role that the concept of the uncanny, as defined by Sigmund Freud and other theorists, plays in queer theoretical discourse and fiction. My research in this area culminated in the publication of *The Queer Uncanny: New Perspectives on the Gothic* in 2012.

With reference to this book, though I refer on occasion to the uncanny, I return in general to my earlier interest in motifs and narrative structures that are distinctively Gothic. As in *The Queer Uncanny*, I discuss works of fiction focusing on different queer sexualities and genders. They include lesbianism, homosexuality, transsexuality and – a topic reference to which has entered fiction relatively recently – intersex.

While writing the book, I've had access to several lively intellectual environments. Discussions that I have held with students while teaching workshops at the City Lit in London have contributed to its production, as has the exchange of ideas at the conferences run by the Contemporary Women Writers' Association and the International Gothic Association. My contribution to the work of Encompass, a Cambridge-based organisation that aims to promote a better quality of life for LGBTQ people in the Cambridge and surrounding areas, has also influenced the book. I'm grateful to Xavier Aldana Reyes, Ann Burgess, Grant Chambers, Patricia Duncker, Ardel Haefele-Thomas, Ruth Heholt, Emma Parker, Maria Romero Ruiz, Robin White, Gina Wisker and other friends and colleagues for their encouragement with writing it. I'm especially indebted to Terry Ryman for his support in this respect.

Although the majority of bookshops cited above are no longer available, Gays the Word is thankfully still flourishing. In fact I discovered some of the novels that I discuss in this study, including Meg Kingston's *Chrystal Heart* and Michelle Paver's *Dark Matter*, on the shelves there. I am grateful to the staff for alerting me to them and taking an interest in my writing.

Contents

1 Introduction: Queering Contemporary Gothic   1

2 Ghosts and Haunted Houses   23

3 Uncanny Others: Vampires and Doubles   65

4 Tracking the Monster   111

5 Regional Gothic: Uncanny Cities and Rural Areas 151

6 Conclusion   175

Bibliography   181

Index   195

CHAPTER 1

Introduction: Queering Contemporary Gothic

QUEERING CONTEMPORARY GOTHIC

Alice Nutter, the protagonist of Jeanette Winterson's *The Daylight Gate* that is a contemporary work of queer Gothic discussed in this study that re-casts events relating to the witch trials that took place in Lancashire in 1612, is portrayed living near Pendle Forest. The location is regarded by the locals as a haunted place where the spirits of the dead allegedly roam and men are transformed into hares. Alice is represented as queer both in terms of her sexuality and the role of social outsider to which the community relegates her. Though born in Pendle, on the death of her husband she moved to London where she assisted Dr Dee, astrologer to Queen Elizabeth, in his experiments to create the elixir of life. While acquiring from him an interest in scientific discourses, associated in the period with magic, she fell in love with Elizabeth Southern, another of his assistants, and lived with her for several years. When the relationship with Elizabeth Southern ended she became involved in an illicit romantic relationship with the Roman Catholic Christopher Southworth. In refusing to re-marry after her husband's death and expressing what today we would call her 'bisexuality', Alice challenges both heterosexual conventions and the view, implicit in the twentieth-century concept of identity categories, that the individual's sexuality is defined in terms of the gender of his partner.[1] In attempting to protect a group of vagrant women who are accused of witchcraft, she lays herself open to a similar charge. Her decision to shelter Southworth, who is accused of being involved in the Gunpowder Plot, in her home hastens her downfall. She finds herself trapped in the cultural and religious contradictions of the period for, as she fatalistically tells her accusers, 'If you cannot try me as a witch, you'll charge me as papist.'[2]

I have opened my study of the queering of contemporary Gothic with reference to Winterson's *The Daylight Gate* since, as well creating a vivid representation of an oppressive episode from early seventeenth-century history, it introduces the reader to some of the themes and narrative strategies that typify fiction of this kind, ones that we shall encounter again in the novels and stories discussed in the following chapters. Teasing out the connections between 'Gothic' and 'queer', Winterson employs a fictional genre familiar to readers for its focus on transgressive sexuality and its association, as Fred Botting describes, with 'liminality' and 'ghosts of the mind',[3] to recount the story of a female protagonist whose behaviour and sexual preferences are regarded by society as disruptive. As is frequently the case in queer Gothic, Winterson's treatment of the tension between fantasy and realism, the uncanny dimension of existence and the material world, metaphorically evokes the tension between queer and hetero-normative perspectives. Whereas queer sexuality is associated in the novel with a secret realm of magic and illicit erotic encounters, heteronormativity is described in terms of the everyday reality of family life and church attendance. The interrogation of the concept of 'the real', in which Winterson engages, and the ambiguities and questions that it provokes, connect queer sexuality to the illicit and the taboo. The reader is uncertain whether the erotic encounter that Alice experiences with Elizabeth in the final chapters of the novel and the transformation of Southworth into a hare while seeking to escape his pursuers that she thinks she sees really take place or whether we should interpret them as examples of what Steven Bruhm terms '"magical" animism',[4] in which emotions of fear or excitement deceive the individual into believing that his fantasies assume material form. Alice herself is unsure whether these events actually occur or not, and, watching them through her eyes, we share her confusion. Ambiguities of this kind are, of course, integral to the operations of the uncanny and the Gothic novels and stories depicting them. It is the ability of Gothic to interrogate the reader's preconceptions about reality and expose the unfamiliar underlying the mundane that, as Rosemary Jackson explains, makes it well suited to treating topics conventionally branded as taboo.[5] Topics of this kind include different forms of queer sexuality for, as Freud, citing Schelling, explains, 'The *unheimlich* is the name for everything that [according to social convention] ought to have remained ... secret and hidden but has come to light.'[6] The Gothic genre, as *The Daylight Gate* illustrates, is admirably suited to representing their relegation to the realm of the secret and taboo and – as illustrated by the public interrogation to which Alice is subjected at her trial – their eventual disclosure.

Winterson's *The Daylight Gate*, as well as illustrating the ability of queer Gothic to explore the interrelation and tension between queer and heteronormative sexualities, furnishes an insight into some of the themes and motifs that fiction of this kind prioritises. They include, in addition to sexualities that tend to be regarded as deviant, the vilification of certain sections of society as monstrous, a topic illustrated in the novel by the demonising of Roman Catholics and the branding of women who exist on the margins of society and reject sexual convention as witches. The grotesque body, another motif frequently employed in Gothic, is also to the fore. It is exemplified on a physical plane by the injured body of Christopher Southworth tortured by the Protestant authorities and, on a supernatural, by the transformation from human to animal that some of the characters enact or fantasise. References to mysterious rural and urban locations also feature in the novel. They are exemplified both by Pendle Forest, described in terms of its treacherous mists and its association with magic, and Dr Dee's laboratory in London where he and his assistants attempt to discover the elixir. In addition, the progress of the narrative is interrupted on occasion by incidents of spectral visitation, as is illustrated by Alice's unexpected meeting with Dr Dee when, prior to her arrest, his ghost appears to warn her of the dangers that beset her. Topics such as these, as well as being significant to Winterson's text, give us a foretaste of their recurrence in the other novels and stories discussed in the chapters below where they assume different manifestations.

Winterson's decision to commemorate a group of women hanged for witchcraft in seventeenth-century Lancaster by re-creating their lives and experiences in a work of Gothic agrees, it is interesting to note, with the emphasis that present-day critics and historians place on the importance of investigating the oppressive, as well as the positive, aspects of queer history. Heather Love, defending her 'decision to look on the dark side', criticises the tendency of 'contemporary critics to describe the encounter with the past in idealising terms'.[7] She argues that, instead of disavowing the difficulties that queer people living in earlier centuries experienced and constructing 'a positive genealogy of queer identity' and 'female experience' (p. 32), as the 1970s lesbian and gay liberation movements, with their emphasis on the celebration of gay pride, tended to do, we need to acknowledge the oppressive aspects of their lives. The historiographer Carolyn Dinshaw, describing her investigation into lives of women in medieval history as motivated 'by a queer historical impulse, an impulse toward making connections across time',[8] describes the aim of her research as the building of an imagined community of the marginal. It is, she admits, necessarily imagined since, due to the fact that the majority of women living in earlier eras lacked literacy skills and could not record their experiences, the researcher has little relevant material on which to draw. Winterson adopts an approach of a similar kind to the histories of the women and queer individuals that she depicts. In representing the persecution of a group of seventeenth-century women who, on account of their unorthodox lifestyles and the fact that their sexualities conflict with hetero-patriarchal conventions, were eventually imprisoned and executed, she foregrounds the dark side of the past and creates a similar community of the marginal. The emphasis that Love and Dinshaw place on the need for writers and historians to address the oppressive aspects of queer history is, as we shall see, also relevant to some of the other works of contemporary queer Gothic discussed later.

FICTION, GOTHIC MOTIFS, AND QUEER SEXUALITIES AND GENDERS

The Daylight Gate, characterised by Winterson's interrogation of 'the real' and her representation of the persecution of a group of women living in the seventeenth-century who were suspected of practising witchcraft, illustrates, of course, only one of the forms that contemporary queer Gothic fiction takes. There are also numerous others. I have selected the novels I discuss with the aim of illustrating its versatility in terms of its treatment of sexuality and gender, as well as its utilisation of Gothic motifs and narrative strategies.

As we might expect from Freud's reference to the individual's experiencing of an uncanny event, such as seeing a ghost, as furnishing a metaphor for the return of his repressed desires and fears,[9] several of the novels examined in the chapters here focus on the topic of spectral visitation. Contemporary writers frequently employ the ghost story as a vehicle to explore queer history and the influence it exerts on the present. Whereas

Steve Berman in *Vintage: A Ghost Story* represents his teenage narrator's encounter with a ghost giving him an insight into male homosexual life in the 1950s and indirectly helping him to clarify his own desires and needs, Louise Tondeur in *The Water's Edge* employs the haunted house narrative to explore family history, elucidating the interplay between heterosexual and lesbian sexualities that it can reveal. Jim Grimsley's version of the haunted house differs radically from the one that Tondeur constructs. Setting it in South Carolina, he depicts the different houses in which the family live as haunted by the father's acts of domestic violence, as seen from the viewpoint of his young son Danny. Also of interest in Grimsley's narrative are the compensatory fantasies of the imaginary figure of 'the River Man' that Danny conjures up, his androgynous persona inspired by the river that runs near his home.

Reference to the Gothic monster and the hybridity and body horror associated with the figure are also to the fore in contemporary queer Gothic fiction. Writers utilise them to represent the way in which society projects on to the homosexual and the transgender individual an image of monstrosity and the grotesque. Peter Ackroyd treats the topic in *The Case Book of Victor Frankenstein*, a metafictional re-working of Mary Shelley's famous novel notable for its innovative re-casting. The shape-shifting abilities that the grotesque figures, such as Richard Marsh's *The Beetle* and Bram Stoker's *Dracula*, who appear in Victorian Gothic display, also furnish writers with a vehicle for queer representation. Kathleen Winter employs them to describe her eponymous intersex narrator Annabel's view of the physical changes that she unexpectedly finds her body undergoing when she reaches puberty, and to represent the ridicule and monsterisation she encounters when she decides to transition.

Reference to different forms of shape-shifting and their uncanny associations also feature, as the reader might expect, in Gary Bowen's *The Diary of a Vampire*. As well as exploiting the sexual potential of the vampire narrative, Bowen employs vampiric existence to metaphorically represent the queer individual's anxieties about coming out and the revelation of his sexuality it will involve. Susan Swan, in addition, employs the Gothic motifs of the double and magical transformation to represent her teenage narrator's incredulous response to the changes in embodiment from female to male that she sees her transsexual friend Paulie unexpectedly enact by means of body movement and gender performance. The queer view of gender as a discursive production dependent on performance and cultural fantasy also informs other works of fiction discussed below.

Geographical locations, as well as contributing significantly to Gothic fiction, are also relevant, as Judith Halberstam argues, to queer people's existence and experience.[10] Although, as she observes, theorists and sociologists have focused considerable attention on documenting the role that urban and metropolitan locations play in the life of the queer community, they have until recently paid little attention to rural areas. However, writers of queer Gothic fiction, in contrast, frequently incorporate reference to them in their texts. Whereas Winterson in *The Daylight Gate* employs Pendle Forest as an appropriately eerie context for her female characters' unorthodox lifestyles, Michelle Paver locates her ghost story *Dark Matter* in the snow-bound landscape of the Arctic.

The novels selected for analysis in this study, in addition to employing a variety of Gothic fictional forms and motifs, differ significantly in the approach towards them they adopt. Whereas Berman in *Vintage: A Ghost Story* focuses his narrative on his protagonist's encounter with a ghost, other writers, such as Alan Hollinghurst in *The Folding Star*, employ spectral references metaphorically to represent queer erotic fantasy. Still others, such as Winterson and Paver, treat the supernatural ambiguously, encouraging the reader to interrogate the paranormal events that the protagonist or narrator thinks that he experiences and queries if they are real or imagined.

As well as being of interest in literary and stylistic terms, the works of fiction discussed in the following chapters introduce the reader to a wide range of topics and experiences relevant to lesbian, male gay, bisexual and transgender people. Topics they address include: Victorian London as the location of lesbian relationships and spiritualist practices, as represented in Sarah Waters' *Affinity*; the gay man's experience of city life, described by Hollinghurst in *The Folding Star*; and the crises that the AIDS epidemic provoked in British and US cities in the 1980s, depicted by Vincent Brome in *Love in the Plague*. Kathleen Winter's *Annabel* is especially innovative in this respect since the theme of intersex, on which it focuses, seldom receives fictional treatment.

The novels and stories discussed, as well as differing in the sexualities and genders on which they focus and the Gothic strategies and motifs they employ, also vary in date of publication ranging from Swan's *The Wives of Bath* published in 1993 to Meg Kingston's *Chrystal Heart* in 2013. They also differ in terms of the fame of the writers who have produced them. Whereas the names of Waters and Ackroyd will no doubt be familiar to readers, other writers such as Kingston, Berman and Winter may be less well known.

Also of interest are the different theoretical perspectives that writers employ in representing the sexualities and genders on which they focus. Do they create a predominantly queer approach that depicts identity as provisional and contingent and foregrounds the mobility of sexuality and the re-signifiable nature of gender or do they write predominantly in terms of identity categories, echoing in this respect the perspectives of the lesbian and gay liberation movements of the 1970s and 1980s? The two approaches are, in fact, not mutually exclusive. As Michael Warner explains:

> Queer politics has not just replaced older modes of lesbian and gay identity: it has come to exist alongside those older modes, opening up new possibilities and problems whose relation to more familiar problems is not always clear. Queer activists are also lesbians and gays in other contexts – as for example when leverage can be gained through bourgeois propriety... or through minority-rights discourse.[11]

Judith Butler, though having played an instrumental role in initiating the growth of queer theory, also supports the use of identity categories when the situation and context require. Though referring to them ambivalently as a 'necessary error of identity',[12] she nonetheless acknowledges their importance as tools for challenging sexism and homophobia. As she argues,

> It remains politically necessary to lay claim to the identificatory terms 'women', 'queer', 'gay' and 'lesbian', precisely because of the way these terms, as it were, lay claim on us prior to our full knowing... in order to refute homophobic deployment of the terms in law, public policy, on the street, in 'private' life. (p. 229)

The novels discussed vary considerably in the approach to sexuality and gender they employ. In addition, the polysemous nature of fiction and its dialogic structure frequently result in them avoiding articulating their ideological perspective explicitly and render their perspective on sexuality and gender to a degree ambiguous. The term 'queer' is, of course, multifaceted in significance and can assume different meanings. Although it is generally employed in academic discourse in accord with the theoretical perspectives of Butler and Eve Sedgwick to foreground the instability of the categories 'hetero' and 'homo', to critique the regulatory nature of identity categories and to foreground sexual mobility, it can alternatively be employed as a shorthand term for 'lesbian', 'gay' and 'trans'.[13] I use it in a similarly versatile way, with the context of the text indicating its significance.

Queer Gothic and Its Development

Before turning to the discussion of the novels referred to above and others that feature in this study, I need to focus on another topic that is significant to it. This is the development of the form of fiction known today as 'queer Gothic' and the contribution that critics and theorists writing in the twentieth and twenty-first centuries have made to it.

Comments voiced by William Hughes and Andrew Smith in the introduction to *Queering the Gothic*, a collection published in 2009 that has helped to establish the importance of fiction of this kind, are pertinent here. Drawing attention to the complex implications of the term 'queer Gothic', they describe Gothic narratives as 'queer' not only in their frequent reference to non-normative sexualities and genders but also, more generally, in foregrounding 'a systematic stylistic deviance from perceived norms'.[14] They alert attention in addition to the fact that, while reference to homoerotic themes and episodes, as illustrated by Matthew Lewis's *The Monk: A Romance* (1796) and Ann Radcliffe's *The Italian* (1797), has characterised Gothic fiction since its advent in the eighteenth and nineteenth centuries, queer Gothic as a specific literary form and the critical texts that analyse and define it have developed relatively recently. They emerged in the climate of debate promoted by the 1970s and 1980s lesbian feminist and gay liberation movements exemplified by the theoretical writing of theorists such as Adrienne Rich and Alan Sinfield, and the focus on queer perspectives on sexuality and gender that appeared subsequently in the late-1980s and 1990s in the work of Sedgwick, Butler and Diana Fuss. These movements and political trends, by promoting an interest in sexual politics and post-modern approaches to literature, have created a fertile ground for the critical re-evaluation of eighteenth- and nineteenth-century Gothic fiction and the references to queer sexuality and gender it introduces. They have also, of course, helped to promote the production of contemporary queer Gothic fiction.

Sedgwick's writing, though referring chiefly to male gay sexuality and making little reference to lesbianism, has been influential in furnishing a theoretical frame for the analysis of Gothic, as well as encouraging the recognition of the genre's importance as a vehicle for representing queer sexuality. After discussing a number of texts produced in the eighteenth and nineteenth centuries, she concludes that 'The Gothic was the first novelistic form in England to have close, relatively visible links to male homosexuality at a time when styles of homosexuality, and even its visibility and distinctiveness, were markers of division between classes as much as between genders'.[15] She also pioneered the concept of paranoid Gothic, employing it with reference to James Hogg's *The Private Memoirs and Confessions of a Justified Sinner* to investigate the emotionally fraught situation of two men entrapped in a relationship in which feelings of aversion and antagonism conflict with homoerotic desire. As she observes, 'The Gothic novel chrystallized for English audiences the terms of a dialectic between homosexuality and homophobia, in which homophobia appeared thematically in paranoid plots'.[16]

The critical writing of George E. Haggerty and the contribution it has made to the development of queer Gothic also merit reference. William Veeder's homoerotic reading of Robert Louis Stevenson's *The Strange Case of Dr Jekyll and Mr Hyde*, as well as being developed by Elaine Showalter with reference to nineteenth-century medical science, is augmented by Haggerty in the Foucauldian context of the tension between behaviour/identity in the analysis of homosexuality.[17] Combining a psychoanalytic reading of fiction with reference to the development of different queer sexualities, Haggerty also usefully demonstrates that the narratives produced by Walpole, Radcliffe and Lewis in the eighteenth century furnished 'a testing ground for many unauthorized genders and sexualities'[18] that, though predating the sexual codification that the sexologists introduced, nonetheless prepared the ground for it. The wide-ranging nature of Haggerty's research interests is illustrated by a recently published essay in which he evaluates recent developments in queer historiography.[19] Some of the observations he makes in it are in fact relevant, as I indicate in the following chapters, to the treatment of history in contemporary queer Gothic fiction.

With reference to transgender and transvestism, although their representation in the Gothic fiction produced in earlier centuries has taken some time to receive critical attention, they are now arousing interest. William D. Brewer discusses the sexual and psychological complexities of transgender in Lewis's *The Monk*,[20] while Kelly Hurley examines the sex changes that the figure of the eponymous beetle undergoes in Richard Marsh's novel.[21] I comment on the representation of female same-sex erotic attachments and gender performativity in Antonia White's *Frost in May* and, with reference to contemporary fiction, the treatment of transsexuality and transgender in Stella Duffy's *Beneath the Blonde* and Patrick McGrath's *Dr. Haggard's Disease*.[22]

As is indicated by the number of different discourses (literary, historical, sexual and psychoanalytic) to which the critics and theorists cited above refer, the critical study of queer Gothic tends to be interdisciplinary in nature, incorporating a variety of different intellectual strands. One particular strand that, since it has played an important role in its development features in some of the contemporary novels discussed below, merits discussion here is 'Female Gothic'. As its name suggests, it refers to female-authored works of fiction and their treatment of the problematics of femininity in phallocentric culture. Critical interest in 'Female Gothic' and the lesbian component that it includes has stemmed partly from the critical intervention that Claire Kahane made in 1985. In a groundbreaking essay developing ideas proposed by Ellen Moers,[23] Kahane challenged the way in which, despite the major contribution that women writers have made to the production of Gothic, Gothic critical studies tended to be dominated in the 1980s by both a focus on male-authored texts and a phallocentric viewpoint. She also drew attention to the fact that, although the majority of critical readings of Gothic, predictably ones produced by men, focus on male writers and characters and 'attribute the terror which the Gothic by definition arouses to the motif of the incest within an oedipal plot', frequently underlying the representation of paternal authority in the text are references to the maternal and 'the problematics of femininity that the heroine must confront'.[24] The latter topic, as Kahane describes, is symbolically represented in several texts by the spectral apparition of the heroine's mother. After discussing in the essay the treatment of mother and daughter attachments in the fiction of Ann Radcliffe, Kahane continues to explore Shirley Jackson's representation of female relationships, lesbian as well as maternal, in *The Haunting of Hill House*. Critics writing subsequently, influenced by the agenda of the lesbian feminist movement, continued Moers and Kahane's 'Female Gothic' project by analysing the treatment of lesbian sexuality in Gothic fiction and film. Bonnie Zimmerman pioneered the discussion of the cinematic representation of the lesbian vampire,[25] while Terry Castle alerts attention to the way in which nineteenth- and early-twentieth-century writers, by portraying the figure of the lesbian in spectral imagery, effectively negated her corporeality and sexuality.[26] As a result of these and other critical and theoretical interventions, the importance of Gothic motifs in female-authored texts and the significant role that female and lesbian sexualities play in Gothic fiction by both men and women are increasingly achieving recognition. The topic of Female Gothic and the debates it has generated are re-evaluated by Diana Wallace and Andrew Smith in the publication *The Female Gothic: New Directions*.

With reference to the present-day critical reception of Gothic fiction with a homosexual, lesbian or trans content, it has of course taken a number of years for works of this kind to receive attention and the topics they treat to be regarded as suitable material for academic and scholarly analysis. Homophobic attitudes, on occasion endorsed by the government, have helped contribute to this neglect, inhibiting the reception and discussion of queer fiction in colleges and, more especially, schools. Section 28,[27] instituted by the Conservative government in 1988, as well as denigrating lesbian families by describing them as 'pretended', prohibited local authorities from 'promoting' homosexuality by devoting funding to educational materials or cultural events with a queer focus. The Section also had the effect of suppressing or limiting the discussion of queer sexuality and gender and the purchasing of texts focusing on them in state-funded schools and colleges, as well as preventing the funding of LGBTQ drama and literary festivals. People such as myself, who were involved in the running of lesbian phone help-lines, queer social groups or arts events that relied on council funding, remember the oppressive effects that the Section had on these organisations and activities, as well as its intimidatory effect on the queer community. Indications exist, however, that, with the repealing of the Section in 2003 and introduction of civil partnerships and marriage, attitudes are now changing. The interest that the topic of queer Gothic is arousing in academia is illustrated by the fact that several major collections of critical essays published in the past fifteen years, as well as studies by individual writers, either intersperse reference to queer topics throughout or include individual chapters focusing on them.[28] However, despite the increasing interest in fictional representations of queer sexuality in academia and society in general, novels and stories with a queer sexual focus continue to be marginalised, as is illustrated by the lack of reviews they receive in mainstream journals and newspapers. This, of course, is unsurprising considering the erasure and neglect that queer culture has habitually experienced. Calvin Thomas refers with a justifiable sense of anger to,

> the thousands of pages of straight literature, the countless reels of mainstream film and hours of compulsorily heterosexual television, that lesbians and gays have suffered through for years without finding any such specific and positive trace of recognition but only the dominant culture's silence, hatred and derision.[29]

Older members of the queer community, though no doubt many younger ones as well, will share Thomas's sense of indignation and endorse his spirited protest.

While the recognition that queer Gothic fiction is now receiving in academia is of course to be welcomed, certain features of its critical treatment, as critics themselves acknowledge, can be problematic. E.L. McCallum, for example, expresses the fear that the critical analysis of fictional representations of queer sexualities and genders in a Gothic context, since it is enclosed within the parameters of a genre that, though in certain respects transgressive, nonetheless has conservative features, may obscure their radical import.[30] Other critics refer to problems relating to the concept 'queer' itself. Iain Morland, for example, criticises what he regards as the concept's increasingly narrow academic connotations and lack of political vigour.[31] Problems also emerge from the limitations that essays discussing works of contemporary queer Gothic, on occasion, display. Whereas critics analysing Victorian novels with a homosexual or homoerotic component, such as Robert Louis Stevenson's *Jekyll and Hyde* and Oscar Wilde's *The Picture of Dorian Gray*, frequently contextualise them by referring to relevant sexual-political events that occurred in the period of their production such as the Oscar Wilde trials, the institution of the closet or the harshness of the sodomy laws,[32] critics discussing present-day novels with a queer content seldom refer to their sexual-political context. Topics that might merit reference in this respect include the emergence of the lesbian and gay liberation movements in the UK and the USA in the 1970s, the AIDS crisis of the 1980s, the advent of the queer movement and the theoretical perspectives associated with it in the 1980s and 1990s, and, of course, the recent introduction of civil partnerships and marriage. Other problems also exist. In contextualising the works of fiction they discuss, critics sometimes mistakenly imply that the years from the 1970s to the present-day in the UK and USA have taken the form of an uninterrupted upward flow of increasing sexual tolerance and social acceptance. This, of course, is by no means the case. They included periods of severe homophobic backlash against the achievements of the lesbian and gay liberation movements, as is illustrated by the oppressive response that the right-wing governments that achieved power in the USA and UK in the 1980s evinced towards people with AIDS. Section 28 was in fact instituted in this era. In addition, any increase in sexual tolerance that has occurred over the years has not happened by chance, as critics sometimes imply. On the contrary, it has been achieved by means of human agency — by struggles waged by queer people and their supporters, frequently at the cost of family divisions, loss of jobs and promotion opportunities.

On moving from the situation of queer people in the past to their lives today, we find that, although, with the institution of civil partnerships and gay marriage, circumstances have certainly improved, many areas of life continue to give cause for concern. The bullying that many children and teenagers with a queer sexuality or gender experience in schools and colleges, the mental breakdowns and suicides that occur as a result, the frequency with which parents continue to evict teenagers from home on discovering their queer orientation and the persecution that trans people frequently suffer, indicate that the situation is not as positive as is often assumed. In addition, in a number of professions such as school-teaching, the law and different forms of industry, coming out as gay, lesbian or trans continues to be problematic or, in some cases, unthinkable. The difficulties that queer people encounter in these and other areas of life, in addition to receiving analysis in books and newspaper features,[33] are explored in some of the queer Gothic fictional texts discussed in this study. Examples include Steve Berman's *Vintage: A Ghost Story*, referred to in Chapter Two, Susan Swan's *The Wives of Bath* in Chapter Three, and Kathleen Winter's *Annabel*, in Chapter Four.

Intersections between 'Gothic' and 'Queer'

The development of Queer Gothic fiction over the years and the critical and theoretical writing that forms its context, as well as being encouraged, as Jerrold Hogle describes, by 'the threats and longings for gender-crossing, homosexuality or bisexuality'[34] that informs numerous eighteenth- and nineteenth-century Gothic texts, also reflects other influences. Important in this respect is the fact that the approaches to sexuality that, as critics observe, characterise Gothic fiction appear especially well-suited to the representation and exploration of queer sexuality and gender.

Stephen Bruhm describes Gothic as signifying 'a narrative of prohibitions and transgressions',[35] while David Punter cites as its 'distinguishing mark' the frequency with which writers focus attention on what he calls 'contradictory characters'.[36] Characters of this kind, as he describes, though, on the one hand, wishing to remain members of conventional society and abide by its familial codes, simultaneously exhibit a contrary desire to enter a less conformist social milieu. Leona Sherman develops this point. Referring to the tendency of Gothic fiction to portray characters who exhibit antithetical passions and interests, she remarks on the contradictory approaches to sexuality they often display. She describes these approaches as signifying 'the symbolization of sexuality as overtly feared but covertly wished'.[37] The emotional conflicts and contradictions that, as Punter observes, writers of Gothic depict their protagonists experiencing, combined with the ambivalent approach to sexuality that, as Sherman describes, Gothic texts frequently display, make the genre admirably suited to treating the tensions and conflicts that the queer individual experiences in coping with the pressures of heteronormative society. Though finding it safer in social terms to conceal his sexuality and accommodate to hetero conventions, he may simultaneously wish to explore the more transgressive world of queer social life and relationships. These contradictions and the tensions and strains they can generate are perceptively summed up by the theorist Sara Ahmed. Commenting on the problematic situation of the lesbian who tries to perform the precarious balancing act of leading a queer lifestyle in the context of mainstream society and perspectives, she refers to what she terms the 'slantwise' nature of lesbian existence and the 'dynamic negotiation between what is familiar and unfamiliar'[38] that it requires. Gothic fiction, with its ambivalent approach to sexuality and its emphasis on the protagonist's conflicted desires, lends itself especially well to representing the tension that the queer individual experiences between his own desires and societal pressures. Several of the novels discussed in this study treat topics of this kind especially vividly. Examples include Sarah Waters' *Affinity* and Michelle Paver's *Dark Matter*. Waters portrays her narrator Margaret moving to and fro between her upper-class home, with its veneer of heterosexual conformity, and Millbank Prison where she succumbs to the erotic spell cast by the spiritualist Selina Dawes who is imprisoned in a cell there. Paver represents her protagonist Jack, on falling in love with his fellow scientist Gus on the expedition to the Arctic on which he has embarked, feeling deeply disturbed by the clash he experiences between the hetero-normative values, with which he has been raised, and the sexual passion he now unexpectedly feels for a male colleague. He finds himself, in fact, for a number of weeks, on account of his conflicted state of mind, incapable of admitting, even to himself, the fact that he loves Gus. Both novels interestingly utilise reference to spectrality, represented in Waters' novel by reference to spiritualism and the séance and in Paver's by an encounter with a ghost, to explore their protagonists' sexual conflicts and dilemmas.

There is also another feature of Gothic, besides the contradictory and ambivalent approaches to sexuality typifying it, which makes it admirably suited to representing queer experience. This is the interaction that is currently occurring between Gothic motifs, on the one hand, and references to queer sexuality on the other. This process of cross-fertilisation is exemplified especially clearly by the infiltration of Gothic tropes and imagery into queer theoretical discourse. Whereas critics working in the field of Gothic discuss the representation of queer sexualities and gender in fictional examples of the genre, theorists working in queer studies employ motifs and tropes with Gothic associations, such as spectrality, secrets and the monster, as vehicles to explore and represent lesbian and male gay sexuality and different forms of transgender. I illustrate, later, some of the key motifs that contribute to this process.

Reference to spectrality plays an especially important role in the intersection between Gothic and 'queer' described above. The motif has, of course, infiltrated several other theoretical discourses besides queer theory. As Andrew Smith observes, 'The ghost, post Derrida, seems to be transformed into a critically mobile figure whose presence helped to illuminate the complex origins and discrete political visions of a variety of intellectual contexts'.[39] Peter Buse and Andrew Stott discuss several key examples of these 'contexts', including Freudian psychoanalysis and Derridean deconstruction, in their collection *Ghosts: Deconstruction, Psychoanalysis, History,* published in 1999.[40] However, frustratingly for the queer reader, although reference to spectrality had been infiltrating queer theoretical writing since the 1990s or earlier, the two critics do not mention this fact. The closest they come to doing so is in their reference in the introduction to the essay by Mandy Merk that discusses Jerry Zucker's film 'Ghost' (1990). Although Merk focuses chiefly on the racial significance of the film, she also includes a brief but insightful lesbian reading of its utilisation of spectral imagery.[41]

Buse's and Stott's lack of reference to the infiltration of spectrality into queer theoretical discourse is perhaps understandable considering the fact that queer studies as a discipline was relatively new to academia in 1999. Despite the innovative work of US theorists such as Sedgwick and Butler, it tended to be marginalised or ignored by the majority of academics. The two critics' neglect of the topic is amply compensated, however, by the numerous references to spectrality that occur in the work of the queer theorists who were writing in the decade. Butler, writing in 1993, describes how the threats of being regarded as subhuman, to which lesbian, gay and transgender people have been frequently subjected, 'haunt those boundaries [of the human] as the persistent possibility of their disruption',[42] while Castle writing in the same year, as mentioned above, describes the way in which writers in earlier centuries rendered the lesbian and her sexuality insubstantial and unreal by portraying her in spectral imagery.[43] Reference to spectrality also furnishes Jay Prosser with a useful metaphor for the transsexual's accommodation to his post-reassignment body and identity. She argues that, in order to be able to 'appropriate the rearranged somatic material as his or her new sex', the transsexual may need to experience 'a prior phantomization of it'.[44] Referring to the spectral double, a motif employed in several of the novels discussed in the chapters in this book, she asks the pertinent question, 'Might the transsexual's post-reassignment body be reconceived as an already phantomized pre-reassignment?'(p. 84).

Spectrality, while being employed by writers in relation to the fantasy image that the transsexual constructs of his post-reassignment body, has also entered the discourse of queer history. The historiographer Carla Freccero utilises it in order to challenge the generally accepted idea that the historian should maintain a sense of emotional detachment from the topics investigated. Rejecting this view, she acknowledges the fact that, 'The past is in the present in the form of a haunting. This is what, among other things, doing a queer kind of history means, since it involves an openness to the possibility of being haunted, even inhabited, by ghosts'.[45] Haggerty welcomes Freccero's unorthodox approach to historical research, exemplified by her acknowledgement of 'the haunting relation between past and present',[46] as inaugurating a new form of historical discourse that has, as he describes 'exciting implications for the history of sexuality' (p. 7). It is exciting in the respect that, as he observes, it encourages historians to cease futilely searching for a developmental model of queer sexuality, as tended to be the practice in the 1980s and 1990s, and gives them the licence to concentrate instead on focusing on the episodic emergence of queer communities and enclaves, ones that resemble metaphorically the episodic appearances of the ghost. Several writers whose novels are analysed in this book, including Berman and Paver, similarly portray the present-day narrator achieving contact with the queer past and the individuals inhabiting it by engaging in an encounter with a spectral figure. They also portray him, as Freccero describes, feeling emotionally and erotically haunted by the experience.

Another motif that plays an important role in Gothic fiction, while also infiltrating queer theory, is that of secrets. It informs, of course, the structure of a number of well-known Gothic novels, including Brontë's

Jane Eyre and the secret of Bertha Mason's incarceration in the attic of Thornfield House around which Brontë structures the narrative, as well as the secret of Dracula's vampirism that Jonathan Harker and his companions, assisted by Van Helsing, discover. Queer theorists frequently employ the motif of secrets with reference to the closeted lives that lesbian and male gay people often feel forced to lead. Sedgwick, linking Gothic with 'queer', interestingly moves from exploring the role that the secret of the closet plays in Gothic narrative to commenting on its importance to the history of homosexuality. After observing, in her critical study *Between Men: English Literature and Male Homosexual Desire* (1985), that there are indications that the unspeakable secret that informs Maturin's *Melmoth the Wanderer* refers to homosexuality,[47] she remarks in her subsequently published queer theoretical work *The Epistemology of the Closet* (1992) that 'There had in fact developed [in the nineteenth-century]one particular sexuality that was distinctively defined *as* secrecy – homosexuality'.[48]

Secrecy is also relevant, as Judith Brown illustrates, to the history of lesbianism. Referring to the prohibition of same-sex female relationships in medieval and early-modern Europe, she observes that, 'Even more than male sodomy, sodomy between females was "the sin which cannot be named"'.[49] The motif of the secret, as well as being significant to male sexuality and lesbianism, also has connections with transsexuality, as is indicated by the effort that the trans individual sometimes makes to conceal his transitioning. However, with transitioning now occurring more frequently and society's increasing acceptance of the mobility of gender, its concealment is starting to appear less necessary.

Reference to the monster, exemplified by the grotesque figures that feature in Gothic fiction and film, has also entered queer theoretical writing. It is employed, as we might expect, to represent the abject treatment and monsterisation of the queer individual by means of verbal or physical abuse. Ellis Hanson, in an essay cryptically entitled 'Undead', employs reference to the vampire and the victimisation that it is portrayed experiencing in novels such as Stoker's *Dracula* to represent the abusive treatment assigned to the AIDS sufferer. He refers to 'the abjected space, that space unspeakable or unnamable'[50] to which 1980s society frequently relegated, as he describes, not only men with AIDS but gay men in general.

Another topic that connects Gothic with queer writing is the multivalent one of death. David B. Morris, commenting on the significant role that it plays in Gothic, refers to the way in which 'Gothic writers [such as Walpole] invest death and dying with new terrors'.[51] The figure of the zombie and the theme of the encounter with a ghost, popular in both fiction and film, also illustrate the importance of the topic. Reference to death features frequently, in fact, in queer writing. In addition to appearing with reference to AIDS, it is employed metaphorically in analyses of male gay eroticism, as exemplified by Georges Bataille's representation of the ecstasy of orgasm, 'as a violation bordering on death, bordering on murder'.[52] The linking of homosexual experience with death in the work of Bataille and other theorists is, of course, at odds both with the concept of gay pride promoted by the 1970s lesbian and gay liberation movements and the trend, apparent in the West today, towards the assimilation of queer people into society by means of civil partnerships and marriage. Jonathan Dollimore, in an effort to defend freedom of expression and maintain a space for the discussion of the transgressive dimension of queer sexuality, in fact concludes his essay 'Sex and Death' by urging the LGBT community, in its eagerness to establish a progressive politics and achieve social acceptance and respectability, not to outlaw the discussion of 'the complexity of the death/desire dynamic'.[53] As he demonstrates, it represents an important *topos* in queer writing.

The final motif connecting queer sexuality with Gothic, one that, especially on account of its utilisation in several of the works of contemporary Gothic discussed in this study, merits reference here is the concept of excess. As well as being exemplified in the complicated plot structure and the excessive display of acts of violence that Gothic novels and films sometimes exhibit, it is reflected in the grotesque image of the Gothic monster. As Max Fincher, commenting on William Beckford's *Vathek* and its treatment of corporeality, observes, 'Excess [in Gothic fiction] is nearly always connected to the body'.[54] Reference to excess is also relevant to queer existence since same-sex partnerships assume connotations of it in the heterosexual imagination. As Halberstam observes, in forming same-sex relationships and in general refusing to abide by conventions of 'reproductive time and familial time'[55] by marrying and having children, they and their lifestyles are regarded as aberrant and excessive.

The view of queer sexuality as excessive and strange is held, of course, not only by heterosexuals but can occur in the view that queer people, influenced by their attitude, have of themselves. Remembering the experience of first discovering herself to be erotically attracted to a member of her own sex and the sense of being unnaturally at odds with society that it evoked, Elizabeth Freeman, employing the term 'queer' in its sexual sense while also hinting at its older meaning of eccentric, observes, 'Wasn't my being queer, in the first instance, about finding sex where it was not supposed to be, failing to find it where it was, finding that sex was not, after all, what I thought it was?'[56] The reader will find other examples of motifs and images with connotations of the odd and the eccentric and carrying Gothic associations infiltrating queer writing in the novels and stories discussed in the following chapters.

NOTES

1. See Annamarie Jagose, *Queer Theory*, p. 69. (Jagose 1996).
2. Jeanette Winterson, *The Daylight Gate*, p. 49. (Winterson 2012) subsequent references are to this edition and in the text.
3. Fred Botting and Dale Townshend, 'General Introduction', in Botting and Townshend (eds), *Gothic: Critical Concepts in Literary and Cultural Studies*, vol. 1, p. 12. (Botting and Townshend 2004).
4. Steven Bruhm, 'The Contemporary Gothic: Why We Need It', in Jerrold E. Hogle (ed.), *The Cambridge Companion to Gothic Fiction*, p. 271. (Bruhm 2002).
5. Rosemary Jackson, *Fantasy: The Literature of Subversion*, pp. 67–72. (Jackson 1981).
6. Sigmund Freud, 'The Uncanny', in Angela Richards and James Strachey (eds), *The Pelican Freud Library*, vol. 14, p. 345. (Freud 1985).
7. Heather Love, *Feeling Backward: Loss and the Politics of Queer History*, p. 32. (Love 2007).
8. Carolyn Dinshaw, *Getting Medieval: Sexualities and Communities, Pre and Postmodern*, p. 1. (Dinshaw 1999).
9. Freud, 'The Uncanny', pp. 371–2.
10. Judith Halberstam, *In a Queer Time and Place: Transgender Bodies, Subcultural Lives*, pp. 34–42. (Halberstam 2005).
11. Michael Warner, 'Introduction', in Warner (ed.), *Fear of a Queer Planet: Queer Politics and Social Theory*, xxviii. (Warner 1993).
12. Judith Butler, *Bodies That Matter: On the Discursive Limits of 'Sex'*, p. 229. (Butler 1993).
13. Donald Morton refers to three other meanings associated with 'queer': 'an oppressed minority's positive re-understanding of a once negative word, the adoption of an umbrella term to encompass the concerns of both female and male homosexuals and bisexuals, and the embracing of the latest fashion over an older, square style by the hip youth generation', 'Birth of the Cyberqueer', *PMML*, 110/3 (1997), 369 (Morton 1997). For reference to the historical context of the emergence of 'queer' and the contestation of the term, see Jagose, *Queer Theory*, pp. 72–126.

14. William Hughes and Andrew Smith, 'Introduction', in Hughes and Smith (eds), *Queering the Gothic*, p. 3. (Hughes and Smith 2009).
15. Eve Kosofsky Sedgwick, *Between Men: English Literature and Male Homosexual Desire*, p. 91. (Sedgwick 1985).
16. Sedgwick, *Between Men*, p. 92.
17. George E. Haggerty, *Queer Gothic*, pp. 123–77. (Haggerty 2006). See also William Veeder, 'Carmilla: The Arts of Repression', in Botting and Townshend (eds), *Gothic: Critical Concepts in Literary and Cultural Studies*, vol. 3, pp. 117–41. (Veeder 2004); and Elaine Showalter, *Sexual Anarchy: Gender and Culture at the Fin de Siècle*, pp. 105–26. (Showalter 1992).
18. Haggerty, *Queer Gothic*, p. 2.
19. Haggerty, 'The History of Homosexuality Reconsidered', in Chris Mounsey (ed.), *Developments in the Histories of Sexualities: In Search of the Normal 1600–1800*, p. 5. (Haggerty 2013).
20. William D. Brewer, 'Transgendering in Matthew Lewis's *The Monk*', *Gothic Studies*, 6/2 (2004), 192–207. (Brewer 2004).
21. Kelly Hurley, '"The Inner Chamber of all Nameless Sin": *The Beetle*: Gothic Female Sexuality and Oriental Barbarism', in Botting and Townshend (eds.), *Gothic: Critical Concepts in Literary and Cultural Concepts*, pp. 241–55. (Hurley 2004).
22. See Paulina Palmer, 'Antonia White's *Frost in May*: Gothic Mansions, Ghosts and Particular Friendships', in Hughes and Smith (eds), *Queering the Gothic*, pp. 105–22 (Palmer 2009); and *The Queer Uncanny: New Perspectives on the Gothic*, pp. 93–103. (Palmer 2012).
23. Ellen Moers, 'Female Gothic', in Moers (ed.), *Literary Women*, pp. 90–110. (Moers 1978).
24. Claire Kahane, 'The Gothic Mirror', in Shirley Nelson Gardner, Claire Kahane and Madelon Sprengnether (eds), *The [M]other Tongue*, p. 336. (Kahane 1985).
25. Bonnie Zimmerman, 'Daughters of Darkness: The Lesbian Vampire on Film', in Barry Keith Grant, (ed.), *Planks of Reason: Essays on the Horror Film*, pp. 153–63. (Zimmerman 1984).
26. Terry Castle, *The Apparitional Lesbian: Female Homosexuality in Modern Culture*, pp. 28–65. (Castle 1993).
27. Section 28 of the Local Government Act was sponsored by a group of Tory backbenchers and, despite major opposition, came into force in the UK on 24 May 1998. It prohibits local authorities from (a) promoting homosexuality or publishing material that promotes it; (b) promoting the teaching in state maintained schools of homosexuality as a pretended family relationship; or (c) giving financial assistance to any person for approval of either of these purposes. As Duncan Fallowell points out it gives 'official approval to homophobia in the country at large',

'Section 28 and its Effects', *The Guardian*, 1 December 1989, p. 36. (Duncan 1989).
28. See Lucie Armitt, *Twentieth Century Gothic* (Armitt 2009); Monica Germana, *Scottish Women's Gothic and Fantastic Writing* (Germana 2010); Jerrold E. Hogle (ed.), *The Cambridge Companion to Gothic Fiction* (Hogle 2014); Catherine Spooner and Roger McEvoy (eds), *The Routledge Companion to Gothic* (Spooner and McEvoy 2007).
29. Calvin Thomas (ed.), *Straight with a Twist: Queer Theory and the Subject of Heterosexuality*, p. 19. (Thomas 2000). See also Olivia Laing's powerful feature 'On the Orlando Shooting and a Sense of Erasure' in which she protests at the attempted erasure of the significance of LGBTQ people from the massacre in the gay club in Orlando, USA, by being told that it had nothing to do with the 'everyday viciousness of homophobia' but was just an attack on Western freedoms in general. (*Guardian Review*, 16 June 2016, p. 19).
30. McCallum, 'The "queer limits" in the Modern Gothic', pp. 71–86. For reference to comments on and critiques of 'queer', see Palmer, *The Queer Uncanny*, p. 9. (McCallum 2014).
31. Iain Morland and Annabelle Wilcox (eds), *Queer Theory*, p. 187. (Morland and Wilcox 2005).
32. Critics who refer to historical events to illuminate the context of earlier queer Gothic fiction include John Fletcher, 'The Haunted Closet: Henry James's Queer Spectrality', *Textual Practice*, 14/1 (2000) 53–60. (Fletcher 2000); and Mair Rigby, '"Do You Share My Madness?" *Frankenstein's* queer Gothic', in Hughes and Smith (eds), *Queering the Gothic*, pp. 42–4. (Rigby 2009).
33. Important examples include Matthew Taylor, 'Schools Accused of Abandoning Thousands of Children to Classroom Bullies', *The Guardian*, 9 May 2005, p. 20 (Taylor 2005); Bella Quist, 'Challenges for LGBT People in the Workplace and How To Overcome Them', *The Guardian*, 28 July 2014. (Quist 2014); and John Browne, *The Glass Closet: Why Coming Out is Good in Business.* (Browne 2014). Jeffrey Weeks's publications *Making Sexual History* (Weeks 1999) and *The World We Have Won: The Remaking of Erotic and Intimate Life* (Weeks 2007) also chart the different forms of prejudice and oppression that queer people continue to encounter in Western society.
34. Jerold Hogle, 'Introduction: The Gothic in Western Culture', in Hogle (ed.), *The Cambridge Companion to Gothic Fiction*, p. 12. (Hogle 2002).
35. Bruhm, 'The Contemporary Gothic: Why We Need It' (Cambridge University Press 2002). p. 12.
36. David Punter, 'The Passions of Gothic', in Allan Lloyd Smith and Victor Sage (eds), *Gothic Origins and Innovations*, p. 233. (Punter 1994).

37. N. Holland and Leona F. Sherman, 'Gothic Possibilities', *New Literary History*, 8/2 (1977), 278–94. (Holland and Sherman 1977).
38. Sara Ahmed, *Queer Phenomenology: Orientations, Objects, Others*, p. 107. (Ahmed 2006).
39. Andrew Smith, *The Ghost Story: 1840–1920: A Cultural History*, pp. 4–5. (Smith 2010).
40. Peter Buse and Andrew Stott (eds), *Ghosts: Deconstruction, Psychoanalysis, History*. (Buse and Stott 1999).
41. Mandy Merck, 'The Medium of Exchange', in Buse and Stott (eds), *Ghosts, Deconstruction, Psychoanalysis, History* (London: Macmillan 1999). pp. 162–74.
42. Butler, *Bodies that Matter*, p. 8.
43. See note 27, this chapter.
44. Jay Prosser, *Second Skins: The Body Narratives of Transsexuality*, p. 85. (Prosser 1998).
45. Freccero, *Queer/Early/Modern*, p. 80. (Freccero 2006).
46. Haggerty, 'The History of Homosexuality Reconsidered', in Chris Mounsey (ed.), *Developments in the Histories of Sexualities*, p. 5. (Haggerty 2013).
47. Sedgwick, *Between Men*, pp. 94–5.
48. Sedgwick, *Epistemology of the Closet*, p. 73.
49. Judith C. Brown, 'Lesbian Sexuality in Medieval and Early Modern Europe', in Martin Duberman, Martha Vicinus and George Chauncey (eds), *Hidden from History: Reclaiming the Gay and Lesbian Past*, p. 75. (Brown 1989).
50. Ellis Hanson, 'Undead' in Diana Fuss, *Inside/Out*, p. 325. (Hanson 1991).
51. David B. Morris, 'Gothic Sublimity', *New Literary History*, 16/2 (1985), 308–19. (Morris 1985).
52. Georges Bataille, *Eroticism, Death and Sensuality*, translated by Mary Dalwood, pp. 16–17 (Bataille 1986). An informative analysis of Bataille's writing and its relation to homoeroticism is to be found in Les Brookes, *Gay Male Fiction since Stonewall: Ideology, Conflict and Aesthetics*, pp. 150–54. (Brookes 2009).
53. Jonathan Dollimore, 'Sex and Death', *Textual Practice*, 9/1 (1995), 49. (Dollimore 1995).
54. Max Fincher, *Queering Gothic in the Romantic Age: The Penetrating Eye*, p. 71. (Fincher 2007).
55. Halberstam, *In a Queer Time and Place*, pp. 6–7.
56. Elizabeth Freeman, 'Still After', in Janet Hallam and Andrew Parker (eds), *After Sex*, p. 32. (Freeman 2011).

CHAPTER 2

Ghosts and Haunted Houses

Queer Spectrality

Andrew Smith, reviewing in his essay on 'Haunting' some of the meanings that spectrality has acquired in post-modern discourse, appropriately reminds the reader that, 'Ghosts are never just ghosts. They provide us with an insight into what haunts our culture', indicating 'what it can only express in oblique terms'.[1] Connotations that the ghost assumes in the different discourses he discusses include the Freudian concept of the return of repressed fears and desires; the Marxist topic of commodity fetishism and surplus value; and oppressive events from earlier eras, such as those represented by Toni Morrison in *Beloved* in which a woman resembling the daughter whom Sethe has killed unexpectedly returns, evoking her personal narrative and the history of slavery in general.

In addition to those that Smith cites, there are, of course, other meanings that contemporary writers attach to the figure of the ghost and his operations. Especially important to queer Gothic are the invisibility of lesbian and male gay sexualities in heteronormative society and the haunting of the present by the repressed and frustrated desires of queer people who lived in earlier periods. These topics receive discussion in the critical writing inspired by the 1970s lesbian feminist and gay liberation movements and by the advent of queer politics in the 1990s. Critical studies referring to them include, in addition to Castle's 'The Apparitional Lesbian', John Fletcher's queer reading of Henry James's ghost stories[2] and the chapter 'Spectral Visitation: The Return of the Repressed' in my earlier publication *Lesbian Gothic*.

The fact that the queer connotations of spectrality have received theoretical analysis relatively recently may lead the reader to assume that their fictional treatment is also new. However, this is not the case. In addition to Henry James's *The Turn of the Screw* and Shirley Jackson's *The Haunting of Hill House*, several short stories produced in the nineteenth and the first half of the twentieth century treat male gay and lesbian sexuality in the context of the spectral. Mrs Gaskell's 'The Grey Woman', that treats what Castle describes as the 'ghosting'[3] of the lesbian in hetero-patriarchal culture, furnishes a poignant example. Gaskell explores from a feminist perspective the erasure of identity that a woman in Victorian England could suffer if she lost the protection provided by a man – either a biological male or a woman performing 'female masculinity'. She portrays the narrator Anna Scherer escaping from the control of her tyrannical husband with the help of a female companion who is also perhaps, as Coral Lansbury convincingly argues,[4] depicted as her lover. The companion, pertinently named 'Amante', dresses throughout in masculine dress. The story concludes on a tragic note. Amante is murdered by the gang of thugs that Anna's husband hires to get rid of her while Anna herself, bereft of both husband and lover, is reduced to a shadowy spectral figure – the eponymous 'grey woman' of the story's title. As Elizabeth Cox, commenting on this text and other of Gaskell's spectral tales, observes, 'In Gaskell's stories the repressed narrative of desire between women acts as a ghostly alternative that haunts the heterosexual narrative'.[5]

Simon Hay argues in his study of British ghost stories that reference to spectrality is especially well suited to the form of the short story. He suggests that stories, since they represent 'narrative fragments',[6] serve to replicate the significance of the ghost as a fragmentary remainder of the past. Whether or not this is the reason for their choice of the story form, several contemporary writers employ it in utilising spectrality as a vehicle for representing queer sexualities and relationships. Stories of this kind appear in the collections that, having initially emerged in the wake of the lesbian and gay liberation movements and appearing in print from around the 1970s to the present day, exemplify a distinctive feature of contemporary queer culture. Although academic critics seldom refer to them, they give a fascinating insight into the queer literary interests that have emerged in different periods. They also serve a sexual political purpose since they encourage writers to publish fiction on queer topics in a socio-political climate in which writing focusing on them still tends to be marginalised. Although the publication of these collections has recently declined in the UK as a result of the collapse of feminist and male gay publishing houses and bookshops, they continue to flourish in the USA. Twenty-first century examples include Catherine Lundoff's *Haunted Hearths and Sapphic Shades: Lesbian Ghost Stories* (2008) and Jameson Currier's *The Haunted Heart and Other Tales* (2009).

Suzan Tessier in 'A Quiet Love', a story published in Lundoff's collection,[7] utilises the figure of the ghost, possibly evoking connotations of the invisibility of lesbian love in hetero-normative society, to comment on the lonely and unfulfilled existence that many women currently lead. Tessier portrays the protagonist Julia working as an assistant at a US heritage museum. While carrying out her duties, Julia is depicted encountering the ghost of Elizabeth Hicks, a founding member of the nineteenth-century New York Women's Suffrage Movement. Though initially finding the meeting disturbing, she becomes increasingly attracted to her. As the weeks pass, she discovers that she in fact prefers Elizabeth's spectral company to that of her dominating husband and her colleagues at the museum. The story concludes with her accepting Elizabeth's invitation to leave the material world, with its male supremacist and heterosexist culture, and share her uncanny, same-sex life. The story is open to different readings. Does it offer a grim comment on the failure of society to recognise same-sex female attraction and relationships or does it celebrate the erotically intense and frequently secret life that two women can create together?

Currier, in contrast, employs spectrality to contrast and explore two different types of masculinity, the romantic and the military. He centres 'The Country House' on the visit that the unnamed male narrator and his partner Scott, who are portrayed experiencing problems in their relationship, pay to a house built in the eighteenth-century that a friend owns. One evening when, as a result of an argument erupting between the couple, Scott abruptly leaves the room, the narrator remains there alone. He is astonished to see, as he tells Scott on his return, two spectral figures wearing nineteenth-century military costume materialise. The two soldiers appear exhausted and battle-weary. Though upset by the sight of their wounds, the narrator resists the temptation to flee. He is astonished to see them, instead of cursing the slaughter that resulted in their deaths or commenting on the battle, lovingly embrace. As he describes, 'The wounds and the blood were gone and there was an unmistakable intimacy between the two men'.[8] The passion that the two ghosts display has, in fact, a positive outcome; it reminds the narrator of his love for Scott and heals the rift between them that had occurred.

The spectral double is another motif with connotations of ghosts and haunting that lends itself to the form of the short story, as Edmund White's 'An Oracle' (1987) illustrates. White opens it by portraying his narrator Ray seeking consolation from the death of his partner George from AIDS by taking a holiday in Crete. While staying on the island, Ray has an affair with a local youth named Marco and, though at first assuming it to be merely a short-lived holiday romance, finds himself becoming increasingly attached to him. In the final stages of his visit he is astonished to hear Marco, on refusing his invitation to live with him, repeat the words that his deceased lover George spoke on his deathbed, 'You must look out for yourself'.[9] Ray responds ambivalently to Marco's rejection. Although, on the one hand, he feels depressed, on the other he experiences an unexpected sense of elation since, as he perceives, his very feelings of disappointment illustrate that his ability to feel emotion, numbed since the occasion of George's death, has revived. White portrays him thinking, 'In pop-song phrases he thought this guy had walked out on him, done him wrong, broken his heart – a heart he was happy to feel thumping again with sharp, wounded life' (p. 350).

The fact that, as illustrated by the texts referred to above, the short story makes an effective vehicle for employing the motif of spectrality as a vehicle to explore queer sexual experience and relationships does not, of course, mean that the novel and its more leisurely style of narration is unsuited to the topic. *Vintage: A Ghost Story* (2007) by the American Steve Berman and *Affinity* (1999) by the British Sarah Waters, the two novels selected for analysis here, illustrate its uses in this respect. Both writers, though treating different periods and employing disparate narrative strategies, focus on the topic of queer history. Whereas Berman locates his narrative in the present in the provincial town of Malvern, New Jersey, and portrays his unnamed teenage narrator experiencing an encounter with a ghost, Waters, in contrast, sets hers in Victorian London. Employing two female narrators, both of whom have recently experienced crises in their lives, she explores their different connections with the spiritualist movement that flourished in the city in the 1870s and 1880s. Both novels have connections with the genre of historical fiction. Whereas Waters' *Affinity* is a neo-Victorian text, Berman's *Vintage: A Ghost Story* interrelates events in the present with ones set in the past. By portraying the narrator forming a relationship with the ghost of a youth who died in an earlier era and, like him, identified as homosexual, Berman furnishes both him and the reader with an insight into the experiences of queer people who lived in an earlier culture.

The urge that present-day writers, whether historians or writers of fiction, feel to investigate queer history is of course understandable. Gabriele Griffin, writing in 1993, remarks on 'the sense expressed by many lesbians in the 1970s that they had no sustained history constructed by themselves'[10] while Martha Vicinus observes that 'The most important and controversial questions [relating to queer history] concern the origins of an individual and group identity'.[11] Despite the efforts that historiographers have made in the past fifty years or so to decipher the mysteries of the queer past, problems with the project continue to exist. They stem from a variety of causes. In addition to originating from scholarly disagreements about what 'homosexuality' precisely signifies, they reflect the changes in the meaning of both the term itself and the words utilised to define homosexual relationships. They also stem from the difficulty that researchers experience in uncovering homosexual and lesbian attachments between people who lived in earlier centuries since the stigmatisation of queer sexuality led them to keep their sexuality and relationships secret. Difficulties of this kind make the project of researching the queer past appear on occasion even more daunting than it did in the 1970s when the study of queer history was still in its infancy. As Haggerty observes in a recently published essay, since the developmental model of queer history that scholars prioritised in the 1970s and 1980s, with its teleological emphasis, has failed to furnish significant evidence of the long-term connections between queer sexualities over lengthy periods of time that historiographers had hoped to uncover, the 'cycles of salience' model, that focuses instead on occasional episodes of queer visibility favoured by the historiographer Valerie Traub, may perhaps prove more useful.[12] Haggerty also welcomes the model of queer historiography that utilises metaphors of haunting and spectrality that, as mentioned in the introductory chapter, the queer historiographer Freccero employs. As we shall see, the different approaches that Freccero and Traub adopt are relevant in different ways to Berman's and Waters' accounts of queer history.

SPECTRALITY AS A VEHICLE FOR REPRESENTING QUEER HISTORIES

Vintage: A Ghost Story by Steve Berman is an appropriate text with which to commence the discussion of the four novels focusing on queer spectrality referred to later, since, as well as combining an account of the problematic nature of contemporary gay teenage life with episodes of humour, it illustrates the range of different discourses, including psychoanalytic, historiographic and socio-political, that can influence and feed into the fictional treatment of queer spectrality. Berman's wide-ranging utilisation of spectral references and imagery also endorses the claim made by Wolfreys that, 'The Gothic is itself one proper name for a process of spectral transformation'.[13]

Berman opens *Vintage* by portraying his unnamed narrator having recently experienced a crisis of the kind that is sadly not uncommon among queer teenagers. His parents, on discovering the fact that he is gay, have peremptorily evicted him from the family home. His unmarried aunt, who has given him refuge in her house, sensitively avoids enquiring about the circumstances that have led to his homeless plight, while he himself rejects the idea of confiding in her – at least in the present early stages of his residence with her. Having been stung twice as a result of his sexual orientation, firstly by a fellow pupil who, on discovering him to be gay, responded by circulating the news round the school and instigating a bout of queer bullying, and secondly by his parents' eviction, he understandably feels nervous about coming out. The only person in whom he has confided his queer sexuality is his friend and co-worker Trace. She works with him at a local shop that specialises in the sale of vintage clothing and, as suits the spectral focus of Berman's story, identifies as a Goth. As the narrative unfolds, Berman humorously contrasts the performative Gothic life-style that Trace employs, dressing in black beaded costumes and frequenting local séances and funerals, with the 'real' world of the paranormal exemplified by the spectral encounter that the narrator himself experiences. While grateful for her companionship and enjoying the anecdotes she tells him about local hauntings, he regrets that his personal shyness, combined with his fear of losing his job at the store, deters him from exploring the local gay scene. As he despondently thinks, 'Hunting down urban legends won't find me a boy'.[14]

Just how wrong the narrator is in making this assumption becomes apparent when, on walking home one night along Route 47 after having supper at the local diner with Trace, he sees a teenage figure appear in front of him. The 'awesome clothes from the 50s' that the figure is wearing lead the narrator to assume that he is returning home from a fancy dress party. Attracted by what he regards as the latter's 'smooth good looks' (p. 18) and blond hair, its silky appearance inviting a caress, the narrator conquers his timidity and, in order to alert his attention, calls out admiringly, 'Cool clothes!' (p. 18). It is only when, with the appearance of the headlights of an oncoming car, the figure vanishes, that he perceives its lack of material substance. Lying in bed that night and pondering 'the strange but beautiful boy' (p. 21) whom he encountered on the highway, he thinks, 'Ghosts aren't real. So then what happened?' (p. 21).

The question prompts the reader to try to decipher the significance of the spectral encounter. The narrator's ambivalent feelings about his own sexuality furnish a clue. Though longing to find a sexual partner, he doubts his ability to attract one, while also feeling nervous of coping with the demands of a gay sexual relationship. As, employing reference to the idiom of Gothic film that the two friends utilise together and that adds an intertextual cinematic dimension to the narrative, he admits to Trace, 'I always thought my life would end up as an Araki film. Not something by Tim Burton. I never imagined any boy would ever like me' (p. 45). His encounter with the ghost invites different interpretations. The most obvious one is the surfacing of the narrator's secret fears and desires, the interpretation that Freud assigns to a spectral encounter.[15] As is indicated by his erotic response to the ghost, exemplified by the thought, 'How would it feel if my fingers brushed over the top of his head?' (p.18), it appears to signify, at this stage in the narrative, a fantasy or, to employ the term that Nicolas Abraham and Maria Torok use, 'the phantom'[16] of his ideal lover. Its materialisation seems to have been inspired by his desire to find a boyfriend, while its image reflects the physical appearance of attractive teenagers whom he has seen in the past. This agrees, in fact, with Abraham and Torok's depiction of 'the secret' that they envisage encrypted in the subject's unconscious as 'the love object' (p. 188).

Other features of the ghost's appearance are also of interest. The narrator's reference to what he initially interprets as the stagey artifice of its 1950s costume recalls the artifice that the governess in Henry James's *The Turn of the Screw* associates with the image of the spectral Peter Quint, a feature of his appearance to which Smith alerts attention.[17] It also develops Berman's representation of the spectral figure in the early stages of the novel as a fantasy construct. Its spectral aspect, though frustrating in physical terms, nonetheless suits the narrator's shyness and the apprehensions he feels about coping with a gay relationship. As he admits to himself, 'I wanted the guy to be a ghost. To be different. Otherwise, I'd be afraid to talk to him again; a ghost I could handle, not someone attractive and normal' (p. 23). On divulging his encounter with the ghost to Trace, he admits with a note of self-irony, 'I've been waiting my whole life to meet a boy different from the rest. Someone special' (p. 30). His wishes in this respect appear to have been fulfilled for, who, as he humorously remarks, could be more different and special than a ghost?

However, as the narrative develops, the ghost takes on a different role. It moves from being represented as an insubstantial phantom reflecting the narrator's personal fears and desires to being portrayed as an autonomous individual who lived and suffered in an earlier period. This shift in representation occurs after the narrator, intrigued by his encounter with his spectral visitor and admitting that he finds him attractive, decides to take the initiative and seek him out. On meeting him again on the highway and engaging him in conversation, he learns that his name is, somewhat unromantically, 'Josh' – and that he met his death by being run down by a car in 1957.

On discussing the information that he has learned with Trace, the narrator discovers that, according to what she authoritatively calls 'the laws of spectrality' (p. 48), the spectral Josh is doomed to walk the stretch of road where he was killed for eternity unless he is fortunate enough to experience some form of psychic release. As well as being thrilled (and a little envious!) to hear of the narrator's supernatural encounter, Trace feels that her role of Goth qualifies her to illuminate the reason why he has been privileged to experience the event. On learning of the suicide attempt that the bullying he experienced at school, combined with his parents' insensitive response to it, resulted in him making, she suggests that it is no doubt this previous brush with death that explains his ability to see and converse with denizens of the spirit world.

At this point in the story events suddenly escalate – a little too rapidly, in fact, for the narrator's liking. Josh, rather than being merely a passive wraith as he initially appeared to be, unexpectedly indicates that he has sexual desires of his own. He materialises one night in the narrator's bedroom and, complaining of being tired of traipsing the highway alone, announces that he fancies him and intends to stay. The narrator, though initially shocked by this turn of events, discovers to his surprise that he enjoys Josh's kisses and caresses. His thought, 'Such kisses break laws' (p. 64) suggests that, at this stage in the narrative, Berman employs spectrality and its transgressive connotations of a metaphor for the taboo connotations of queer sexual practice. Berman represents the couple's love-making in terms of contraries of hot and cold. The narrator describes the sensation of 'Josh's tongue in my mouth as like sucking an ice cube' (p. 92) and his fingers probing the warm flesh around his heart as evoking the sense of 'cold drops'(p. 93). The orgasm that he experiences leaves him, as he tells the ever-curious Trace, feeling 'like he left ice inside of me' (p. 96). He finds himself looking forward with pleasurable anticipation to the nightly visits from the spectral Josh, whom he now proprietorially calls 'my ghost'(p. 93), and the thrilling sexual practices he enjoys with him. He finds the pang of desolation that he experiences when Josh de-materialises and vanishes, as he invariably does each morning, giving place to a sudden surge of compassion. Remembering how he himself has 'known loneliness, the fear of being pushed away... of having no one' (p. 35), he sympathises with his spectral lover's desolate plight.

After some months, however, the pleasure that the narrator takes in Josh's romantic visits wanes when he begins to recognise, as Berman humorously describes, the social limitations of a spectral love-affair. Admitting that, 'The idea of romancing a ghost now seemed like a silly plot from a late-night movie', the narrator gloomily thinks, 'You can't bring a spectral boyfriend for a night on the town or to a coffee house to share a mocha' (p. 42). In addition, he experiences a sense of panic at the thought of his love affair with Josh taking place in his bedroom within earshot of his aunt: 'All I could think of was my aunt's reaction if I told her a ghost followed me home. And, oh yeah, we're both hot for each other, so don't mind the sounds you might hear behind closed doors' (p. 35). However, though eager to terminate the relationship, he continues feeling sorry for Josh. In an attempt to put an end to the latter's endless traipsing along Route 47, he visits the town library. From the research he conducts there and the conversations that he holds with Josh, he discovers that, in the year 1957, the latter engaged in an angry altercation with his ex-lover Roddy on Route 47 on account of him having outed him at school in revenge for his sexual infidelities. Feeling scared, in the homophobic climate of the period, of seeking adult assistance, he proceeded to court death on the highway by entering the path of an oncoming car and, as a result, got run down by a drunken driver.

Despite the gloomy topics of suicide and the eviction of the queer teenager from home that the novel treats, Berman concludes the narrative on a positive note. He describes Trace, encouraged by her supposition that it is the narrator's close encounter with death in his act of attempted suicide that led to him to make contact with Josh, trying to find a means to release latter from his traipsing along Route 47. With the narrator's assistance, she succeeds in contacting some of Josh's former friends, whom are now, of course, middle-aged. By organising a séance and summoning up Josh's spectral presence, they succeed, or so it appears, in enabling him, as Trace optimistically describes, to 'pass on to the next plane' (p. 189).

Berman's account of the difficulties that Josh experienced at school and his death on Route 47 in which they culminated gives both the narrator and the reader an insight into the oppressive experiences that homosexual teenagers could encounter in the homophobic climate of the 1950s. However, as Berman indicates in his reference to the narrator's eviction from home and suicide attempt, the situation of the queer teenager living today, though preferable in certain respects to that of his 1950s counterpart since the narrator, on being evicted, succeeds in finding friends and alternative living accommodation, nonetheless continues to be beset with difficulties.

An interesting feature of Berman's novel from a literary point of view is the connections it reveals with Hay's observations in his study of the ghost story about the different forms of suffering that writers associate with the figure of the ghost. Although, like many critics discussing fiction of this kind, Hay ignores its treatment of homosexuality, he mentions that writers frequently depict 'the spectral presences that haunt society'[18] as representing certain 'traumatic events from the past, some piece of past human suffering, that has not been successfully dealt with, and returns to haunt the present' (p. 87). Berman's account of Josh's unhappy experiences at school and his death on the motorway exemplifies a queer version of the topic.

The emphasis that Berman places on the fleeting and episodic nature of his teenage narrator's connection with the spectral Josh, as well as the erotic response and feelings of compassion he expresses toward him, are also of interest since they display connections with the ideas articulated by contemporary queer historiographers. The links they reveal with Freccero's model of historical research are especially pronounced. Admitting that researching the lives of individuals living in earlier centuries can be a 'profoundly erotic experience',[19] she defends her unorthodox approach to history on the grounds that it furnishes a space for 'the ghosts to speak' (p. 21). Endorsing Derrida's concept of a hauntology and the commitment it makes to what she describes as 'responding ethically within history and acknowledging the force of haunting by the voices of the deceased', she urges fellow historians to show a similar sense of ethical responsibility in their research (p. 73). Certain features of Berman's novel, such as the emphasis that it places on allowing 'the ghosts to speak', as the narrator permits the spectral Josh to do, as well as the portrayal of the narrator displaying a sense of responsibility towards Josh and assisting in his spiritual liberation, are illuminated by reference to her work.

In addition to representing Josh signifying ambiguously both an erotic fantasy originating from the narrator's unconscious and an individual from an earlier historical period who experienced a violent death, Berman interestingly assigns to him a third role in the narrative. Scattered throughout the novel are references to another male character. This is Trace's brother Mike. Mike is portrayed as a similar age to the narrator and drops occasional hints that he fancies him. An episode portraying the two characters enjoying a kiss is followed by another in which, despite the fact that spectral Josh unexpectedly intervenes in a fit of jealous rage in an attempt to spoil their romantic tryst, they succeed in spending the night together. The novel concludes, as the reader by now assumes it will, with Berman depicting the two teenagers embarking on a relationship. In this respect, Berman represents the narrator's love affair with Josh as forming a fantasy prelude to the relationship that, having conquered his fears of a gay relationship, he goes on to form with the flesh-and-blood Mike. As Berman portrays him optimistically remark, 'What's the chance my luck has finally changed?' (p. 198).

Sarah Waters's *Affinity* differs radically from Berman's *Vintage* in the approach to history that it adopts, as well as in its treatment of spectrality. Instead of locating her narrative in the present and introducing a reference to characters and events from an earlier historical period, as Berman does, she creates a work of historiographic metafiction set in Victorian London. Her representation of the emergence of spiritualism in the 1970s and the role that the séance played as a vehicle for expressing lesbian desire, rather than resembling Freccero's focus on the haunting relationship between past and present, has more in common with Valerie Traub's model of queer history that she describes in 'The Present Future of Queer Historiography' (2007). Instead of representing an unbroken line of queer activity, it takes the form of an occasional occurrence that briefly emerges but subsequently disappears when the historical circumstances alter.

In representing the Victorian spiritualist movement, Waters focuses on teasing out the contradictions of power/powerlessness that it exemplified for women, as well as the potential that it displayed for subverting class-structures, though at the cost of the advent of female conflicts and divisions. She in fact trained as an historian and one of her key projects as a writer of fiction, as is illustrated by the novels located in different historical periods that she has produced, is the recovery of women's history. Describing

Affinity as one of her 'most genuinely historical novels', she represents it as exemplifying 'an attempt to recover the Victorian lesbian voice'.[20] In it she focuses on the emotionally complex relationships that develop between the three key female characters whose trajectories she depicts: the working-class medium Selina Dawes, her lover Ruth Vigers and the upper-class Margaret Prior. Selina is portrayed spending the major part of the narrative incarcerated in a cell in Millbank Prison. She has been sentenced to five years' imprisonment there on account of the role that she allegedly played in the death of a woman who attended a séance she held. She argues in court in self-defence that she did not directly cause the woman's death but it occurred as a result of her spirit control Peter Quick behaving aggressively. His role in the séance, as the reader eventually perceives, is surreptitiously enacted by Ruth Vigers, Selina's maid and her lover.

While imprisoned in Millbank, Selina happens to encounter the upper-class Margaret Prior who has access to the prison in the role of 'Lady Visitor'.[21] Margaret, though initially distrusting Selina's protestations of 'affinity' (p. 275), is erotically attracted by her beauty and the air of mystery she evokes and, as result, becomes sexually infatuated with her. Deceived by her charm, she eventually agrees to assist Selina financially with the escape from the prison that she is planning to make. The novel concludes with Selina and Ruth, the latter having secretly maintained contact with Selina during her months in prison, eluding capture and escaping together to Italy. Margaret meanwhile, forced to recognise the trick that the two women have played on her, is left alone and emotionally desolate. As well as being deceived in love, she faces penury since she has spent a major part of her inheritance on financing Selina's escape. As the reference she makes in the final pages of the novel to the River Thames and its 'deep...black water' (pp. 350–1) indicates, she appears to envisage suicide as her only means of escape from penury and shame.

In constructing *Affinity* as a Gothic novel structured on spectrality and the connotations the motif held for women living in the 1870s, Waters employs a genre that is admirably suited to representing the topic of female social invisibility in the Victorian era. Hilary Grimes, discussing the Victorian ghost story and its production, argues that its popularity with women writers stemmed not only from the fact that fiction of this kind sold well but also because it furnished 'a transgressive space which allowed women to write in politically coded terms about their ghostly role in society'.[22] Waters also foregrounds in her neo-Victorian novel the topics of female de-realisation and spectralisation. She portrays women, separated from one another by class divisions and patriarchal structures, existing, as the French feminist theorist Luce Irigaray describes, in a state of *dereliction* like lonely phantoms.[23]

Margaret is portrayed on the initial visit that she pays to Millbank Prison as a solitary, depressive figure. Though eager to help the female prisoners and comfort them by listening to their accounts of their lives, she is no conventional do-gooder. The personal tragedies that she has experienced are conveyed to the reader by reference to her memories and personal thoughts. The recent death of her father, an historian with whom she was planning to travel to Italy, combined with the loss of her lover Helen who, wearying of a life of sexual subterfuge, has accepted an offer of marriage from Margaret's brother Richard, have left her feeling desolate and bereft. Visiting the reading room at the British Museum where her father used to research, she is struck by the number of other apparently single women who are studying there. Introducing the topic of female invisibility that features prominently in the novel, Waters portrays her thinking, 'Perhaps, however, it is the same with spinsters as with ghosts; one has to be of their ranks in order to see them at all' (p. 58). In episodes such as this, Waters, in a similar way to the nineteenth-century women writers whom Grimes describes as foregrounding 'woman's ghostly role in society',[24] utilises spectral imagery to emphasise their marginalised existence.

Thoughts of female invisibility and its connotations of spectrality assail Margaret again when she enters Millbank Prison. She is first made aware of the existence of the female prisoners who inhabit the building by hearing the sound of their boots as they trudge from the exercise yard into the building. On recognising the import of the sound, she thinks that 'They might be ghosts!' (p. 20). As well as being associated with spectrality throughout the narrative, in one particular episode Margaret even assumes the appearance of a ghost. On walking through the mysterious fog-bound London streets in the winter prior to the visit that she pays to the Reading Room of the British Association of Spiritualists, she notices, 'There might have been a dome about me – a dome of gauze' (p. 126).

Waters also foregrounds the way in which friendships and sexual involvements between women tend to be rendered, as a result of the phallocentric culture of the period, insubstantial and invisible in social terms. She portrays Margaret noting with resentment how quickly her mother appears to 'forget', perhaps deliberately, the fact that Helen was initially her own 'friend' and it was, in fact, she herself who initially introduced her into the family.

However, in addition to foregrounding the negative aspects of female and lesbian invisibility, and their metaphorical spectralisation, Waters, unlike many writers, also illustrates their advantages. As she indicates in the episodes focusing on the séances that Selina holds with the assistance of her lover Ruth, who acts the role of the spirit guide, the séance furnishes a space that enables women to enjoy same-sex contact. Although the séance's role in furnishing a means of contacting the spirits of the dead, as Waters illustrates, is illusory and fake, its function as a vehicle for secretly articulating female same-sex desire is authentic. As Tatiana Kontou perceptively writes, 'Tricks allow desires to be realised...There is a psychical reality in deceit'.[25] Regarded in this context, Selina's role as a medium is not a form of pretence but signifies, as Kontou describes, 'a way of expressing or, more accurately *performing*, her passion for Ruth' (p. 195).

Waters's representation of the séances that Selina holds and their erotic dimension furnishes a connection between *Affinity* and Berman's *Vintage*, different though the two novels obviously are. Whereas Berman portrays his unnamed narrator engaging in or possibly fantasising a same-sex love affair with a ghost, Waters depicts the séance furnishing a vehicle for erotic contact between spirit guide, medium and participants. However, in contrast to Berman, who portrays his teenage narrator eventually terminating his involvement with the spectral Josh in exchange for forming a relationship with the physically tangible Mike, Waters concludes her narrative on a significantly grimmer note. Though intimating that Selina and Ruth succeed in escaping to Italy together, she portrays Margaret being rendered broken-hearted and suicidal by the loss of Selina and the recognition of the cruel trick that she has played on her. In addition, in contrast to her subsequently published novel *Fingersmith*, representations of lesbian love scenes, are notably absent from *Affinity*, reflecting the lonely and frustrated situation of both Margaret and Selina. Female erotic contact is depicted as existing for both women either as a memory from the past or a tantalising fantasy located in the future. And, although same-sex desire is powerfully evoked both in Margaret's nostalgic memories of her relationship with Helen and the erotic gaze that she directs at Selina when visiting her in her cell at Millbank, lesbian sexual practice remains, as suits its significance as the unrepresentable of phallocentric culture and a figure for the Lacanian real, undescribed. The sexual encounter between Selina and Ruth that Margaret suspects takes place at her home in Cheyne Walk where, after Selina has escaped from Millbank Prison, the two are depicted spending the night prior to fleeing to Italy together, is also undescribed.

Uncertainty, in fact, exists as to whether it actually takes place or if it is a product of Margaret's imagination that she fantasises as a means to torment herself mentally.

During the months that she spends in Millbank Prison, Selina is described by the warders, ironically considering her lesbian relationship with Ruth, as a 'queer one' (p. 42) on account of the mysterious sounds they hear emanating from her cell at night indicating, they suspect, her communication with the spirit world. Rachel Carroll remarks on the historical accuracy with which Waters employs the term 'queer', employing it 'in keeping with late nineteenth-century usage to denote the odd, the peculiar and the strange'.[26] The word also evokes, of course, connotations of queer sexuality for the present-day reader and, although Carroll does not mention this, Waters also deserves credit for the wit and subtlety with which, while utilising the word chiefly in its nineteenth-century sense, she occasionally hints, as the reference to Ruth as a 'queer one' illustrates, at its present-day sexual meaning. In 're-shaping material (in this case the past) in the light of the present',[27] a strategy that Linda Hutcheon specifically associates with historiographic metafiction, Waters briefly acknowledges the existence of the lesbian reader of her novel and her viewpoint.

Another of Waters's achievements in constructing *Affinity* is the tantalising game with genre and ideology that she plays in teasing us about the kind of novel we are reading and the ideological perspectives that the text inscribes. Is *Affinity* a Gothic romance that endorses the existence of the paranormal or a Gothic thriller that exposes it as fake by furnishing a rational explanation for Selina's apparently paranormal powers? Will the narrative leave us on the plane of Gothic fantasy or will it shatter the web of spectral illusion that Waters skilfully creates by giving us a materialist feminist explanation of events? In fact it does the latter – though it may take some time for the reader, depending on her attentiveness to the text and her familiarity with Waters's sexual-political perspectives, to discover it.

Whereas Selina's and Margaret's associations with spectrality are revealed relatively early in the novel, Ruth's become apparent in later chapters. However, in the role of maid that she performs, represented by the behind-the-scenes activities that the maid typically enacted in the running of the Victorian household and the opportunity for spying on her upper-class employers that it furnished, Ruth too assumes connotations of spectral invisibility. Selina signals her skills in this respect by observing how 'quietly...like a real lady's maid, like a ghost' (p. 119) she performs her duties in the household. When, after Selina has been incarcerated in Millbank Prison, Ruth accepts under the name of 'Vigers' the position of maid at Margaret's home in Cheyne Walk with the aim of keeping her under observation, Margaret ironically fails to perceive her spectral import. Sitting in her room alone at night, conscious of the fog enshrouding the streets outside the window, she despondently thinks, 'How my mind runs to ghosts, these days' (p. 126). On hearing Vigers moving in the attic room overhead, she wonders why she should be so restless. She is unaware that the house in fact harbours a 'spook' – a spy that Selina has planted there in order to keep an eye on her and observe her activities.

Waters's description of the acts of trickery and deceit that Ruth adeptly performs in enacting the role of the spirit guide Peter Quick in Selina's séances and serving as go-between linking Millbank Prison with Margaret's home extends the socio-political scope of the novel by alerting attention to the ambiguous position that the maid assumed in the Victorian household. Hélène Cixous, complaining that 'Freud didn't give the servant-girl enough recognition' in his case-study 'Dora',[28] astutely describes the maid as the 'little character on whom rested the family structure' (p. 150). Jane Gallop also refers to the maid's ambiguous significance. She describes her as a 'threshold figure'[29] who, by living physically inside the upper-class family unit, though remaining from a social point of view outside it, exemplifies the threat of anarchy that the Victorian bourgeoisie associated with the working-class. The role that Ruth plays under the assumed name of Vigers in assisting Selina's escape from Millbank Prison and, by so doing, contributing to Margaret's demise, illustrates the power that the maid could exercise in the Victorian upper-class home.

Affinity also introduces the reader to another form of spectrality besides those with which Selina, Margaret and Ruth, as illustrated above, are associated. Jacques Derrida describes literature as having spectral import since, by continuing to signify and 'act' after the death of the writer, it enacts, like the ghost, a process of repetition and return. Commenting on what he evocatively calls the 'phantom-text',[30] he remarks on the way in which, in a work of fiction, intertextual references to literature produced earlier create 'ghostly traces' that 'phantomize the text itself' (p. 80). Gothic is a genre noted for its abundance of intertextual allusions. On reading a Gothic text, we frequently perceive, as Wolfreys describes, 'the ghost of another text haunting and inhabiting the narrative', creating 'the sense of the unfamiliar within the familiar'.[31] His comment is especially pertinent to *Affinity* since, as I illustrate in an earlier publication,[32] the novel is notable for the number of references that it makes to Victorian literary texts, both popular and upper-class. I shall conclude my discussion of it by commenting on another text that haunts the novel and the effects that this promotes. The text is Charles Dickens's *Bleak House*.

Affinity, as well having generic links with *Bleak House* in sharing with it conventions of Gothic and the sensation novel, also reveals narrative connections. The latter relate to the references Dickens makes to emotional attachments between women, both cross-class and erotic. As Holly Furneaux observes in her study *Queer Dickens*, *Bleak House* is notable for 'the diversely classed inter-female relationships explored in the novel'.[33] Examples Furneaux cites include 'the highly eroticized genteel reunion' (p. 219) that occurs between Esther and Ada after the former's recovery from an illness; and Caddy's explicit expressions of affection for Esther. The latter are on occasion so excessive that Esther fears they will provoke a response of jealousy from Caddy's husband. Another cross-class attachment between servant and mistress that Dickens depicts, one that Furneaux does not mention, is the intense infatuation that the French maid Hortense develops with her mistress Lady Dedlock. The threat of violence that it harbours becomes apparent when Hortense, on discovering that the pretty young Rosa has supplanted her in Lady Dedlock's affections, resigns from the latter's service in a fit of pique and, in order to achieve revenge, tries to incriminate her in the act of murder she herself has committed. Although Hortense's acts of deceit are unsuccessful, they look forward to the trick that the working-class Selina and Ruth play on Margaret, manipulating her into assisting Selina's escape from Millbank Prison while also defrauding her of her wealth. Feminine dress features prominently, it is interesting to note, in both Dickens's and Waters's account of the attempt that the maid makes to deceive and entrap her mistress. Whereas Hortense in *Bleak House* attires herself in a dress belonging to Lady Dedlock in order to incriminate her in the murder that she herself committed, Selina and Ruth in *Affinity* dress themselves, as a form of disguise, in the expensive garments that Margaret purchased for herself and Selina to wear when, so she had hoped, they travelled together to Italy.

Affinity also reveals another narrative connection with *Bleak House*. The law clerk William Guppy, on looking at the portrait of Lady Dedlock on the wall at Chesney Wold in Dickens's novel, is surprised to recognise in it a familiar face, though he is unable to recall to whom it belongs. The face is, in fact, that of Lady Dedlock's illegitimate daughter Esther, whom Guppy, though unaware of the familial connection between the two women, has in fact previously encountered. Esther herself, on gazing at Lady Dedlock in church, while unaware of fact that she is her mother, is also puzzled to glimpse what she terms 'scraps of old remembrances'[34] in her face. She feels disturbed by the intensely emotional response that the act of recognition provokes in her and is at a loss to understand, 'Why I should be so fluttered and troubled... by having casually met her eyes?' (p. 268). These two episodes in Dicken's novel are echoed in Waters's description of the visit that Margaret pays to the Spiritualist Reading Room in *Affinity*. On gazing at the pencil drawing of the spirit guide Peter Quick, Margaret experiences the uncomfortable sensation that, though she has never attended a séance, his 'dark eyes... seemed – how odd it sounds! – they seemed *familiar* to me – as if I might have gazed on them already...' (p. 154). As is the case in Dickens's description of the subliminal act of recognition that Esther experiences on gazing at the woman who, unbeknown to her, is her mother, it is the eyes that are focus of attention in Margaret's partial recognition of Ruth in the picture of the spirit guide Peter Quick. She has previously encountered him, of course, in his female manifestation as the maid Vigers.

The intertextual connections with *Bleak House* referred to above, rather than being merely ornamental, are significant in the respect that they serve to strengthen *Affinity*'s connections with nineteenth-century fiction. They assist, as a result, in explaining the novel's success as a work of neo-Victorian fiction. They also illustrate how the motif of spectrality, as well as informing Waters's representation of sexuality, femininity and class, is reflected in the ghostly traces of Dicken's novel that Waters' narrative introduces.

Haunted Houses

Discussing the haunted-house narrative and the role that it plays in Gothic fiction, Ruth Parkin-Gounelas refers to the emphasis that writers place on the significance of the home as the domain of secrets, frequently transgressive in nature and generating spectral events.[35] Secrets of this kind differ in origin. They can stem, as is the case in Elizabeth Gaskell's 'The Old Nurse's Story' from the father's ejection of his daughter from the family home on account of her giving birth to an illegitimate child – and the acts of haunting that his tyrannical action set in motion. In M. R. James's 'The Mezzotint' they relate, on the contrary, to an act of violence (the abduction of a child) that an intruder to the property perpetrates in revenge for an act of injustice committed by the owner. Walter De La Mare's 'Out of the Deep' introduces yet another source of spectral visitation. Here the secrets and the ghostly events to which they give rise hinge on the protagonist's memories of his unhappy childhood. On returning as an adult to his former home, he finds himself disturbed by the ghosts of family servants who return eerily from the region below stairs.

The emphasis that the haunted-house narrative places on familial secrets, especially ones of an illicit kind, makes it admirably suited, of course, to treating themes relating to queer sexuality and experience. However, whereas texts produced in the nineteenth-century, such as Henry James's *The Turn of the Screw*, tend to concentrate attention on the disruptive effects that queer sexuality has on heterosexual members of the household, while hinting at their sexual origins, contemporary writers frequently approach the topic directly from the viewpoint of the queer individual. Rebecca Buck's *Ghosts of Winter*, published in 2011, exemplifies this approach. The lesbian narrator, on inheriting the rural property of Winter Manor, finds her dreams disturbingly haunted by images of the same-sex couples who inhabited the house in the eighteenth century. She learns that, rather than leading a contented life there, they were forced, as a result of conventions relating to marriage and patrilineal property inheritance, to terminate their same-sex partnerships and succumb to the force of heterosexual social codes. Jameson Currier's story 'The Country House' in his collection *The Haunted Heart and Other Tales* (2009) also utilises the haunted-house narrative to explore the effect of oppressive events on the homosexual resident. The male gay couple whom Currier portrays owning the house in the present-day, on finding their life together disturbed by incidents of paranormal activity, search the interior for clues to their origin. The discovery of human bones dating from the eighteenth century buried in the chimney stack prompt the two men to investigate the history of the house. They discover, in so doing, information about an eighteenth-century labourer who inhabited it. After leading a life of sexual subterfuge, he was apprehended on a sodomy charge in 1765. Rebecca Brown's *The Haunted House* also merits attention. Like Buck's *Ghosts of Winter*, it represents a same-sex relationship disintegrating under the burden of hetero-patriarchal pressures. Assigning to the haunted-house narrative psychological significance, Brown portrays her lesbian narrator, as a result of unconsciously identifying with the egocentric alcoholic father who raised her and re-enacting his dominating behaviour, alienating her female lover and eventually forcing her to terminate the relationship. In this instance the house that the two lesbian women inhabit together, in addition to representing an actual property, moves in the course of the narrative to metaphorically signifying their relationship haunted by the oppressive attitude of one of the partners – and, as the chain of familial relationships unravels and their origin is perceived, by the oppressive influence exerted by the narrator's father.

Several of the stories treating queer relationships referred to above hinge, as the reader will have perceived, on secrets or mysteries of a sexual and emotional nature relating to the home and its members' histories. The emphasis they place on the home is, of course, unsurprising. As Fincher observes, 'The queerness of Gothic often resides where it is in fact least expected: in the family, not least because the Gothic has always been partly about dysfunctional families'.[36] The stories, as indicated above, generally conclude with the secrets on which they focus, though initially concealed, being discovered and, as the German nineteenth-century philosopher Friedrich Schelling observes, 'brought to light'[37] – as generally occurs with the uncanny and its workings. *The Water's Edge* (2003) by the British Louise Tondeur and *Winter Birds* (1984) by the American Jim Grimsley, the two queer haunted-house narrative selected for analysis here, display a similar movement.

Whereas Tondeur's novel explores the interrelation between lesbian and heterosexual relationships in the history of a rambling seaside hotel situated in the provincial town of Bournemouth on the English south coast, Grimsley re-works traditions of American Gothic and its rural associations. He also breaks with convention by employing as the construct of the house not a single property but a series of lodgings in North Carolina that, as the circumstances of the family renting them deteriorate on account of the father's alcoholism and bouts of violence, become increasingly bleak and dilapidated. Both novels, as is often the case in works of fiction focusing on the haunted house, though differing in location and the aspects of familial relationships on which they focus, employ children as narrators, utilising them as a mouthpiece for the occurrence of spectral events and uncanny fantasies. Tondeur assigns the role of narrator to an orphaned female relative of the family that runs the Water's Edge Hotel, the house that furnishes the setting for her narrative, whereas Grimsley employs a son of the family. Together, the two novels give us an insight into the differing approaches to sexuality and gender that the queer re-casting of the haunted-house narrative can create, as well as its treatment of spectral events and imagery.

Louise Tondeur is by no means unusual in focusing a work of haunted house fiction on a hotel, as she in fact does in *The Water's Edge*. As a spectral visitor to the Overlook Hotel in Stephen King's *The Shining* laconically observes, 'Every big hotel has a got a ghost. Why? Hell, people come and go'.[38] Ghosts also play a role in several earlier Gothic novels and stories that centre on hotel life, including Wilkie Collins's *The Haunted Hotel: A Mystery of Modern Venice* and M. R. James's atmospheric story 'Number 13' set on the British east coast. Tondeur's treatment of the form, however, differs from these three texts not only in its queer content but also in the significant use that it makes of other genres and forms of fiction. Classical myth, the family saga, fairy tale, the ghost story and, in keeping with the novel's queer dimension, the lesbian coming-out novel, all contribute to its structure.

Another feature that contributes to the complexity of Tondeur's treatment of the haunted-house narrative, besides the different genres and fictional forms that her novel incorporates, is the interplay of storylines she constructs in treating the lives of the family members who manage The Water's Edge Hotel, as well as their friends and lovers. She also foregrounds the theme of the concealing and revelation of illicit familial secrets, such as illegitimate births, jealousies between sisters, and lesbian involvements. She represents the latter as emerging unseen in the context of heterosexual family life and interacting with it in complex and unpredictable ways. The production of ghosts and uncanny events that this interplay of different sexualities creates contributes to the representation of the hotel as, to cite Freud in his discussion of the topic in 'The uncanny', an intriguingly imagined '*unheimlich* house'.[39]

The theme of the interrelation between lesbian and heterosexual familial formations and relationships that Tondeur explores in the novel has received attention in contemporary sociological studies. Commenting on the changes that have recently occurred in the discourse of kinship theory, Elizabeth Freeman describes how, whereas in earlier periods kinship tended to be defined chiefly in terms of relationships between heterosexual couples and their biological or adoptive offspring, the limitations of this model are now beginning to be recognised. Anthropologists increasingly acknowledge that, as she describes, 'Kinship is social and not biological, a matter of culture rather than nature'.[40]

Kath Weston in *Families We Choose*, a study to which Freeman refers, argues that queer people construct their social groupings and partnerships in terms of 'families of choice'.[41] Families of this kind, though frequently emerging in the context of heterosexual family life, do not necessarily merely imitate or copy heterosexual structures and formations but, on the contrary, sometimes creatively transform them. Ideas of this kind, especially the concept of a queer 'family of choice' that develops in the context of heteronormative familial relationships, form, as we shall see, the socio-sexual hub of Tondeur's haunted-house narrative.

The title *The Water's Edge* that Tondeur selects for her novel is of interest from a queer point of view. As well as referring to the coastal location of the hotel on which the novel focuses and the point of border-crossing between material and spectral worlds that it represents, it signifies the role that the hotel plays as a site of intersection between different sexualities – heterosexual, lesbian and bisexual. As well as tracing the way in which queer kinship formations develop within the context of the heterosexual family life of the hotel, Tondeur describes the interconnections and antagonisms existing between them.

As suits the plurality of characters and storylines that she introduces, Tondeur employs in the novel two narrators, one divine and the other human. The goddess Persephone who, on account of her immortality, is familiar with the hotel's long-term history, furnishes a frame for the narrative as a whole. Acting as a benevolent tutelary spirit, she arrives from Hades on the beach at Bournemouth each spring to keep an eye on the Hotel and record the activities of the family who run it, as well as those of the guests. Rice, the niece of Beatrice who manages the hotel in the 1980s, also acts as narrator, though, in contrast to Persephone, she gives the reader a personal and limited view of events. She is aged fourteen when she arrives at the hotel in 1984, and eighteen when she leaves in order to attend art school. Like Jane Eyre, dispatched to the care of Mrs Reed in Charlotte Brontë's novel, she is sent there on account of her orphaned situation. Her mother Suzie, Beatrice's sister, has recently died and Beatrice, though having broken off contact with her on account of her having had an affair with her ex-boyfriend, nonetheless feels duty bound to care for her daughter.

The goddess Persephone and the teenage Rice are portrayed as especially sensitive to paranormal influences, Persephone on account of her immortality and connection with Hades and Rice as a result of her maternal bereavement and the association with death that it signifies. Tondeur in fact opens the novel by portraying Rice, on embarking on the journey to the hotel where she is to live, as intuitively aware of the role that the ghosts inhabiting it and the secrets to which they have access will play in her future life. As Rice, on stepping into the train to Bournemouth, thinks, 'I felt like I was getting into the red carriage of a ghost train with my suitcase and pulling the safety bar down, and even though I didn't want to I was heading into the tunnel'.[42] Her reference to 'the ghost train', with its connections, on the one hand, with spectrality and, on the other, with the carnivalesque site of the funfair and its unorthodox associations, looks forward to the encounters with the spectral that she will later experience while living at the hotel and the transgressive secrets she will encounter there. It also evokes, in intertextual terms, echoes of Shirley Jackson's famous Gothic novel *The Haunting of Hill House* and her comparison of the architectural irregularities of the structure of Hill House to the 'crazy house at the carnival'.[43]

Like the lesbian relationships that emerge secretly from within their midst, the heterosexual attachments in which the three generations of women who run the hotel from the 1940s to the late-1980s in Tondeur's novel engage are by no means conventional. They illustrate the changing attitudes to sex and the socio-cultural movement from puritanical to permissive that the period reflected. The goddess Persephone describes how in the 1940s era of World War II, with the Hotel premises having been requisitioned by the Army to furnish accommodation for personnel on leave from the Front, Margaret, the daughter of Grace who managed the hotel at the time, had a love affair with an officer who was billeted there and became pregnant by him. To avoid the scandal of an illegitimate birth, Grace insisted that Margaret move to the attic bedroom known as 'Room Fifteen' and live there in hiding during her pregnancy. The goddess Persephone, commenting playfully on the puritanical mores of the period and representing Margaret's incarceration in terms of an episode from a fairy tale, describes how she 'was stashed away like Rapunzel because she had let down her hair down. Room Fifteen was her home for six whole round and heavy months' (p. 151). When Margaret eventually gave birth to her daughter Beatrice, Grace, as a further precaution against gossip, promoted the fiction that she herself was the mother of the baby. However, the secret of Beatrice's parentage eventually comes to light. As Persephone, continuing the fairy-tale analogy, observes, 'Gradually, I watched Beatrice grow up and find out who her parents were, or rather who they weren't, first her mother, then her father, as though she was in a fairy tale with a tower, a wolf and a peasant princess' (p. 152).

The hotel also furnishes the site of another illegitimate birth. Margaret's daughter Beatrice, on entering her teens in the era of free love of the 1960s, becomes infatuated not with a soldier but, influenced by the alternative culture of the era, a hippy-style youth called Timothy who works on the hotel premises as a cook. When Beatrice's daughter Esther is born, Timothy promptly leaves her, observing that he has no wish to being be tied down by family life. The goddess Persephone, indicating her Greek origins by comparing him to the hero Theseus who was faithless in love, describes how, 'In June 1970, he dumped Beatrice high and dry on an island, like Ariadne. He told her he was coming back, but he never did' (p. 200). Instead, on returning to Bournemouth after his travels abroad, he transfers his affections to Beatrice's sister Suzie and, when she too becomes pregnant, leaves before the baby Rice is born. The sisters Beatrice and Suzie avoid disclosing to their daughters, Esther and Rice, the fact that they share the same father, and it is only as teenagers, towards the end of the narrative, that the two girls discover the fact that they are half-sisters.

The culture of secrecy in which these familial events take place creates, as Tondeur describes, a fertile breeding-ground for ghosts. When Margaret's officer lover is killed in combat, his ghost appears in Room Fifteen. Margaret glimpses his face in the mirror and Grace, though telling people that she has decided to move to a room on the ground floor on account of her rheumaticky legs, in actual fact decides to do so, as she privately admits, 'because she had seen one too many ghosts... and didn't want to be kept awake any more' (pp. 151–2). From that point on the majority of family members and hotel visitors, sensing the room's spectral associations, make a point of avoiding it.

One of the few people who frequent Room Fifteen is the teenage Rice when, as a result of Beatrice offering her a home on her mother Suzie's death, she commences her new life at the hotel. On choosing it as her private retreat, she thinks, sensing its spectral atmosphere, 'I liked Room Fifteen because it had a ghostly feeling, as if all the people who had once slept in there had left a bit of themselves behind to haunt it' (pp. 35–6). In containing discarded items left by family members, Room Fifteen, although Rice is initially unaware of the fact, also has connections with lesbian relationships. Assuming that Rice would like to see a picture of her mother Suzie, Esther shows her a photo from Beatrice's photograph album. Unlike the typical family photo that, as Freeman observes, generally inscribes a heterosexual ideology and omits images of queer family members, this one interrelates images of queer people with heterosexual. It portrays the teenage Beatrice and Suzie sitting on the beach in front of the Hotel with their friend Meredith. Although Esther and Rice regard Meredith merely as Beatrice's friend, she is, as the two girls are subsequently to discover, her lover.

Queer sexuality, as mentioned in the introductory chapter, evokes on account of its transgressive and aberrant associations connotations of excess. To foreground this, Tondeur introduces in the novel references to other representations of excess. In addition to constructing the narrative around an excessive interplay of narrative lines and genres, she foregrounds the architectural complexity and superabundance of the hotel interior, with its hidden rooms and winding corridors. On initially exploring the building at the age of twelve, Rice thinks, 'The corridors seemed impossibly twisted, rooms were hidden in alcoves and cupboards tucked in next to fire doors' (p. 21). Her description reveals further echoes of Shirley Jackson's *The Haunting of Hill House* and the latter's reference to the eccentric and confusing architectural structure of Hill House's interior. Rice continues, hinting at the mysteries that the hotel conceals and her desire to discover the clues to them, 'I felt like I was inside a gigantic crossword puzzle. As we went I wondered about all the things that had happened in this new place I had come to live in and whether I would ever find out about them' (p. 21). Her observation, as well as reflecting her curiosity about the hotel's history, is also directed at readers of the novel. It encourages us to read on with the aim of discovering the mysterious 'things' that the pages will disclose.

On account of the role it plays as the hub of the spectral presences that haunt the hotel, Room Fifteen itself also evokes connotations of excess. It resembles in this respect Jean Copjec's account of what he terms 'the forbidden room'.[44] He describes how a room of this kind 'allows the house to constitute itself as a whole – but a whole from which this room is absent' (p. 23). Foregrounding its connections with the spectral, he dramatically states, 'It is the opening up of this empty space that makes the wind whistle and the living dead blow through the uncanny house' (p. 23). In addition Room 15 has associations, in the context of Female Gothic, with the 'red-room'[45] in Brontë's *Jane Eyre*, where the young Jane, on being imprisoned there, thinks that she sees the ghost of her uncle and, on account of this event and her aunt's unsympathetic response to her expressions of distress, collapses. The bedroom of the deceased Rebecca in Daphne Du Maurier's novel is also relevant here on account of the secrets that it harbours. The second Mrs De Winter, on surreptitiously entering it, is discovered there by the witch-like housekeeper Mrs Danvers. By showing her Rebecca's personal possessions such as her nightdress, the folds of which draped her body when she was alive, Mrs Danvers symbolically conjures up the presence of her former mistress.

It is, in fact, the goddess Persephone, the immortal keeper of the hotel records, who clarifies, for the benefit of the reader, the lesbian dimension of the hotel's history by describing the details of the sexual involvement that exists between Beatrice and Meredith. As she discloses, the two girls shared their first kiss as teenagers at the foot of the steps leading to the beach adjacent to the hotel in 1956. After separating for several years while Beatrice was living with Timothy and giving birth to Esther and Meredith was studying music at a college in London, they subsequently secretly renewed their relationship. Although Meredith currently spends much of the year touring abroad with the orchestra to which she belongs, she visits Esther regularly at the hotel. On encountering the teenage Rice, in the process of mourning her mother's death, she perceives that Rice needs help with coping with the traumatic effects of her bereavement. Rice responds with gratitude to Meredith's expressions of sympathy, welcoming the encouragement she gives her to unburden herself of the distress she feels at the terminal illness that her mother suffered. Eager to keep her memories of her mother alive, she thinks, 'I felt excited because Meredith had seen through me. She'd seen my dead mother underneath my skin and was making her come back to life a little with each word, and I wanted the words to tumble out of me and not stop' (p. 65). However, she feels incapable of revealing to Meredith the full intensity of her grief. In a statement recalling the psychoanalytic theory of Abraham and Torok,[46] she explains, 'I couldn't tell Meredith how I was feeling because it was like when you cut yourself really badly and then you get a scar... I couldn't tell Meredith all of the stuff about scars because it was secret' (pp. 75–6).

Irigaray, commenting on what she regards as the failure of male-authored traditions of psychoanalytic theory to analyse female relationships adequately, complains that, 'One thing has been singularly misunderstood, scarcely sketched out in the theory of the unconscious: the relationship of woman to mother and the relationship of woman to woman'.[47] The confidences that Rice shares with Meredith in her conversations with her centre on topics of this kind. She moves from divulging her deep emotional attachment to her mother and her response of intense distress at her death to confiding to her, as she moves into puberty, secrets relating to same-sex desire. Unaware of the fact that Esther is her half-sister, tells Meredith that she finds her 'bewitching' (p. 15) and thinks she would like to kiss her. Meredith understandably finds Rice's unexpected disclosure problematic since Beatrice has forbidden her to reveal to Rice her sororal relationship with Esther. Though feeling uneasy about doing so, Meredith respects

Beatrice's wishes and keeps the relationship between the two girls secret. The situation of Rice, unaware that Esther is her half-sister yet sensing she has some form of close emotional tie with her, echoes Abraham's theory. He posits the concept of an intergenerational secret – he calls it 'the phantom' – that is subliminally transferred from one familial generation to another, without the members consciously perceiving it. As he observes, 'What haunts us are not the dead, but the gaps left within us by the secrets of others'.[48] Rice appears unconsciously to intuit the fact that she and Esther are intimately related, though at this point in the narrative she is unaware precisely in what way.

The emotional bond that develops between the teenage Rice and the older Meredith, as well as being of interest from a feminist and psychoanalytic perspective, encourages the reader to perceive the difficulty that queer people experience in finding an appropriate terminology to describe their relationships with one another and the different forms and degrees of attachment they signify. Meredith is unrelated biologically to Rice. She is neither her aunt, nor her sister, nor her mother. The term 'mentor', sometimes employed to depict a relationship between an older and a younger homosexual man, has predominantly male associations and also appears too formal. Whereas heterosexual society is notably rich in the terms that it employs to define familial relationships, both lateral and relating to descent, the queer community, as a result of its relationships having been stigmatised and treated as unspeakable, has notably few. As Freeman observes, 'We lack names that would individuate participants within larger formations like affairs, ménages a trois, cliques or subcultures' (p. 296). Dismissing the term 'queer "extended family"' as inappropriate since it 'collapses into amorphous and generic "community"', she perceptively observes that, on account of this deficiency, 'Sexual minorities are stranded between individualistic notions of identity on the one hand and on the other a romanticized notion of community' (p. 297).

The eventual revelation of the secret of Rice's and Esther's sororal connection, combined with Meredith's and Beatrice's lesbian relationship, with which Tondeur concludes the novel, transforms its denouement into a thrillingly double-stranded coming-out narrative. This, of course, suits the novel's Gothic dimension for, as Eleanor Salotto observes, commenting on the role that the motif of blocked narration plays in Gothic fiction, the revelation of the secret, though delayed, will inevitably take place, returning 'to haunt the narrative'.[49] Derrida too endorses the fact that the secret, as he writes, 'does not conceal itself' and, as a result, is discoverable.⁵⁰ It is Meredith who, as suits the emotionally supportive role that she has played in Rice's life, divulges to her the important news that she and Esther are half-sisters. Rice, who by now has transferred the sexual attraction that she felt for Esther to another girl and, as Tondeur hints, subsequently adopts a lesbian lifestyle, responds gladly to the news. She senses that it explains the emotional closeness that she feels to Esther, the conviction that, as she states, 'We were sisters underneath our skin' (p. 307). Her feeling in this respect connects with a comment voiced by Dennis Flannery who, in his study of sibling love and queer attachment, refers to the way in which writers such as Willa Cather and Herman Melville frequently treat sibling affection 'as a model for ethically validated intimacy and as a route to queer life'.⁵¹

In addition Esther, who has just that moment received the news from Beatrice, excitedly announces to Rice the fact that Beatrice and Meredith are in fact sexual partners. Bounding up to her ebulliently, she announces, 'My Mum swings both ways!' (p. 188). Rice, who is unfamiliar with the phrase, admits that 'I had only a vague idea what she meant. I pictured Beatrice swinging from tree to tree above a jungle floor, orange like an orang-utan' (p. 194). However, on understanding its meaning, she joyfully embraces the two women 'with a new kind of excitement' (p. 188).

The exorcising of kinship secrets, both lesbian and heterosexual, from the life of the family running The Water's Edge Hotel has the effect of introducing a new era of openness and honesty. Tondeur registers its importance by consigning the present building, representing, as it does, an earlier culture of sexual prejudice and secrecy, to the flames. The fire that she describes destroying the building echoes the concluding episodes of Brontë's *Jane Eyre* and its daughter text Du Maurier's *Rebecca*, two female Gothic novels that feature prominently in the intertextual structure of *The Water's Edge*. Brontë's *Jane Eyre* and the 'daughter' novels that it has inspired, have played, in fact, an important role in contributing to the intertextual structure of contemporary lesbian and queer fiction. *Cereus Blooms At Night* by the Trinidadian Shani Mootoo, that I discuss in my earlier publication *The Queer Uncanny*, also alludes to Brontë's novel, as well as to Jean Rhys's *The Wide Sargasso Sea* and the motif of the burning down of the family mansion that features in the conclusion of the two novels.

Tondeur aptly concludes her narrative by portraying Persephone describing how, 'The hotel's ghosts and monsters, who usually hid in dusty cupboards and corners' (p. 236) leave the ruins of the building and wander down to the beach waiting to be 'taken down to Hades through the gateway that lies just beneath the surface of the sea' (p. 239). They carry with them the remnants of the culture of sexual secrecy and hypocrisy that, as Tondeur imaginatively depicts, has oppressed the previous residents of the hotel and their friends and lovers.

Jim Grimsley's *Winter Birds*, as well as creating a very different version of the haunted-house narrative, in both geographical setting and the treatment of spectrality, from Tondeur's *The Water's Edge*, also raises a key question relevant to the ghost story. Can a novel validly be termed one if it does not refer, however fleetingly, to a ghost or to spiritualist practices? The critics Leon Edel[52] and T. J. Lustig[53] argue that it can. Referring to stories by Henry James that do not refer to a ghost, they argue that the emphasis they place on secrets, combined with the introduction of passages with spectral significance, relate the texts to the fictional form. Smith, discussing E. T. A. Hoffmann's 'The Sandman', endorses their argument. He observes that, although 'Hoffmann's tale is not a ghost story as conventionally understood', the fact that Freud, in analysing it, alerts attention to its 'ghostly symbolism' gives it, in metaphorical terms, spectral significance.[54] Developing Freud's reading of Hoffmann's story, Smith argues that the protagonist Nathaniel is 'in thrall to a spectral, oedipal past and so is ghosted by a particular oedipal anxiety that is represented in symbolic form' (p. 15).

Grimsley develops the tradition of the ghostless ghost story imaginatively in *Winter Birds*. After having initially failed to find a publisher on account of the disturbingly violent image of American family life that it portrays, he eventually published the novel in 1994. He focuses the narrative of domestic violence that it relates on the series of derelict houses in rural North Carolina that the poverty-stricken Crell family rent, as its members move down the social scale as a result of their internal conflicts and diminishing finances. The different properties they inhabit are haunted not only by poverty but also by the father Bobjay's alcoholism and the violent rampages and incidents of sexual harassment, generally directed at his wife Ellen, in which he engages. Grimsley portrays Bobjay as both a perpetrator of male violence and a victim of misfortune. He earns a living as a labourer, and the loss of one of his arms in a machinery accident while he was working on an agricultural site limits his ability to obtain work. The sense of humiliation this provokes, rather than encouraging him to treat his family more caringly, serves only to exacerbate his sense of frustration and anger, increasing the frequency of his fits of rage.

A distinctive feature of the novel, helping to account for its poignancy and emotional power, is the tension that Grimsley creates between the material world and the spectral. Whereas he describes Bobjay's physical assaults on Ellen and the rooms and the yard in which they occur in realistic detail, his introduction of spectral imagery, employed especially in relation to Bobjay and the eerily oppressive influence he exerts on the household, gives the novel a significantly Gothic dimension.

Reference to the patriarchal home as a site of violence receives attention in both radical feminist and post-modern writing. Adrienne Rich observes that, though the word 'Motherhood calls to mind the home',[55] encouraging us to envisage it as a cosy, peaceful environment, the term in fact often signifies a place of danger and physical brutality. Mark Wigley goes further. He grimly describes the home as 'not simply a site of a particular subordination, a particulate kind of violence' but, on account of the hierarchically gendered relationships on which it is traditionally structured, 'the very principle of violence'.[56] The representation of the home in these terms, as well as featuring in feminist and gender studies, also occurs in Gothic. The acts of domestic violence that works of Gothic fiction frequently depict are generally represented as originating, as Fred Botting describes, 'in the failings or tyrannical impostures of the paternal figure'.[57] As he illustrates, discussions hinging on the difference between the benevolent father and the tyrannical have informed examples of the genre since its advent in the eighteenth century. Ann Radcliffe's *The Castle of Udolpho* and Maria Roche's *Clermont*, published in the eighteenth century, and Stephen Kings' *The Shining*, published in the twentieth, furnish illustrations.

Although all six of Bobjay's children are portrayed as victims of his erratic fits of rage, it is the eight-year-old haemophiliac Danny, employed by Grimsley as narrator, who appears especially entrapped in the crossfire that his parents' conflicts and marital breakdown generate. Danny's narrative, like that of Nathaniel in Freud's commentary on Hoffmann's 'The Sandman', has oedipal connotations. Grimsley contrasts Danny's hatred of Bobjay and the brutal form of masculinity that his father exemplifies with his intense love for and identification with his mother Ellen. Danny's distress at the misery and hopelessness of his situation are reflected in the macabre names that he privately assigns to the ramshackle properties where he and his family have lived. They include 'the Snake House'[58] infested with rattlesnakes, 'the Ice House' (p. 26), memorable for its lack of heating and the ominously named 'Blood House' (p. 34) where, in an attempt to protect Ellen from Bobjay's violence, he fell over and bit his tongue. His efforts to protect her on this occasion nearly cost him his life since he almost bled to death and had to spend some weeks in the local hospital.

In addition to portraying Danny expressing his distress at his familial situation by describing the houses where he has lived in images redolent of a horror film, Grimsley employs spectral imagery to evoke Danny's view of his view of his father as a monstrous apparition who haunts their lives. Danny describes his conversations with his brothers while walking in the fields near their home as interrupted by the ghostly sound of Bobjay's voice echoing scarily across the fields. He ominously depicts it as 'a flat thread of sound' that, rather than appearing human, resembles 'a sound like an animal would make' (p. 3). Referring to the terror that it inspires, he adds, 'You feel yourself go empty listening to it... You walk to the river, hoping you will find a place there to hide from the noise' (p. 3). On hearing the sound transmitted across the landscape by the wind in the trees, he thinks, 'But the pines cannot hold back Papa's voice. When you hear it, you stand still' (p. 17). Danny's representation of the terror that Bobjay's voice inspires in him has the effect of representing Bobjay as a monstrous supernatural force rather than a human being. It looks forward to King's description in *Pet Sematary*, published the year after Grimsley's novel, of the terror that the sound that the supernatural Wendigo emits inspires in Louis, as he follows his elderly neighbour Jud to the native American burial ground. Louis similarly describes, 'How the sound seemed at first distant, then very close; moving away and then moving ominously toward them.'[59]

Danny associates Bobjay with spectrality not only in an outdoor environment but also in the claustrophobic interior of the home. His description of how, on approaching Ellen, Bobjay's 'large, dark body cast a sudden gloom on her, and she was almost afraid to look up at him' (p. 100) makes him resemble an oppressive phantom haunting the living room. Representing his body as paradoxically signifying both excess and lack, Danny describes how he himself and the other children fall silent in his presence 'because he was always frowning, and because the place where his whole arm used to be looked vacant and strange' (p. 26). Here the scrutiny to which Danny subjects his father has the effect of transforming the latter into the passive object of his gaze, de-masculinising him and making him appear deformed and deficient. Despite the tyranny to which

Bobjay subjects the family, he is represented in this instance not as a powerful and physically vigorous figure but as abject and grotesque – though nonetheless frightening as a result of his very strangeness. The contrary representations of him that Grimsley creates in the novel recall the representation of the figure of the monster in Gothic fiction and the contrary images, both powerful and abjectly pathetic, that writers such as Mary Shelley assign to him.

Whereas the spectral references that Danny applies to Bobjay have the effect of transforming him metaphorically into a phantom or monster, those he applies to Ellen evoke, on the contrary, fragility and a pathetic heroism. When, in a desperate attempt to avoid Bobjay's attack, she escapes outdoors and tries to conceal herself in the yard, Danny, on momentarily catching sight of her, describes her as 'a paler shadow in the light that drifts under the house's raised ledge' (p. 129). In addition, after Bobjay has attacked her in a fit of rage, he observes how, in the haze from the latter's cigarette smoke, 'Breath shivering into her, she leans up on thin arms, a swirl of smoke twining round her and light filling her hair' (p. 144). The description serves to transform Ellen from the fragile victim of physical violence to a figure evoking angelic connotations, with her hair magically transformed into a gleaming halo. Despite the efforts that she makes to elude or repel Bobjay's physical assault and protect the children from him, even resorting on occasion to locking them in the car, her efforts, as Danny painfully recognises, are futile. As is the case with many women, her financial dependence on her husband deters her from seeking help. As she rhetorically asks the doctor at the hospital when he urges her to contact the police and charge her husband with criminal assault, 'If he were in jail, who would feed the family?' (p. 66).

However *Winter Birds* does not only tell a story of domestic violence and the damaging physical and psychological effects that it has on Danny, his mother Ellen and the other members of the Crell family. Enriching and complicating the narrative is Grimsley's treatment of the theme of the boy's 'introduction into the symbolic order of masculinity'[60] by means of identification with a male adult that the queer theorist David M. Halperin describes it as frequently involving. Grimsley treats this topic in the subsidiary storyline he introduces that focuses on Danny's fantasy construction of an idealised individual whom he names 'The River Man'. Arguing that 'the renewal of manhood has to take place, to a significant extent, outside the family' (p. 151), Halperin refers to the important role that a male figure who is unrelated to the family, such as a teacher or mentor, can perform in this respect (p. 158). Since Danny, on account of his biological father's brutal behaviour, has no actual individual in his life to perform this role, he invents a fantasy construct. Grimsley's portrayal of Danny walking by the river that runs near his home and singing to himself the consolatory words of the hymn 'Shall we ga-ather at the ri-v-er, the be-oo-tiful ri-i-ver' (p. 9), the melody of which features in the 1950s and 1960s Westerns directed by John Ford, with their focus on constructs of masculinity and male antagonisms, indicates the role that the river plays as a source of inspiration in his personal mythology. Its banks furnish a temporary respite from his father's rages and, as a result, he names The River Man after it. Constructing the persona of The River Man on the images of the heroes in the films that he and his siblings watch on television, one of the few forms of entertainment to which they have access in rural North Carolina, Danny pictures him as a model of ideal masculinity who exhibits generosity, patience and tenderness – all the attributes, in fact, that his biological father Bobjay lacks. He describes The River Man as 'tall and brown-skinned' (p. 10), with a voice that is 'warm and deep' (p. 11) and a body that, in contrast to Bobjay's, is physically intact. He foregrounds his protectiveness, describing his mysterious underwater cave as furnishing a shelter from Bobjay's violence. By portraying The River Man as Bobjay's polar opposite in character and appearance, Grimsley develops the debate about paternal authority and the differences between the tyrannical and benevolent father figure that features frequently in Gothic.[61]

Grimsley describes Danny's emotional attachment to The River Man as chiefly filial in nature. As indicated by Danny's observation, 'You see in his eyes every minute he cares for you' (p. 10) and by his description of The River Man promoting his interest in sport and encouraging him to protect and fondle the deer and rabbits that his older brothers habitually shoot, he appears to regard him primarily as a surrogate father figure. However, since fantasy is mobile, Danny also endows The River Man with a maternal aspect. After picturing him in heroic terms, 'rising out of the black water, ice dripping from his muscular chest and arms' (p. 204), he describes how he 'kneels, finds you wounded in the honeysuckle and carries you down to the bottom of the river' (p. 204). Here The River Man places Danny gently in his own bed in his underwater cave and, as Danny describes, tenderly 'gets a blanket...maybe the fur of a big animal, spreads it over you and you sigh at its engulfing heaviness and warmth' (p. 15). The River Man destabilising of gender boundaries recalls the transsexual theorist Kate Bornstein's reference to the queer significance of the 'transgressively gendered individual' and the 'gender ambiguities'[62] he displays. It also echoes Sedgwick's inclusion of 'feminist men' and 'other criss-crossings of definitional lines'[63] in the account that she gives of 'the mesh of possibilities, overlaps, dissonances and resonances' (p. 8) that the concept 'queer' can encompass.

Whereas writers of Gothic generally associate the fantasy world with spectral imagery while representing the material world realistically, Grimsley on occasion does the reverse. He represents the fantasy underwater world, where Danny pictures The River Man living, as free from the taint of the spectral, while describing Danny's family life, as illustrated by his representation of Bobjay and Ellen, cited above, in imagery redolent of it. This indicates the way in which, regarded from Danny's traumatised viewpoint, his home and familial relationships appear increasingly illusory and uncanny while his excursions into the compensatory fantasy realm of The River Man's cave strike him as real.

However, as Danny's references to the river's depth and its dark appearance indicate, the fantasies that he creates around it alternatively assume on occasion an ominous aspect. He associates the river at times with the thoughts of drowning that intermittently haunt him, since, as he perceives, suicide, as well as enabling him to escape Bobjay's act of violence, would liberate him from his guilt-feelings about his mother Ellen's predicament and his inability, on account of his youth, to rescue her. Gazing at his own reflection in the river, Danny thinks, 'You're so white you might as well be a ghost' (p. 16). His self-portrayal is ambiguous in effect. Though intimating his fear of death, it simultaneously indicates his longing for it since it would allow him to escape his conflicted familial situation by enabling him to collapse into a state of entropy and un-differentiation. In referring to entropy Grimsley re-works a theme that, as Rosemary Jackson illustrates,[64] has significant Gothic associations, featuring especially powerfully in the work of Edgar Allan Poe.

Reference to entropy occurs again in the context of the bleeding that Danny suffers, when the doctor who is attending him at the hospital experiences difficulty in staunching the flow of blood. Envisaging his transformation into a corpse and personifying the blood as it oozes from his body, Danny fatalistically thinks, 'Your blood had always wanted to be free of your body... it wanted to leave you flat and empty' (p. 60). His desire for self-annihilation reaches a peak when, one wintry night when Bobjay is absent from home, he leaves the house and wanders out into the fields. Gazing in fascination at the snowy expanse of 'perfect whiteness', he thinks, '[w]hile you watch it, part of you is dissolved into it and you are not afraid, you are blank' (p. 174). His personal musings are interrupted, however, by the recognition that the sensation of 'absolute emptiness' he is experiencing 'will never last' (p. 174) and, when Bobjay returns, he will again experience a response of fear.

Whereas certain episodes in Grimsley's novel, such as those focusing on the river, are constructed around the element of water, others centre on fire. He portrays Danny, while burning the rubbish in the yard, unconsciously re-enacting his father's macho behaviour, seeking to destroy him. Picturing himself, in an image that, though appropriated from the patriarchal context of the Old Testament, also has associations with the genre of Horror, as an agent of divine retribution, he describes himself as 'angry as God was when Moses struck the rock' (p. 148). Turning to a pagan reference, he proceeds to portrays himself as a witch, 'a master of fire', while envisaging 'this bag of trash' that he is about to throw into the blaze as 'a city you mean to level' (p. 148). Picturing his father's face at the centre of the fire, he watches the flames ignite the margarine wrappers that he is burning and, as he ghoulishly describes, 'curl the flesh inward like this paper, till it burns him and blackens him to the eyes' (p. 148). The images of body horror that Grimsley employs in the episode furnish him with a powerful vehicle to represent Danny's intense hatred of his father and the pain that he longs to inflict on him. It endorses Aldana Reyes's account of the role that reference to the genre of Horror can perform in representing anguish and intense passions.[65] Although Danny's vindictive utterances are emotionally disturbing, since they portray him emulating his father's violence in his imagination and indicate the brutalising effect it is having on him, their performative aspect indicates that they also furnish him with a strategy to articulate and survive the misery of his family life.

The novel concludes with a description of Danny walking home with his mother from the river bank where, knowing the attraction that the site holds for him and possibly nervous of the river's dangerous implications, she has come to seek him. Foregrounding the archetypal dimension of both the scene itself and the bond between mother and son that it evokes, Grimsley portrays Danny thinking, 'You are a little boy following your Mama across the field. She has found you by the river and brought you home'. Hinting at the idea of suicide that he appears for the moment to have rejected, he thinks, 'You did not go down to the black water where The River Man was waiting' (p. 209). However, referring indirectly to the ambiguous role that The River Man's underwater cave assumes in the narrative as a protective environment or alternatively a site of death, he fatalistically adds, 'But you will return to the river as long as you live in this house' (p. 209). His comment alerts us to the fact that Danny's narrative, as Grimsley recounts it, remains open-ended and unfinished, encouraging the reader to complete it, for good or ill, in his own imagination. In addition, by throwing it open to his readers, Grimsley foregrounds the generic nature of Danny's story, alerting attention to the fact that other boys may experience oppressive familial contexts of a similar kind.

The novels discussed in this chapter furnish an insight into the role that spectrality and the motif of the haunted house associated with it play in contemporary queer Gothic fiction. As Berman's *Vintage: A Ghost Story*, that interrelates a narrative set in the present with ones in located in the past, and Waters's neo-Victorian novel *Affinity* illustrate, reference to spectrality furnishes writers with a vehicle to treat different forms of male gay and lesbian history. Berman's *Vintage: A Ghost Story* represents the teenage narrator's encounter with a ghost from the 1970s introducing him – and the reader – to the problems and oppressive experiences encountered by a homosexual teenager living in an earlier period. As indicated above, Berman's treatment of spectrality reveals interesting connections with present-day queer historiography. Freccero's reference to the erotic dimension of historical research and the claim she makes that it provides a site for 'the ghosts to speak' is important in this respect.[66]

Instead of interrelating episodes set in the present with ones from the past, as Berman does, Waters locates *Affinity* in 1870s London, focusing on the spiritualist movement that flourished in the era. While illustrating the importance of the séance as furnishing an area in which the participants can make same-sex erotic contact, she also utilises spectrality metaphorically to depict the different forms of social invisibility that the lesbian, the spinster and the house maid experience in male-dominated society. She also foregrounds the Victorian context of her novel by introducing intertextual allusions to Dickens's *Bleak House*. The version of history she constructs in the novel interestingly reveals connections with the historiographer Traub's 'cycle of salience' model.

Turning to Tondeur's *The Water's Edge* and Grimsley's *Winter Birds*, we find that the structure of the haunted-house narrative they both employ furnishes a context for writers to explore the emotional tensions and sexual secrets, both heterosexual and queer, that infiltrate the world of the family. Tondeur utilises reference to spectrality to explore the interrelation between lesbian, bisexual and heterosexual relationships in the history of a family running a hotel on the English south coast. The complexity of her narrative is increased by her utilisation of two narrators, the twelve-year-old Rice and the omniscient goddess Persephone, as well as by the interplay between different fictional genres that she constructs. They include the fairy tale, the bildungsroman and the lesbian coming-out narrative. In employing the fourteen-year-old Rice as narrator and referring to her feelings of erotic attraction to other girls, Tondeur continues the trend, one that, as Margareta Georgivia describes, features in nineteenth-century Gothic fiction, of employing a child as narrator or protagonist and associating her with the homoerotic.[67]

Rejecting the conventional connection of the haunted-house narrative with a rambling Gothic-style mansion, Grimsley selects as the location for *Winter Birds* the series of derelict homes that the American Crell family are reduced to renting, as their fortunes decline on account of the father Bobjay's alcoholism and violent behaviour. Depicting these disturbing events from the viewpoint of the eight-year-old haemophiliac Danny, Grimsley foregrounds the boy's sense of helplessness in being unable to protect his mother from his father's attacks. Grimsley also focuses attention on the fantasy construct of 'The River Man', inspired by the local river, that Danny creates, exploring the ambiguous role that it plays in his imagination.

Spectrality and the haunted house, though assuming, as illustrated above, a major role in queer Gothic fiction, exemplify, of course, only two of the motifs that feature prominently in it. Chapter 3 introduces the reader to two other motifs that also play a key role: the vampire and the uncanny double. The vampire, as we shall see, is significant for the changes in representation that it has undergone, largely as a result of being utilised as a vehicle for the depiction of queer sexualities in texts inspired by the 1970s and 1980s lesbian and gay liberation movements. The shift from monstrous predator to 'sympathetic vampire' it has experienced, one initiated to a large extent by queer theorists and writers, is especially important in this respect. The uncanny double, as I shall also illustrate, is notable for the versatile contribution it makes to different forms of queer fiction, including the AIDS narrative and novels focusing on transgender and transsexuality.

Notes

1. Andrew Smith, 'Hauntings', in Catherine Spooner and Emma McEvoy (eds), *The Routledge Companion to Gothic*, p. 153. (Smith 2007).
2. John Fletcher, 'The Haunted Closet: Henry James's Queer Spectrality', *Textual Practice* 14/1 (2000), 53–80. (Fletcher 2000).
3. Castle, *The Apparitional Lesbian*, p. 5.
4. Coral Lansbury, *Elizabeth Gaskell: The Novel of Sexual Crisis*, p. 211. (Lansbury 1975).
5. Liz Cox, *'Bridling her neck of ivory, and curling her lip of carmine': Gothic Narratives of Lesbian Identity and Desire in British Women's Fiction, 1840–1890* (PhD Thesis, January 2008, Warwick University), p. 2. (Cox 2008).
6. Simon Hay, *A History of the British Ghost Story*, pp. 86–87. (Hay 2011).
7. Catherine Lundoff, *Haunted Hearths and Sapphic Shades*, pp. 69–82. (Lundoff 2008).
8. Jameson Currier, 'The Country House', in Currier (ed.), *The Haunted Heart and Other Tales*, p. 52. (Currier 2009).
9. Edmund White, 'An Oracle', in Adam Mars-Jones and Edmund White (eds), *A Darker Proof: Stories from a Crisis*, p. 250. (White 1988).
10. Gabrielle Griffin, *Heavenly Love? Lesbian Images in Twentieth-Century Women's Writing*, p. 69. (Griffin 1993).
11. Martha Vicinus, 'They Wonder to Which Sex I Belong: The Historical Roots of the Modern Lesbian Identity', in Dennis Altman and Carole Vance (eds), *Homosexuality, Which Homosexuality?*, p. 172. (Vicinus 1989).
12. George Haggerty, 'The History of Homosexuality Reconsidered', in Chris Mounsey (ed.), *Developments in the Histories of Sexualities*, pp. 1–5. See also Valerie Traub, 'The Present Future of Lesbian Historiography', in George Haggerty and Molly McGary (eds), *The Blackwell Companion to Lesbian, Gay, Bisexual, Transgender and Queer Studies*. (Traub 2007).
13. Julian Wolfreys, *Victorian Hauntings: Spectrality, Gothic, the Uncanny and Literature*, p. 7. (Wolfreys 2002).
14. Steve Berman, *Vintage: A Ghost Story*, p. 15 (Berman 2007). Subsequent references are to this edition and in the text.
15. Freud, 'The Uncanny', pp. 371–2.
16. Nicolas Abraham and Maria Torok, *The Shell and the Kernel: Renewals of Psychoanalysis*, translated by Nicholas T. Rand, p. 171. (Abraham and Torok 1994).
17. Smith alerts attention to this in his discussion of James's story in *The Ghost Story 1840–1920*, p. 131.
18. Hay, *A History of the British Ghost Story*, p. 9.

19. Carla Freccero, *Queer, Early, Modern*, p. 80 (Freccero 2006). See also Valerie Traub, 'The Present Future of Lesbian Historiography' in Haggerty and McGarry (eds), *The Blackwell Companion to Lesbian, Gay, Transgender and Queer Studies*, p. 126.
20. Sarah Waters, 'Hot Waters', *The Guardian*, G.2, Thursday, 26 September 2002, p. 9. http://wwww.guardian.co.uk/books/2002/sept26/ arts feature. (Waters 2002).
21. Waters, *Affinity*, p. 46. Subsequent references are to this edition and in the text. (Waters 1999).
22. Hilary Grimes, *The Late Victorian Gothic: Mental Science, the Uncanny and Scenes of Writing*, p. 91. (Grimes 2011).
23. Margaret Whitford (ed.), *The Irigaray Reader*, p. 9. (Whitford 1991).
24. Grimes, *The Late Victorian Gothic*, p. 91.
25. Tatiana Kontou, *Spiritualism and Women's Writing: From the Fin de Siècle to the Neo-Victorian*, p. 194. (Kontou 2000).
26. Rachel Carroll, 'Rethinking Generational History: Queer Histories of Sexuality in Neo-Victorian Feminist Fiction', *Studies in the Literary Imagination*, 39/2, (2006), 143. (Carroll 2006).
27. Linda Hutcheon, *A Poetics of Postmodernism: History, Theory, Fiction*, p. 137. (Hutcheon 1988).
28. Hélène Cixous, 'Exchange', in Cixous and Catherine Clement, *The Newly Born Woman*, translated by Betsy Wing, p. 152. (Cixous 1986).
29. Jane Gallop, *The Daughter's Seduction: Feminism and Psychoanalysis*, p. 146. (Gallop 1982).
30. Jacques Derrida, *Memoires for Paul de Man*, translated by Cecile Lindsay, Jonathan Culler and Eduardo Cadava, p. 80. (Derrida 1986).
31. Julian Wolfreys, *Victorian Hauntings*, p. 110.
32. Paulina Palmer, '"She began to show me the words she had written, one by one": Lesbian Reading and Writing Practices in the Fiction of Sarah Waters', *Women: A Cultural Review*, 19/1 (2008), 69–86. (Palmer 2008).
33. Holly Furneaux, *Queer Dickens: Erotics, Families, Masculinities*, p. 219. (Furneaux 2009).
34. Charles Dickens, *Bleak House*, ed. Stephen Gill, p. 268. (Dickens 1996).
35. Ruth Parkin-Gounelas, *Literature and Psychoanalysis: Intertextual Readings*, p. 123. (Parkin-Gounelas 2001).
36. Fincher, 'Queer Gothic', p. 535.
37. See Freud, 'The Uncanny', p. 345.
38. Stephen King, *The Shining*, p. 158. (King 1987).
39. Freud, 'The Uncanny', p. 364.

40. Elizabeth Freeman, 'Queer Belongings: Kinship Theory and Queer Theory', in George E. Haggerty and Molly McGary (eds), *A Companion to Lesbian, Gay, Bisexual, Transgender, and Queer Studies*, p. 299. (Freeman 2007).
41. Kath Weston, *Families We Choose: Lesbians, Gays, Kinship*, pp. xv–xix. (Weston 1977).
42. Louise Tondeur, *The Water's Edge*, p. 9. Subsequent references are to this edition and in the text. (Tondeur 2003).
43. Shirley Jackson, *The Haunting of Hill House*, p. 44. (Jackson 1987).
44. Jean Copjec, 'Vampires, Breast Feeding and Anxiety', in Botting and Townshend (eds), *Gothic: Critical Concepts in Literature and Cultural Studies*, vol. 4, p. 23. (Copjec 2004).
45. Charlotte Brontë, *Jane Eyre*, p. 10 (Brontë 1940). Brontë's 'red-room' and its Gothic significance was powerfully recreated in visual terms in Louise Bourgeois's installations on show at Tate Modern Art Gallery, London, in 2007.
46. Rice's reference to the secret 'scar' that she feels concealed within her is illuminated by reference to Abraham's and Torok's concept of the crypt. Reworking the Freudian concept of repression, the analysts envisage the crypt as a secret realm within the subject's psyche where the lost object is buried and preserved. See Abraham and Torok, *The Shell and the Kernel*, pp. 174–5.
47. Helene Vivienne Wenzel, 'Introduction to Luce Irigaray's "And the One Doesn't Stir without the Other"', *Signs: Journal of Women in Culture and Society*, 7/1 (1981), 57. (Wenzel 1981).
48. Abraham, 'Notes on the Phantom: A Complement to Freud's Metapsychology', *Critical Enquiry*, 13 (1986/7), 287 (Abraham 1986). See also Royle, *The Uncanny*, p. 280.
49. Eleanor Salotto, *Gothic Returns in Collins, Dickens, Zola and Hitchcock*, p. 20. (Salotto 2006).
50. Jacques Derrida, 'Passions: "An Oblique Offering"', in David Wood (ed.), *Derrida: A Critical Reader*, p. 21. (Derrida 1992).
51. Dennis Flannery, *On Sibling Love, Queer Attachment and American Writing*, p. 14. (Flannery 2007).
52. Leon Edel, 'Introduction' in Edel (ed.), *The Ghostly Tales of Henry James*, p. xvii. (Edel 1948).
53. T. J. Lustig, *Henry James and the Ghostly*, p. 2. (Lustig 1994).
54. Andrew Smith, *The Ghost Story 1840–1920: A Cultural History*, p. 14. (Smith 2010).
55. Adrienne Rich, *Of Woman Born: Motherhood as Experience and Institution*, p. 274. (Rich 1977).
56. Mark Wigley, *The Architecture of Deconstruction: Derrida's Haunt*, p. 137. (Wigley 1995).

57. Fred Botting, 'The Gothic Production of the Unconscious', in Glennis Byron and David Punter (eds.), *Spectral Readings: Towards a Gothic Geography*, p. 28. (Botting 1999).
58. Jim Grimsley, *Winter Birds* (1984), p. 19. Subsequent references are to this edition and in the text. (Grimsley 1997).
59. Stephen King, *Pet Sematary*, p. 128. (King 1983).
60. David M. Halperin, 'Deviant Teaching', in George E. Haggerty and Molly McGarry (eds), *A Companion to Lesbian, Gay, Bisexual, Transgender and Queer Studies*, p. 158. (Halperin 2007).
61. See note 57, this chapter.
62. Kate Bornstein, *Gender Outlaw: On Men, Women, and the Rest of Us*, p. 98. (Bornstein 1984).
63. Eve Kosofsky Sedgwick, 'Queer and Now', in Sedgwick, *Tendencies*, p. 8. (Sedgwick 1994).
64. Rosemary Jackson, *Fantasy: The Literature of Subversion*, p. 80. (Jackson 1981).
65. Xavier Aldana Reyes, *Body Gothic: Corporeal Transgression in Contemporary Literature and Horror Film*, pp. 17–19. (Reyes 2014).
66. Freccero, *Queer, Early, Modern*, p. 21.
67. See Margarita Georgieva, *The Gothic Child*, p. 91. (Georgieva 2013).

CHAPTER 3

Uncanny Others: Vampires and Doubles

UNCANNY OTHERS

The motifs of the vampire and the other weird and monstrous figures who shadow the narrators and protagonists of Victorian fiction in the form of uncanny doubles, exemplified by the creature that Frankenstein constructs and Jekyll's alter-ego Hyde, have been key components of Gothic since the nineteenth century. Although their present-day representation, especially that of the vampire, has prompted expressions of disapproval from critics working in both earlier forms of Gothic[1] and contemporary[2] who complain that their image is being trivialised and rendered over-familiar, they continue to flourish in fiction and film. There is, in fact, one particular readership and audience who, remembering their own oppressive history and the persecution that their fellows in countries abroad continue to experience, responds positively to the representation of these figures and identifies with their outcast status. This is the queer community. As Greg Herren and J. M. Redmann, writing in 2012 in the introduction to their collection of queer Gothic tales *Night Shadows*, observe, 'Gays, lesbians, bisexuals, and the transgendered, as members of both a repressed and a suppressed community pushed to the margins by the mainstream, can understand and identify with these works – for they focus on the marginalized and outsider'.[3]

Critics working in the field of film also remark on the sense of identification that the vampire and monstrous double evoke in the queer spectator. As Richard Dyer and his fellow critics, discussing the cinematic image of the vampire in an essay in *Sight and Sound*, observe, 'If the vampire is an other, he or she was always a figure in whom one could find oneself'.[4] The fact that, in addition to that produced by Herren and Redmann, other collections of queer Gothic tales focusing on the vampire and the monster continue to appear in print[5] indicates the appeal they continue to hold.

A sense of identification with the role of the oppressed or persecuted outsider that these monstrous figures evoke is, of course, not the only attraction that they exert on queer readers and cinema audiences. We also respond positively to the pleasure and power that the shape-shifting abilities they are frequently portrayed as manifesting enable them to enjoy. These features rescue them from the unitary role of abject outcast and attract our imaginative identification in another way. The queer individual, living as he does in a minority subculture and existing, as Ahmed writes, 'slantwise'[6] and in oblique relation to hetero-normative society, resembles them since he too is, in metaphorical terms, a shape-shifter who moves to and fro between the queer community and heteronormative society. The act of reading Gothic, as Judith Halberstam describes, involves the reader in a similar form of mobility. Referring to the way in which Gothic texts tend to erase the boundaries between the reader and the uncanny creatures whose adventures he peruses, she asks, 'Do I read or am I written?...Am I monster hunter or the hunted? Am I human or other?...Who / what do I desire?'.[7] The novels discussed in this chapter and the imaginative attraction they exert provoke similar questions. Writers appear on occasion to construct their stories and novels with this in mind. In reading Michael Rowe's 'All the Pretty Boys'[8] published in Herren and Redmann's collection, though we are positioned to empathise with the protagonist Dale and his desire to provide sustenance for his lover Derek who, we learn, as a result of having been transformed into a monster, now eats only human flesh, we also sympathise with the innocent young lad, newly arrived in the city, whom Dale, in an effort to feed Derek, entraps to provide his dinner. Since Derek's physical appearance is not described and almost the only fact we know about him is his gruesome diet, the precise nature of his metamorphosis remains ambiguous. Has he been transformed into a ravening beast, a blood-thirsty troll or a vampire? This ambiguity illustrates the imaginative mobility of Gothic. The monstrous creatures that feature in novels exemplifying the genre, rather than being represented in terms of a single unitary persona, are often portrayed, as Halberstam also observes, as 'mobile, permeable and infinitely interpretable'.[9] Rowe exploits this mobility, creating a space for the reader to use his imagination to construct his own image of Derek.

The uncanny figures represented in the novels and stories discussed in this chapter, as well as attracting the reader for reasons of this kind, are also of interest from a historical viewpoint. They shed light on the developments that have occurred since the 1970s in lesbian, male gay and transgender history and the sexual political and cultural developments they reflect. The changes in representation that the vampire and monster have experienced since the 1970s and 1980s furnish an insight into the sexual political agendas of the lesbian and gay sexual liberation movements in the past fifty or so years and the modifications they have undergone. Significant here is the shift that took place in the 1980s from a predominantly lesbian feminist perspective to the sexually explicit interests of the lesbian sexual radical movement that occurred around that time. Another important development, one originating from the advent of queer theory in the late 1980s and the 1990s, is the movement from an emphasis on identity categories, such as lesbian, male gay, bisexual and transgender, to a focus on queer perspectives foregrounding sexual mobility and the performative dimension of gender. Both, as we shall see, along with the debates they have promoted, have influenced the representation of the vampire and uncanny double and the modifications that have taken place in their fictional and cinematic image. Also of interest are the dates at which the motifs of the vampire and the double entered queer fiction, as well as the facets of queer experience writers utilise them to represent. These topics and their impact on queer culture receive analysis in this chapter.

The Vampire and its Changing Representation

The portrayal of the vampire as a signifier of queer sexuality, though generally associated, as mentioned above, with the lesbian and gay liberation movements of the 1970s and 1980s, emerged, in fact, considerably earlier. The nineteenth-century sexologist and pioneer of the German homosexual movement Karl Heinrich Ulrichs in fact wrote a vampire story. Centring it on the relationship between Har, a member of the fishing community living in the Faeroe Islands off the coast of Norway, and his vampire lover Manor, Ulrichs describes the sexual pleasures that the two enjoy together and depicts the persecution they experience when Manor's vampiric identity is discovered. The islanders accuse Manor of torturing Har, while rejecting the latter's insistence that 'He did not torment me'.[10] Subjecting Manor to the penalty traditionally assigned to members of the undead, they cruelly impale him on a stake. This punitive act, however, rather than serving to release Har from Manor's erotic spell results, on the contrary, in keeping with the emphasis that Ulrichs places on the unhappy effects of sexual repression, in his death.

Another nineteenth-century vampire text with queer associations, one probably more familiar to present-day readers, is Bram Stoker's *Dracula* (1897). A key episode in the novel portrays the eponymous Count, on seeing his vampire women embracing Jonathan Harker and about to penetrate him with their fangs, command them to release him with the performative utterance, 'This man belongs to me!'[11] Though the women obey Dracula's command, they do so grudgingly, rebuking him with the accusation, 'You yourself never loved; you never love!' (p. 39). Their words appear to imply, as Christopher Craft suggests,[12] that, in rejecting female embraces in favour of male, Dracula prefers same-sex relationships. Although Stoker does not develop this theme but portrays Dracula relating indirectly to the members of the Crew of Light by means of sexually appropriating their women, it nonetheless resonates throughout the narrative. Craft also remarks on the fact that Harker himself, instead of rejecting the erotic embraces of the female vampires, gives signs of enjoying them. Though feeling guilty at his own erotic response, he appears to relish the pleasure of '"feminine" passivity'[13] and the respite that it furnishes from Victorian conventions of masculine assertiveness.

Whereas Stoker signals in *Dracula* his male vampire's homoerotic tendencies, Sheridan Le Fanu's 'Carmilla', published twenty-five years earlier, focuses on the figure of the lesbian vampire. William Veeder comments in his analysis of the story on the unexpectedly sympathetic approach that Le Fanu adopts towards the eponymous female vampire on which it centres. Veeder convincingly argues that, although Le Fanu's narrative, if read superficially, appears to create a conventional 'tale of a Victorian heroine saved from a deadly predator',[14] it treats, in actual fact, themes of female sexual repression and emotional and social isolation. As he illustrates, by referring to Laura's passionate response to the vampire Carmilla's overtures of love and her occasional enactment of 'aggressor' (p. 126) in the relationship, Le Fanu both rejects the image of her as a passive victim and implicitly criticises Victorian ideals of female sexual purity. Veeder also exposes the way in which, throughout the narrative, men tend to be assigned the role of custodians of knowledge, both sexual and medical, while women are left in ignorance. As a result, both Laura and Carmilla emerge as victims of hetero-patriarchal social and intellectual dominance. As Gina Wisker, commenting on the story, observes, 'Contemporary feminist critics and those influenced by queer theory might find in Carmilla a literary role model for questioning patriarchal power relations'.[15]

On turning from Stoker's portrayal of Dracula to the representation of the vampire in present-day fiction and film, we perceive the significant changes that it has undergone. As well as no longer being depicted as merely a threatening alien, its portrayal frequently reveals a greater degree of psychological complexity. And, instead of being distanced from the reader or viewer by being represented by the other characters in the text, it is often assigned the role of protagonist or narrator. These developments have met with a mixed response. Joan Gordon and Veronica Hollinger writing in 1994 welcome them. They remark approvingly on the fact that, though 'stories, novels and films continue to be produced in which the vampire enacts its familiar role as life-consuming threat, there are nonetheless others in which the creature, if not completely sympathetic, is at least portrayed with empathy'.[16] They also welcome the fact that the vampire is no longer depicted as a figure of 'relatively uncomplicated evil' (p. 2), as previously tended to occur, but is given the space to present his own viewpoint and recount his own story. Other critics, however, resent these modifications and view them unfavourably. Fred Botting, making no reference to the contribution that, as illustrated below, lesbian and male gay theorists and writers have made, in the course of their sociopolitical struggles, to its shift of image, complains that the vampire's 'sympathetic' representation has the adverse effect of 'rendering its strangeness familiar' and 'diminishing its otherness'.[17] Catherine Spooner, though endorsing certain post-modern re-workings of the motif, also expresses the fear that the motif may be in danger of 'being sucked dry of invigorating life' and 'doomed to replicate itself as an empty cliché'.[18] In fact certain of the modifications that the vampire has undergone in contemporary fiction, rather than being unprecedented, as critics sometimes imply, are signalled in Victorian fiction. Le Fanu's representation of the vampire Carmilla, as Veeder indicates, interrelates features of both monster and victim. And, although she is not permitted by the conventions of vampire fiction in the period to perform the role of narrator and recount her own history, she indicates a wish to do so. The remark she voices to Laura that, since she has taken a vow of secrecy, 'I dare not tell my story yet ',[19] suggests that she has a story that she would like to tell. She also drops intriguing hints about her earlier life, even hinting at her vampiric initiation. The fascination she holds for both Laura and the reader, in anticipating the image of the 'sympathetic vampire'[20] in contemporary fiction and film stems both from her performative abilities and the intriguing interplay of contraries that she embodies – the grotesque and the poignant, the scary and pathetic. Her portrayal also displays a degree of ambiguity. Does she actually experience the fear and disquiet that she describes or is she deliberately performing these emotions with the aim of winning Laura's sympathy and sexual compliance?

Whatever the responses that readers and critics make to the changes that have occurred in the vampire's portrayal, it appears that, to judge from the frequency with which they appear in fiction and film, the motif of 'the sympathetic vampire' is here to stay. Although the history of the emergence of the motif has been to a degree investigated, with critics referring to the role that the vampire plays in contemporary fiction and film as rebel, outsider and protagonist in heterosexual romance narrative, it is frequently not represented adequately. Critics frequently downplay or ignore the contribution that lesbian and male gay theorists and writers, especially those associated with the sexual liberation movements of the 1980s and 1990s, have made to the initiation and development of the motif.[21] Here I plan to redress the balance by discussing the roles that the vampire plays in queer fiction and exploring their history.

Although representations of the vampire sometimes appeared in the lesbian fiction produced in the 1970s as a signifier of rebellion and liberation, they increased considerably in number in the 1980s and early 1990s, replacing in popularity the figure of the witch[22] that had previously been to the fore in this respect. Their popularity coincided with the advent of the lesbian sexual radical movement[23] in North America and the UK – and the critique that its members directed at what they regarded as the unadventurous and sometimes puritanical attitude to sex evinced in some examples of lesbian feminist writing. Jessica Benjamin accuses lesbian feminists of attempting to 'sanitize or rationalize the erotic, fantastic components of human life' and responding to female fantasies of domination 'with moral condemnation rather than understanding'.[24] Comments such as this help to explain the increasing popularity that the vampire acquired in the lesbian fiction of the period. In contrast to the motif of the witch that chiefly exemplifies an image of female self-assertion and rebellion, representations of the female vampire, while signifying these attributes, generally have, in addition, an explicitly sexual component. The varied metaphorical uses that lesbian theorists make of the vampire in the writing of the 1980s and 1990s illustrate this. Whereas Sue Ellen Case describes the lesbian as resembling the vampire in her sexually transgressive lifestyle,[25] Barbara Creed observes that, like the vampire who rejects convention by destabilising the boundary between the living and the dead, lesbians and gay men challenge taboos by forming same-sex relationships. Introducing ideas from psychoanalytic discourse that were entering lesbian writing at the time, Creed describes the lesbian vampire as more transgressive than the male since, in taking a female lover, she makes a forbidden return to the pleasures of the mother–daughter relationship. Creed also radically interprets the image of the female vampire seducing victims with a deadly kiss as symbolically enacting the moral contagion that homophobes associate with lesbian sexuality.[26]

Reference to the vampire also features in the male gay theoretical texts produced in the 1980s and 1990s. Writing in 1988, the year in which the UK Conservative Government, in a backlash against the socio-political successes of the 1970s gay and lesbian liberation movements, instituted the repressive Section 28, Richard Dyer appropriately observes, that like the vampire who dares disclose his identity only after dark, gay men and lesbians feel coerced into passing as hetero during the day, daring to reveal their sexuality only at night in the dimly-lit world of clubs and bars.[27] The vampire also furnishes writers with a vehicle for commenting on the homophobic treatment that victims of the epidemic and gay men in general encountered during the AIDS crisis of the 1980s and 1990s. Hanson compares the vilification directed at them with the persecution that the vampire experiences in Gothic fiction and film.[28]

References to the metaphorical connections between the lesbian and gay individual and the vampire have also of course entered fiction, with writers developing in novels and stories the connections that theorists introduce in their analyses. Pat Califia, a supporter of the lesbian sexual radicals, portrays the eponymous protagonist of her story 'The Vampire' (1988) transgressively engaging in S&M sex, while Anna Livia in *Minimax* (1991) playfully instructs the lesbian reader to 'think of all those beautiful heads rising superbly from between their lover's thighs, mouths dripping with menstrual blood. Triple taboo: no oral sex; no sex during periods; no female to female sex'.[29] Jody Scott in *I, Vampire* (1986), interrelating the vampire storyline with a sci-fi narrative, utilises the interplay to create a humorously constructed comparison between lesbian and vampiric behaviours and lifestyles. The vampire motif also furnishes writers with a vehicle to treat the intersection between sexual and racial oppression. Jewelle Gomez centres *The Gilda Stories* (1991) on the adventures of three lesbian vampires, an African American, a Creole and American Indian, describing the socio-political network that they create in order to challenge racism and lesbophobia.

The fictional representation of the vampire also furnishes writers with a vehicle to represent and explore male gay sexuality and experience. Paul Magrs in *Could It Be Magic?* refers to Dracula in his account of the party, attended by several gay revellers, that takes place on the Phoenix Court housing estate in Newton Aycliffe, while David Leavitt in *The Page Turner* employs vampiric imagery to critique the exploitive sexual relationships that he portrays teachers forming with pupils at a New York music school. Ann Rice in *The Vampire Chronicles* (1976–2014) employs the relationship between Louis and his vampire creator Lestat to depict male homoerotic bonding and, in representing the couple giving a home to the child vampire Claudia, focuses attention on male gay parenting. The motif of the queer vampire is also popular with film directors, with films such as Sam Dragoti's *Love at First Bite* and Tony Scott's *The Hunger*, produced in the late 1970s and the 1980s, receiving critical acclaim.

The utilisation of the motif of 'sympathetic vampire' as a vehicle for exploring topics relating to sexual politics and lesbian and male gay experience, pioneered by lesbian and male gay theorists and fiction writers in the 1980s and 1990s, continues to flourish in contemporary queer fiction. *Chrystal Heart* by the British Meg Kingston and *Diary of a Vampire* by the American Gary Bowen, the two novels selected for discussion below, illustrate some of the facets of the vampire motif that writers, working in different periods, prioritise, as well as the narrative strategies they employ. Kingston, writing in 2013, creates a playfully post-modern text that advertises the fictionality of her storyline. Illustrating that the vampire narrative continues to furnish a vehicle for sexual-political analysis and comment, she introduces in one episode a debate between the concept of identity categories, with its prioritising of lesbian and gay identification, on the one hand, and the queer emphasis on the mobility of sexuality, on the other. Bowen, in contrast, writing earlier in 1995, powerfully foregrounds his vampire narrator's anxieties about coming out and his fears of homophobic persecution, topics significant to the oppressive situation of the gay community in the era. However, different though the two writers' representations of the vampire are, they nonetheless display a point of connection. Though foregrounding the vampire's recently acquired sympathetic persona and giving him a personalised identity and voice, they nonetheless also refer in some episodes to his monstrous aspect, illustrating that, despite the changes he has undergone, he is still capable of using his fangs.

Meg Kingston's *Chrystal Heart*, published as mentioned above in 2013, makes eclectic use of different literary styles and traditions. In addition to interweaving the sympathetic image of the vampire with its traditionally monstrous persona, the novel reveals connections with the lesbian vampire fiction produced in the 1980s and 1990s. The interweaving of humour and sexual politics that Kingston creates recalls the similar interplay that Jody Scott and Anna Livia construct in their novels *I, Vampire* and *Minimax* published in the earlier period. In addition, in constructing the persona of her protagonist Philomena Carstairs, Kingston develops the connections between vampire and sci-fi narratives that Scott helped to initiate in her novel. Whereas Scott portrays her vampire protagonist Sterling O'Blivion encountering the visitor Benroya who comes from outer space, Kingston introduces references to the evil snake-like Geb and his troops who live on a distant planet in the galaxy. Recognising that the ancient Olmec calendar is about to expire threatening to bring about the destruction of the world, and assuming that no one exists who is capable of re-starting the clock that controls it, they look forward gleefully to the demise of the human race. However their assumption in this respect, as the reader discovers, is incorrect. Kingston's vampire protagonist Philomena, or 'Chrystal' as she informally calls herself, is at hand to combat him and put the clock to rights, thus saving the world from destruction.

The vampire Chrystal also plays another role in Kingston's narrative in addition to combating the evil Geb. She achieves the unusual feat of combining the roles of vampire, sci-fi adventurer and romantic heroine with that of cyborg. Her cyborg connection originates from the crystal heart she has had implanted in her chest. It was placed there, as the reader learns in the opening chapters, by a group of Tibetan mystics who saved her life when she suffered a near-fatal stab wound after visiting the British exhibition at the Crystal Palace in London in 1851. Before leaving, her rescuers informed her that, in order for her to survive, her new heart will require a regular supply of blood. Their words convey to her – and the reader – the news of her metamorphosis into a vampire.

Kingston portrays Chrystal, in combatting Geb and striving to prevent the Olmec calendar from expiring, employing two significant tools – the magic properties invested in the crystal heart and her knowledge of Victorian steam punk technology. An instrument relating to the latter that plays a key role in the struggle she wages is her trusty aetheric resonator.[30] As well as furnishing her with a weapon to save the world, it plays a contributory role in the same-sex female romance plot that Kingston introduces early on. It is exemplified by the love affair on which Chrystal embarks in the opening chapters of the novel with 'Sam-of-the-boy's name',[31] as she playfully calls the twenty-first century lesbian feminist whom she takes as her lover.

Chrystal's initial encounter with Sam is distinctly unpromising. It is represented taking place in 2012 in a London tube station where Sam, who is currently destitute and in urgent need of cash to pay the rent, makes a ham-fisted attempt to steal Chrystal's purse. However, despite the inauspicious nature of their meeting, the erotic attraction the two experience, combined with their mutual interest in steam-punk technology, results in them falling in love. In an episode commenting parodically on the imperialistic role played by the British Museum as the depository of exotic items pilfered from different races and cultures around the world, Sam assists Chrystal in surreptitiously retrieving her precious aetheric resonator from the display case where it has been housed since the nineteenth-century. On perceiving that the energy Chrystal has used in carrying out the raid on the Museum has left her exhausted and learning of her vampiric transformation, Sam offers to give her a few drops of her own blood to re-vitalise her heart. From this point on, as well as helping her in her mission to save the world, she acts as Chrystal's blood donor.

Chrystal is not in fact the first vampire to reject the vampire kiss in exchange for the technology of the blood transfusion. The protagonist of Mary Braddon's story *The Good Lady Ducayne* (1896) furnishes a nineteenth-century precedent, while Caleb in Kathryn Bigelow's film *Near Dark* (1987), who is cured of his vampirism by receiving a transfusion from his father, exemplifies a twentieth-century example. As Aspasia Stephanou, in discussing Braddon's novel and Bigelow's film, illustrates, blood can assume different meanings in the vampire narrative. Though traditionally representing 'a symbolic or supernatural fluid', it can alternatively signify, as it does today, 'an empirical material'.[32] Kingston's representation of the properties that blood exemplifies is somewhat ambiguous. Although the syringe and sterile needle that Chrystal gives Sam to furnish her heart with blood indicate that she has some understanding of present-day medicine, she appears unconcerned about whether Sam's blood-type will conflict with her own. Blood is alternatively represented in a later episode in the novel as assuming its traditional magical significance of familial or erotic affinity. In finding herself on one occasion accidentally separated from Sam, Chrystal succeeds in tracing her whereabouts since her own heart, infused with drops of Sam's blood, guides her towards her.

Whereas the heroic role that Chrystal plays in attempting to re-start the mechanism that controls the movement of the world and combatting Geb's efforts to prevent her, combined with her romantic involvement with Sam, connect her with the figure of the sympathetic vampire who attracts the reader's identification and sympathy, other features of her portrayal link her, on the contrary, with the monstrous image that Victorian writers such as Stoker create. Important in the latter respect is Chrystal's grotesque cyborg body and the intersection of human with machine it exemplifies. Rosemary Jackson, though describing the vampire, as represented in nineteenth-century fiction, as a monster with no fixed form, acknowledges that the uncanny physical transformations it can assume, though 'outside human categorisation',[33] are capable, as Stoker's *Dracula* and Le Fanu's 'Carmilla' illustrate, of attracting humans sexually. Kingston innovatively re-works these contradictions. Though portraying Sam, on unexpectedly discovering Chrystal's cyborg component, nervously wondering if she is 'some kind of inhuman monster' (p. 93), she subsequently portrays her, influenced by the dictates of her 'treacherous heart' (p. 93), falling in love with 'this strange woman' (p. 95). The anxiety about Chrystal's monstrosity that Sam initially experiences, as well as her speedy capitulation to the imperative of desire, relate her in fact to Billie, the protagonist of Winterson's *The Stone Gods* (2007), who, despite her reservations and fears, becomes erotically infatuated with the cyborg Spike. The passion that Sam feels for Chrystal, like Billie's for Spike, turns out in fact to be more in consonance with feminist ideology than she initially assumed. Chrystal's cyborg body, though relating her from a phallocentric perspective to the image of the monster, associates her, from a feminist viewpoint, as Donna J. Haraway argues in 'A Cyborg Manifesto', with post-modern femininity. As Haraway illustrates, postmodern woman, in rejecting 'the myth of originary wholeness'[34] and exemplifying the intersection between nature and culture, in fact resembles the cyborg since it too lacks an essential identity and interrelates human with technological.

The interplay that Kingston creates between the sympathetic representation of the vampire and its traditionally monstrous persona is especially in evidence in the episode in which Sam first catches a glimpse of Chrystal's naked body. On stepping out of the shower and raising her towel to dry her hair, Chrystal accidentally reveals to the astonished Sam the 'unlikely combination of flesh and mechanics' (p. 63) that her cyborg form, with the crystal heart implanted in her chest, reveals. Sam is uncomfortably aware of the fact that 'Chrystal noticed me looking. Not that it was hard – I must have been staring' (p. 63). However, the gaze she directs at Chrystal quickly moves from reflecting astonishment and alarm to – as indicated by the speed with which she responds to her embraces – one of sexual desire. The feminist significance of the episode is clarified by Sue Ellen Case's analysis of the role that the motif of the gaze plays in the vampire film. Re-working Linda Williams's classic essay 'When the Woman Looks',[35] in which Williams interprets the gaze that woman and monster share in horror films as reflecting a sense of identification stemming from their mutual association in phallocentric culture with spectacle and castration threat, Case argues that, in the lesbian vampire film, the gaze signifies not identification but, on the contrary, desire.[36] The passionate gaze that Sam directs at Chrystal endorses Case's reading.

Kingston's novel, as well as responding to Haraway's discussion of the cyborg's feminist significance and Case's innovative interpretation of the relationship between woman and monster, also introduces a debate about the different merits of queer theoretical perspectives and identity categories. Since the novel focuses on a sexual relationship between a woman and a female cyborg vampire, reviewers generally classify it as 'lesbian'. However, as is indicated by the ease with which Chrystal is portrayed moving from her relationship with Sam to engaging in brief affairs with men, she does not, in fact, identify as lesbian. She is bisexual or, since the term is more appropriate, sexually mobile. Whereas 'bisexual', as Jagose explains,[37] implies a binary division to exist between homosexual and heterosexual, queer theory endorses the mobility of sexuality. Chrystal's unexpected reference to her love affairs with men understandably upsets Sam since she had assumed her, like herself, to be attracted only to women. As well as feeling jealous of Chrystal's male lovers, she resents the superior manner in which Chrystal dismisses her own belief in fidelity in love as old-fashioned – especially since Chrystal was born in the Victorian era and, as Sam discovers, is 188 years old! She is also puzzled by Chrystal's incongruous choice of male lovers. They include a fifty-six-year old Army Colonel whom Chrystal picked up in the tea room at the British Museum (She assures him that she does not mind the age difference!) and the third officer of the ship in which the two women sail to Barbados in order to prevent the expiry of the Olmec calendar. Chrystal, however, is unmoved by Sam's protests. She defends her decision to accept the Colonel's invitation to a tea-dance with the humorous observation, 'Men can be just as much fun as ladies. They are different, as I'm sure you are aware – but they have their attractions none the less' (p. 105).

Chrystal, speaking from personal experience while also adopting a Foucauldian viewpoint, also lectures Sam on her limited and incorrect view of the Victorian approach to sex. She informs her that it was considerably less narrow than she appears to assume, since it included a number of non-orthodox sexualities and genders, including homosexuality, transvestism and, of course, sapphism. The humour stemming from the two lovers' contrary attitudes to sex and the arguments they use to support them, with Chrystal, though born in the Victorian era, defending ideals of 'free love' and the twenty-first century Sam advocating monogamy, is wittily handled. It resembles the humour that the sparring between the vampire Sterling and the visiting alien Benaroya triggers in Scott's *I, Vampire*. However, Kingston's novel, though resembling Scott's both in tone and in its utilisation of the vampire motif, differs from it in one important respect. Chrystal, unlike Scott's protagonist Sterling, does not identify as lesbian. Her sexuality is, on the contrary, mobile.

This raises the question, how do we interpret the emphasis that Kingston places on Chrystal's sexual mobility? In the lesbian feminist fiction of the 1970s and 1980s, the coming-out novel in particular, a female character who admits to being attracted to both women and men, on the rare occasions that she is portrayed, is generally assigned the role of the sexually politically flawed foil to the lesbian feminist narrator or protagonist.[38] In employing Chrystal as protagonist and representing her affirming her right to enjoy affairs with both women and men, she appears to be adopting a queer approach to sexuality and possibly protesting, as the writer Jan Clausen did in the 1990s,[39] at the practice of defining the individual's sexuality in terms of the gender of her object choice.

Another question that Kingston's novel provokes is, how do we interpret the odd assortment of colonels and ship's officers whom she portrays Chrystal taking as lovers? Is she commenting humorously on the inconsistencies and contradictions that human or, in Chrystal's case, vampiric/cyborg nature, can involve? Or is she perhaps signalling that, although Chrystal is a heroic vampire who succeeds in outwitting the evil Geb and saving the world, as she eventually does, she nonetheless has a streak of old-fashioned Victorian Toryism in her? Or is she playfully mocking the current literary vogue for neo-Victorian fiction and culture, that her own novel in fact exemplifies, by indicating the sexual-political contradictions that it can involve?

As well as utilising the episode in which the Major invites Chrystal to a tea-dance to illustrate the latter's incongruous choice of lovers, Kingston also employs it to comment self-reflexively on the neo-Victorian dimension of her narrative and the popularity that social activities relating to the trend play in twenty-first century social life. She portrays the Major as observing, in response to Sam's expressions of incredulity, that such antiquated forms of entertainment should still take place, 'You'd be surprised. There are even a number of young people getting interested in such old-fashioned activities.' He adds conspiratorially, 'They tell me they call themselves *Neo-Victorians*!' (p. 104).

Chrystal, as well as enjoying the neo-Victorian entertainment of the tea-dance, also takes pleasure in the dressing-up and attiring herself in rare Victorian jewellery that preparation for it involves. This connects her with another form of vampire, besides the 'sympathetic' kind, that features currently in fiction and film. This is 'the sparkly vampire'. Although vampiric sparkliness is generally associated with the gleaming appearance of the creature's skin, as illustrated by the vampires portrayed in Stephanie Meyer's *Twilight* novels and the films re-casting them, rather than their jewellery, Chrystal's persona suits the term in another respect. As Spooner explains, 'The sparkly vampire has come to be regarded as representative of a "de-fanged" vampire, a vampire more likely to be regarded as a desirable romantic partner than a bloodthirsty killer'.[40] The description suits Kingston's portrayal of Chrystal since, despite the militant role that Chrystal plays combatting the evil Geb and saving the world, she appears in fact more attracted to romance than violence.

Kingston concludes the novel on a romantic note by portraying her neo-Victorian sparkly vampire Chrystal and her lesbian feminist lover Sam achieving a truce and accepting each other's sexual differences. She portrays them walking harmoniously out of the narrative frame together not, as usually occurs with lovers, into the sunset but, appropriately for a vampire and her mate, as Sam describes, 'with our backs to the lowering sun' (p. 307).

The Hungarian Rafael, whom Gary Bowen employs as narrator in *Diary of a Vampire*, as indicated by the novel's publication date of 1995 and the fact that he is male, differs significantly from the sparkly vampire Chrystal whom Kingston portrays in her text of 2013. The two novels, however, reveal features in common since, as well as interrelating the vampire's sympathetic image with his traditionally monstrous one, Bowen, like Kingston, introduces features from earlier vampire fiction. Whereas Kingston's text has connections with the lesbian vampire fiction produced by Scott and Livia, Bowen's reveals intertextual links with Victorian works such as John Polidori's 'The Vampyre' and Le Fanu's *Carmilla*. Bowen opens his novel by portraying his Hungarian narrator Rafael being transformed against his will, in the chaotic events that followed the Russian Army's invasion of Budapest in 1956 to crush the national rebellion, into a member of the vampiric undead. Rafael describes how one of his fellow countrymen, having undergone a similar transformation and desperate to obtain food, attacks him in a churchyard while he is placing flowers on the grave of his lover Valentin who was killed by the Russian soldiers when they entered the city. Although these events resonate throughout the narrative in subsequent episodes in Rafael's disturbing memories, Bowen interestingly locates the major part of the novel not in Hungary but in the USA. He portrays Rafael, since he has no emotional ties to keep him in Budapest and is eager to escape his unhappy past, deciding to join the other members of his family, unaware though they are of his vampiric metamorphosis, by emigrating to Baltimore.

Exhausted by the disturbing events he has previously experienced in Hungary, Rafael commences his new life in Baltimore by enjoying a lengthy sleep in the basement of the house that his father has purchased for him there. He is awakened thirty or so years later in 1991 by the sound of loud knocking on the front door. Though nervous of whom he will find there, he discovers with relief that the visitor is his nephew Michael. Although this is first occasion he has set eyes on him, Rafael deciphers Michael's identity from his familial resemblance. Describing himself as an artist by profession, Michael tells Rafael that he is seeking accommodation, including a space to use as a studio, and wishes to rent rooms in his house. The request perturbs Rafael. Though impressed by Michael's friendly manner and good looks, he fears that sharing his home with him will force him to reveal both his homosexual orientation and vampiric identity. Although he eventually decides to act the role of supportive uncle and agree to his nephew's request, he impresses on him the fact that he requires privacy and needs to remain undisturbed. His observation, rather than diminishing Michael's curiosity about him, understandably has the effect of exacerbating it.

Bowen proceeds to exploit in the narrative the utilisation of the vampiric identity as a metaphor for a homosexual identification, and the anxieties that the gay man living in the 1980s and 1990s experienced about revealing it. The period was especially problematic for the homosexual community, gay men in particular, since on account of the AIDS crisis and the unsympathetic or abusive response often accorded it, homophobia was especially rampant. In portraying Rafael, as his friendship with his nephew Michael develops, wishing to divulge his sexuality to him but scared of doing so, Bowen foregrounds the topic of secrets and their revelation, one that, as mentioned in the introductory chapter, links queer fiction with Gothic. As Sedgwick, describing the queer significance of the secret, observes, 'Every encounter with a new boss, social worker, loan officer, landlord, doctor, erects new closets which exact from gay people... new requisitions of secrecy or disclosure'.[41]

Another strategy Bowen employs to emphasise the fear that the thought of the discovery of his homosexuality arouses in Rafael is to represent the murder of his lover Valentin by the Russian soldiers as having been especially brutal on account of the fact that they suspected him of being gay. Rafael, as he remember only too painfully, was forced to witness the event. As a result he finds it difficult to credit the fact that responses to gay men in 1990s Baltimore, though sometimes taking the form of ridicule or verbal abuse, do not generally involve killing.

Bowen's portrayal of Michael fearing the scrutiny of the people he encounters in his new life in the USA, in addition to foregrounding the theme of secrets, also introduces the related topic of homosexual legibility, one that achieved prominence in nineteenth-century writing. As Fincher observes, 'The fear of the exposure of a secret to a public, penetrating eye'[42] is a topic that features frequently in texts of the period, especially with reference to homosexuality. Arguing that 'One might compare the queer body to a script or a text that needs to be translated or interpreted, to be understood and ultimately controlled' (p. 45), he suggests that 'Translation and transgression – the two are related through reading the body of the queer man' (p. 86). Lee Edelman also refers to homosexual legibility in his study *Homographesis*, citing John Addington Symonds's representation of the homosexual as a man with his 'lusts written on his face'.[43]

In addition to employing vampirism as a metaphor for Rafael's homosexual identification, Bowen also utilises it in a specifically Gothic context to foreground Rafael's fear of the discovery of his vampiric identity.

He renders credible the anxiety that Rafael feels in this respect by portraying him mentally reliving the terrifying events he experienced prior to leaving Budapest. Rafael vividly remembers the occasion when two men, on perceiving the pallor of his face, a signifier of vampirism in texts ranging in time from Polidori's nineteenth-century 'The Vampyre' to Meyer's twenty-first century *Twilight*, threateningly accused him of belonging to the fraternity of the undead. He succeeded in allaying their suspicions and escaping death only by reciting verses from Psalm 23. The details of the episode remain imprinted on his mind. In fact so scared is he that his vampirism will be discovered that even when, in a sudden fit of lust, he recklessly seduces a student in the reading room of the Enoch Pratt Free Library in Baltimore and, with his consent, punctures his neck and sucks the blood, he forbids him to say the word 'vampire'. He dramatically insists, in an emphatically performative utterance, 'Don't say it!'.[44]

Rafael's vampiric identity comes under scrutiny again when his nephew Michael, whom he is beginning to find increasingly attractive and, ignoring the incest taboo, eventually takes as his lover, tells him that he looks too young to be his uncle and expresses astonishment at his apparent ability 'to vanish and materialize into thin air' (p. 107). Like Carmilla who, on being interrogated by Laura about her history, maintains, as Le Fanu describes, 'an ever-wakeful reserve,'[45] Rafael resists the temptation to divulge the secret of his longevity. He laughs off Michael's question about his youthful appearance and attributes his ability to perform a sudden vanishing act to 'being light on my feet' (p. 107). Although rationally aware that, in 1990s Baltimore, the discovery of his vampirism is unlikely to result in his death, he is scared of suffering a more sophisticated and long-term penalty, such as being confined for life in a laboratory and forced to undergo frequent blood tests.

The interplay Bowen creates between the fears that Rafael experiences about the discovery of both his homosexuality and vampirism recall the interrelation between the two that occurs in certain nineteenth-century vampire texts. In addition to informing Le Fanu's representation of the vampire Carmilla's erotic relationship with the heroine Laura, it features in John Polidori's treatment of male homoerotic relations in 'The Vampyre'. Polidori centres the story on the relationship that develops between the narrator Aubrey and the aristocratic Lord Ruthven whom Aubrey, in fact, suspects of being a vampire. The connection that develops between the two men, as Fincher describes,[46] is intriguingly ambiguous since Ruthven, while pursuing Aubrey, also appears to be the focus of Aubrey's interest.

Although Aubrey ostensibly cultivates Ruthven's company in order to protect the women whom the latter pursues, he also gives occasional signs of being attracted to him erotically. Bowen's narrative, as well as sharing with Polidori's text a focus on anxieties relating to both vampiric and homosexual legibility, portrays Rafael, in a manner resembling the shifting relationship between Aubrey and Ruthven, relating to his nephew Michael in a series of emotional moves involving a process of advance and retreat. However Bowen's representation of his relationship with Michael differs from Polidori's treatment of Aubrey and Ruthven in one significant respect. Whereas Polidori distances the vampiric Ruthven from the reader by portraying him from Aubrey's viewpoint, Bowen, adopting the present-day practice of utilising the vampire as narrator and exploring his subjectivity, allows Rafael to tell his own story and express his emotions directly.

In treating Rafael's vampirism as a metaphor for his homosexuality, Bowen re-works certain motifs that appear traditionally in queer vampire fiction. The episode in which Michael shows Rafael the portrait that, attracted by his good looks, he has secretly painted of him while renting rooms in his house, furnishes an example. Portraits feature significantly, in fact, in several vampire novels. Le Fanu describes Laura seeing a portrait of Carmilla's alleged ancestor the Countess Karnstein (the two vampiric women are in fact one and the same), while Hannah Hart opens her contemporary novel *The Vampire's Portrait: Winters' Curse* by portraying the protagonist Jake discovering a picture of the vampire Dominic Winters in the ancestral house that he has recently inherited and, as romance convention dictates, falling in love with his image. Although Michael is unaware of Rafael's vampiric identity when he shows him the portrait of him he has painted, the image he has created of Rafael's elegantly sexy appearance with his 'old fashioned ruffled white shirt open to one button above the waist' (p. 106), resembling, as it does, that of the vampire Louis in Neil Jordan's film of Rice's *Interview with The Vampire*, nonetheless hints at it. The pleasure with which Raphael responds to his nephew's flattering portrayal, exclaiming approvingly, 'That's quite a painting!' (p. 106) and singling out for praise the artistic representation of his face, resembles Dorian Gray's delighted response to Basil Hallward's famous portrait in Oscar Wilde's novel. As Wilde describes, 'A look of joy came into Dorian's eyes, as if he had recognised himself for the first time'.[47] Although Wilde does not treat the vampire motif explicitly in *The Picture of Dorian Gray*, the theme of monstrous transformation the novel treats has connotations of it and critics have, in fact, compared Dorian's portrayal to that of a vampire.[48]

Unlike the homosexual characters in nineteenth-century fiction who are generally represented remaining closeted, refusing to reveal their homosexuality, Bowen's twentieth-century Rafael, having spent some months worrying about the visibility of both his sexuality and his vampirism, suddenly succeeds, inspired by the intense sexual attraction that he feels for his nephew Michael, in overcoming his fears and coming out to him. On discovering to his astonishment that Michael appears unperturbed by both revelations, he admits with a response of relief, 'I'm out of the closet now!' (p. 188).

Despite the success with which Rafael's revelation of his sexuality concludes, Bowen's frequent references in *Diary of a Vampire* to the act of coming out, both gay and vampiric, and the anxieties they arouse, powerfully foreground the onerous nature of the revelation of gay and lesbian identity in a culture that is homophobic or that the queer individual fears to be so. As Sedgwick observes,

> The closet is for many gay people the fundamental feature of social life and there can be few gay people, however courageous and forthright by habit, however fortunate in the support of their immediate communities, in whose lives the closet is not still a shaping presence.[49]

Whereas Bowen constructs his portrayal of Rafael in general on the blueprint of the post-1980s 'sympathetic' vampire, he punctures it on occasion by portraying him as the traditional blood-thirsty monster. As well as introducing descriptions, some extremely gory, of the murders Rafael commits in order to obtain the supplies of human blood that he requires, Bowen also represents him engaging after the deed in fits of anguished remorse. Indulging in a performative outburst of guilt, Rafael melodramatically describes himself as, 'an insane, ravenous monster doomed to shamble through a miserable unlife until the sun caught me or a stake impaled me' (p. 14). As if compensating for the lack of emotional self-analysis that the vampires portrayed in earlier texts have been permitted, Bowen perhaps allocates Rafael a little too much space in the narrative for these excessive expressions of guilt and self-pity.

Like the anxieties he experiences about Coming Out, the concerns that Rafael experiences about obtaining supplies of human blood are also unexpectedly alleviated. With the assistance of contacts in the medical profession, he succeeds in contacting the services of a blood bank – a facility, of course, unavailable to the eighteenth and nineteenth-century vampire. Although the blood that Rafael purchases is genuine and not synthetic, his obtaining of it looks forward to the Alan Balls television series *True Blood* and the novels by Charlaine Harris they re-work. Aldana Reyes, analysing the ideological significance attached to blood in the series, describes how, 'The articulation of a blood business points towards the predatory nature of financial logic whereby lack of choice is prevalent'.[50] Although Bowen handles the topic with less wit and political acumen than the television series *True Blood*, he too signals the way in which the vampire's access to a blood bank serves as a metaphor for the capitalist economy. Only the lucky few who are financially affluent or, like Raphael, have friends who are doctors or lab researchers, are in a position to obtain these supplies.

Another feature of Rafael's portrayal, besides the murders he commits to obtain human blood, that assumes connotations of the monstrous, one that Bowen treats especially dramatically, are the animal transformations in which, in a manner resembling the shape-shifting abilities of the traditional Gothic monster, he engages. Elisabeth Grosz describes the monster as 'an ambiguous being whose hybridity endangers and problematizes categories and oppositions dominant in social life',[51] and the shape-shifting that Raphael enacts echoes her description. Robert Azzarello suggests that the ability to transform himself into a bat and a dog that Stoker ascribes to Dracula would probably have struck readers who encountered the novel on its initial publication in the 1890s as especially disturbing on account of the anxieties that the readings and misreadings of Darwin's *On the Origin of Species* and *The Descent of Man* promoted in the Victorian reading public.[52] The sight of Dracula making a lizard-like descent down the wall of his castle in Transylvania in fact prompts Jonathan Harker to ask, 'What manner of man is this, or what manner of creature is it in the semblance of a man?'.[53] However, on account of the present-day reader's familiarity with animal transformation scenarios in Gothic film and the fact that the majority of us no longer find the implications of Darwinian evolutionary theory so alarming, Rafael's animal metamorphoses strike the reader as exhilarating rather than monstrous, reflecting the pleasure he takes in becoming animal. On transforming himself into a cougar after fasting for some days, he buoyantly observes that, 'My shrunken body was easy to change; I could rearrange it without adding or subtracting any mass.' He continues, 'My face lengthened into a blunt snout and my ears grew triangular and erect while my legs and arms shortened until I stood on four strong paws' (p. 19). The impression of physical strength and vitality the description evokes recalls Patricia MacCormack's observation that, interpreted from a Deleuzian viewpoint, vampires should be regarded not 'as monsters as spectacle forms but as events, not as molar entities but as hybrid becomings' and 'transformative potentialities'.[54]

Transformations into animal form are not the only form of shape-shifting with which Rafael experiments. In order to please his lover Michael, who is bisexual, he agrees, though a little unwillingly, to adopt a female form. However, unlike Michael who enjoys making love to him as a woman, Rafael feels uncomfortable about his sex change, temporary though it is. Though enjoying metamorphosing into animal form, he feels – dubiously perhaps – that his transformation into a woman conflicts with his transgressive gay male identity (p. 185). Trevor Holmes, commenting on the reception of Bowen's novel, alerts attention to the chauvinistic response that the episode provoked from certain male readers. They reacted to it, as he describes, 'with rancor and disdain as if such an inclusion [that of a woman] in a sex scene . . . automatically disqualifies the novel from being a gay vampire novel'.[55] The episode gives an interesting, though depressing, glimpse of the chauvinism that can infiltrate the readership of queer Gothic.

Strategies of Doubling in the AIDS Novel and the Transsexual Narrative

References to motifs of the double and doubling, as critics agree, feature frequently in Gothic fiction. Day, after discussing some of the examples of fractured identities and the divided self that proliferate in nineteenth-century examples of the genre, arrives at the conclusion that 'Doubling, then, is not simply a convention, but the essential reality of the self in the Gothic world'.[56] Marshall Brown, supporting his view, observes that 'There can be few traditions so beset with second selves and *doppelgangers* as the Gothic novel'.[57] Freud, writing in 1919 and discussing 'the figure of the double', remarks on 'the extraordinary strong feeling of something uncanny that pervades the conception'.[58]

Works of eighteenth- and nineteenth-century Gothic, as well as referring to doubling and doubles, frequently utilise motifs of this kind with reference to queer gender and sexuality. Commenting on transgender (used as an umbrella term for people who do not conform to conventional gender roles), Dale Townshend observes that, in Matthew Lewis's *The Monk*, Ambrosio's feelings of erotic attraction for the temptress Matilda appear to be enhanced by her masculine style of behaviour and by the fact he previously encountered her in the persona of the male Rosario.[59] Regarding transvestism (the individual dressing in clothing associated with the opposite sex), David Stuart Davies alerts attention to the fact change to the way in which in Richard Marsh's *The Beetle*, published in 1897 when gender roles and their relevance to the figure of 'the New Woman' were topics of debate, the eponymous creature transforms Marjorie into her male double by dressing her in masculine clothes and cutting her hair.[60]

As well as utilising motifs of doubling with reference to transgender and transvestism, writers working in the nineteenth- and early-twentieth centuries employ them as a vehicle for exploring male and female same-sex attraction. Eric Daffron describes the creature that Victor Frankenstein constructs in Mary Shelley's novel, in evoking connotations of Frankenstein's homoerotic desires, as 'the period's most celebrated instance of doubling'.[61] In addition Haggerty[62] and Elaine Showalter,[63] discussing Robert Louis Stevenson's depiction of Dr Jekyll's doppelganger Hyde, both refer to the fact that Dr Jekyll's friends appear to regard Hyde as his sexual partner.

The examples of psychic fragmentation and sexual displacement that, as indicated above, the introduction of the motifs of the double and doubling generates in Gothic, become increasingly complex in the latter years of the nineteenth century. This is illustrated by Henry James's portrayal of the spectral Peter Quint, the valet with a pale face and queer whiskers whom the governess encounters at Bly in *The Turn of the Screw*. As well as portraying Quint as a socially inverted image of the Master of the house, as indicated by him wearing the Master's clothes, James implies that he may also duplicate a sexually predatory male whom the governess encountered in her earlier life. James portrays her thinking, in a sentence that, while striking a chill into the heart of the female reader who has had a similar experience, appears to furnish a clue to the governess's determination to prevent what she interprets as Quint's attempted possession of Miles, 'It was as if I had been looking at him for years and had known him always'.[64] The utilisation of dress as a signifier of doubling that occurs with reference to Quint in *The Turn of the Screw* also acquires queer significance in Shirley Jackson's *The Haunting of Hill House*, published in 1959. Theodora, on dressing in the clothes of Eleanor, to whom she is erotically attracted, when her own have been ruined by the psychic disturbances emanating from the House, observes that they are now twins. When the disturbances re-commence, the terrified Eleanor grasps hold of Theodora's hand – whereupon further displacements occur. The hand, she is terrified to discover, is not Theodora's but belongs to somebody else.

As a result of the theoretical writing of Butler in the 1990s and the focus she places on the performative dimension of gender and the unstable, re-signifiable nature of all gender roles,[65] interest in transgender and gender-role experimentation is flourishing at the present time, encouraging writers to treat topics of this kind. Novels introducing them include Jonathan B. Coe's *What a Carve Up* and Julie Anne Peter's *Luna*. Whereas Coe interweaves the storylines of several characters who, dissatisfied with their existing gender identities, either embark on a sex-change or consider doing so, Peters explores what the sister of the transsexual protagonist calls 'the girl in Liam',[66] the female double whom Liam regards as entrapped inside him and determines to liberate. Although neither Coe's nor Peter's novels can be described as Gothic, the emphasis they both place on the mismatch the characters experience between the gender identity with which they were born and what they see as their 'real' selves evokes a strong sense of the uncanny.

Vincent Brome's *Love in the Plague*, in contrast, one of the novels discussed in this section, is emphatically Gothic both in the themes it employs and the mood of fear and uncertainty the narrative evokes. Utilising the concept of the double as the frame for an AIDS narrative and juxtaposing episodes situated in London in the period of the 1980s AIDS crisis with ones set in the city in the 1660s during an outbreak of bubonic plague, he compares and contrasts the responses of present-day and seventeenth-century communities to the two epidemics. He examines, in his treatment of AIDS, the effect of the HIV virus on the lives of gay men, as well as the impact that it had on the heterosexual population, especially mothers and women of child-bearing age. Gothic tropes that he introduces include, in addition to the double and doubling, the uncanny city and the representation of the house haunted by an uncanny presence.

Susan Swan's *The Wives of Bath*, the second novel discussed, also makes significant use of the double and strategies of doubling, though employing them to very different effect. As well as focusing on the topic of female to male transsexuality and different forms of gender role inversion, Swan portrays her characters encountering doubles in mirror images, pictures and dreams. The novel also introduces a number of other motifs with Gothic associations such as spectrality, the grotesque body and transformations evoking magical connotations.

The literary form of the AIDS narrative that Vincent Brome employs in *Love in the Plague* first emerged in the 1980s in response to the devastating effect that the epidemic was having both on individuals and the gay community in general, as well as the anger queer people felt at the negligent and homophobic response that the pharmaceutical industry and governmental agencies adopted to the crisis. In addition to failing to allocate sufficient funds for testing and research, the Reagan government refused to permit the advertising of safe sex strategies.[67] The British prime minister Margaret Thatcher, as has recently been disclosed in official documents, adopted a similarly blinkered and oppressive policy.[68]

As Emmanuel S. Nelson describes in *AIDS: The Literary Response*, novels focusing on the epidemic take numerous different forms and differ significantly in literary and socio-political perspective.[69] Robert Ferro's *Second Son*, critiquing the uncaring attitude that families that are predominantly heterosexual frequently adopt towards the AIDS sufferer, describes how a member who is homosexual and, a cause of even greater stigma, HIV positive, tends to be excluded from its supportive structures. Other novels represent the familial in a more positive light. The members of the Irish family whom Colm Toibin represents in *The Blackwater Lightship*, though initially separated geographically and emotionally, on learning that the son Declan is in the terminal stages of AIDS, are prompted by force of circumstance to temporarily overcome their differences and unite. Alice Hoffman in *At Risk* employs yet another approach. She centres her novel not on a gay man but on the eleven-year-old Amanda who has contracted the HIV virus from a contaminated blood transfusion. Emotions of anger and distress conflict in her parents' response to her situation, while she herself struggles to come to terms with it. Geoff Mains in *Gentle Warriors*, rejecting a familial context for his novel, creates a dystopian narrative representing the struggle waged by a group of gay men to challenge the conspiracy that the CIA is depicted as having instigated to exterminate the male gay population by rounding them up and incarcerating them in death camps. The anger inspiring his novel and the accusations of genocide that it levels at the political establishment are directed at what the activist Douglas Crimp calls the 'murderous regime of silence and disinformation that virtually ensures the death of sexually active young people – gay and straight',[70] promoted by the Regan government in its refusal to provide essential drugs and advertise information about safe-sex practices. Brome's *Love in the Plague*, while resembling Mains's novel in being indebted to the genre of dystopian fantasy, reveals, in addition, a Gothic component. Gothic motifs that it introduces include, in addition to the double and doubling, the haunted house and the representation of the city as an oppressive location permeated by the fear of contagion and death.

In comparing the AIDS virus and its effects with the bubonic plague that ravaged the population of London in 1665, *Love in the Plague* also has connections with historical fiction. Brome's description of the outbreak of the plague and the strategies that the seventeenth-century population employed to prevent it spreading, such as the locking up of infected houses, appears to be indebted to Daniel Defoe's *Diary of the Plague Year* (1722). The historian Laurel Brodsley, in an essay comparing the twentieth-century AIDS epidemic and its effects with those associated with the plague in the seventeenth-century, focuses attention on the different socio-political contexts of the two epidemics and the public responses they provoked.[71] Her comparison may have influenced Brome's novel.

Brome centres the narrative of *Love in the Plague* on Lucille, an academic living in 1980s London who is writing a book on seventeenth-century history. By portraying her developing what she calls 'another self'[72] that inhabits the seventeenth-century city, he utilises her to link the two historical periods and comment on the different epidemics that they harboured and their socio-political effects.

Brome opens the novel in a dramatic manner by describing Lucille waking one morning in her London home in a state of terror on account of the disturbing dream she has just experienced. As she tells her husband Richard, she believed herself to be standing in a street in seventeenth-century London in the company of a man, whose name she later learns was Barnaby, at the edge of a pit containing the corpses of plague victims. In fact so vivid was the experience that, on waking, she is convinced that her arm bears a red plague spot. Although Richard eventually succeeds in convincing her that the apparent symptom is a product of fantasy, she refuses to touch him for fear of infection. On dressing, she is alarmed to read in the newspaper the first reference to the AIDS virus that she and her husband have up to then encountered. Whereas Richard, whom Brome portrays at this stage in the narrative as sexually faithful to her, is unperturbed by the news, Lucille, on account of her memory of the plague pit and the mistaken assurance she gave Barnaby that 'I come from a place where there is no Plague' (p. 5), finds the newspaper feature deeply troubling. She strives to impress upon Richard the fact that, from this moment on, they must be totally honest with one another, especially with reference to their sex lives.

As the narrative unfolds, Lucille is portrayed experiencing further dreams about visiting seventeenth-century London. The impressions she gains of both the city and Barnaby himself are so vivid that, as she confides to the incredulous Richard, she is convinced that she does not merely dream about the location but visits it in person. In portraying her moving to and fro between 1980s and 1660s London, Brome employs what John Herdman in his study of the double describes as the 'divided personality'[73] version of the motif. The individual, instead of discovering that he has a doppelganger, represented by a figure who is physically distinct from himself, carries his alter ego inside him and leads, as a result, a double life.

Commenting on the complex role that the double and doubling can play in the representation of the Gothic protagonist and his psychology, Day argues that

> Because the self embodies within itself both the dynamics of all relationships in the Gothic world [a realm Day describes as evoking mystery and terror], and because the self manifests this duality through the creation of doubles, we can see that the encounter of the self with the Gothic world leads to its transformation of the self into its opposite, into its own hidden double'.[74]

This is the effect that the encounter with seventeenth-century London has on Lucille, helping to explain the compulsion she feels to visit it. The vivid descriptions she gives of the location, with the boarded-up houses, fires illuminating the streets and the atmosphere of corruption generated by the plague pits, evoke the typically uncanny image of the Gothic city, a topic that Robert Mighall vividly describes.[75] Despite its plague-infected aspect, Lucille becomes fascinated by it. She is attracted by the sense of mystery pervading it and the difference it evinces from the twentieth-century world with which she is familiar. On one occasion, while exploring the site, she loses her way in the maze of narrow streets and alleys. The event appears to metaphorically represent her increasing emotional involvement or, to cite the term that Day employs, 'enthrallment',[76] with the city and its residents, Barnaby in particular. He serves as her guide in her explorations and, although he is married and his wife Anna is expecting a baby, he and Lucille become increasingly emotionally involved.

Meanwhile in twentieth-century London and North America, as Brome describes, the effect of the AIDS virus is beginning to assume crisis proportions. Richard works in the field of cybernetics and, while visiting Massachusetts to lecture at MIT and assist with a research project, he becomes infected by the virus. Though identifying as heterosexual and having never before felt sexually attracted to a man, he has unprotected sex with his US colleague Luke in the aftermath of a party that the two men attend. Lucille, of course, is appalled by Richard's news. She has been considering becoming pregnant by him but, on his return to London, refuses to have sex for fear that the baby will be born HIV positive.

As well as employing the episode of Richard's visit to Massachusetts to explore his personal trajectory, Brome utilises it to depict the effect of the AIDS crisis on US queer subculture. Richard perceives with disquiet that, as the epidemic gains momentum, gay relationships are becoming increasingly fragile and deceit between partners and friends commonplace. As Luke informs him, people frequently lie about their sex lives, concealing the fact that they are HIV positive or have experienced unprotected sex.

Lucille's experience of travelling back in time to seventeenth-century London, in which, lured by the attraction that the city and Barnaby exert, she finds herself engaging with increasing frequency, enables her to compare the effects of the twentieth-century AIDS crisis with those of the bubonic plague. The two epidemics, she discovers, are different in the way they operate. Whereas the plague generally kills its victims relatively speedily, AIDS works more slowly. The latter, as Joseph Dewey describes, originates in 'a retrovirus... that slumbers until, after stretches of years, it begins the steady work of destroying the body's fragile defences against illness'.[77] However, different though the two epidemics are, the responses they evoke in seventeenth and twentieth-century societies reveal marked similarities. Both societies resent the restrictions that the fear of infection imposes on their lives. As Luke's sister Vanessa observes, 'In the plague years they had inspectors who locked up people in their houses. They made sure they remained locked up. How long before we have inspectors?' (p. 14). In fact, as Richard has discovered from the party at MIT that he attended with Luke, informal 'inspections' of this kind are already taking place. The guests at the party, on discovering in their midst a man who is rumoured to have engaged in unsafe sex and to be HIV positive, frogmarched him outside and subjected him to impromptu punishment. Luke reacts to the event with disgust, remarking that, 'AIDS has made people vicious' (p. 112), while Vanessa, on hearing of the episode, sharply retorts,

'The disease has infected the whole sexual snake pit' (p. 146). The situation in seventeenth-century plague-stricken London, Lucille observes, is similar to that in the US in certain respects. The citizens, terrified of contagion, punish victims of the disease who leave their homes in search of food as well as accusing neighbours of being infected, even if they are healthy. She also hears unverified accounts of women having killed their babies for fear that they may have been infected in the womb. Uncertainty also exists in both societies about the means by which the two epidemics are spread. On learning that the baby belonging to the seventeenth-century Barnaby is ill, despite the fact that his mother Anna appears heathy, Lucille, perturbed by the event, asks, 'How can the baby be infected but not the mother?' (p. 24). Barnaby helplessly replies in a sentence that sums up the climate of ignorance and fear currently pervading the city, 'We do not understand' (p. 24). A similar state of confusion exists in twentieth-century London and Massachusetts in relation to HIV and AIDS, since 'one medical expert claims that semen is contagious, another saliva' (p. 109). As Laurel Brodsley, commenting in 1992 on the imperfect medical understanding of both the bubonic plague and AIDS in the early years of the epidemics, observes, 'Plague was not fully understood in the eighteenth century, AIDS is not fully understood now'.[78]

Brome leaves ambiguous the question of whether Lucille actually does travel back in time to the seventeenth-century or whether she fantasises the event, preserving, as a result, the mystery on which the narrative hinges. He portrays her exploring the different areas of the plague-ridden city with Barnaby who, with the schools having closed, is unable to practise his profession as a teacher. Attracted by her charm and intrigued by the cultural and behavioural differences she exhibits from his wife, he feels privileged to act as her escort. Lucille, depressed by her husband Richard's infidelity and the discovery that he is HIV positive, eventually takes Barnaby as her lover, regarding her relationship with him increasingly real. The fact that, on returning to her 1980s home, she discovers on her breasts bruises from his passionate lovemaking and finds herself on one occasion wearing a cotton smock of the kind that women wore in seventeenth-century England, appears to verify her claim that this is the case. Both phenomena are, however, open to rational explanation. The psychoanalyst she visits diagnoses the bruises as 'hallucinations' resulting from 'psychological conversion' (p. 46) while, as Richard points out, smocks of the kind she is wearing were fashionable in 1960s London.

She may have had one in her wardrobe or been given it by a friend. Brome frames these events and the questions they raise with debates about the concept of the de-centered self and the fragmentation of the psyche. Whereas Richard insists that, 'There's no such thing as an integrated, continuing I, which remains consistent and goes on experiencing life', sardonically adding that he regards humanity's desire to believe there is to be 'another of God's tricks' (p. 32), Lucille veers between endorsing and rejecting his view. While understanding both her analyst's and husband's insistence that the visits that she believes she makes to the seventeenth-century London are insubstantial fantasies, she nonetheless harbours a conviction – and a secret desire – that they are real.

Other examples of doubling, besides those associated with Lucille and the visits she pays, in the role of her 'other self' to seventeenth-century London, also occur in the narrative. Elisabeth Bronfen, connecting the utilisation of the double in Gothic fantasy with Freud's famous dictum that, 'The finding of an object is always a refinding of it',[79] argues that since, as he claims, the current objects of our affection tend to repeat, with displacements and differences, features of our earlier ones, so, in fiction, 'the second term doubles by copying the first'.[80] This is the case, as Lucille recognises, with her second love, the seventeenth-century Barnaby, since he in fact mirrors attributes of her first love, her twentieth-century husband Richard. The two men, as well as valuing Lucille for her intellect as well as her sensuality, also resemble one another in the fact that they both have prior emotional commitments in their lives. Although both feel themselves to be in love with Lucille, Barnaby remains emotionally attached to his wife Anna, while Richard is involved intellectually and emotionally with the cyborg 'Albertine' that he has invented in his cybernetic researches.

Richard, though having initially regarded Albertine in a purely academic manner as an interesting research project, finds himself, like Nathaniel, the protagonist of E.T.A. Hoffmann's story 'The Sandman' who becomes infatuated with the puppet Olympia, becoming over the months emotionally obsessed with her. Lucille, in consequence, though recognising the folly of her response, discovers herself becoming jealous of Albertine and regarding her, non-human though she is, as her rival in love. With Richard absent in Massachusetts researching concepts of artificial intelligence with Luke, she finds the thought of Albertine, domiciled in the laboratory in the basement of her home, disturbing and eerie. She feels that the building, uncannily dominated by Albertine's presence, is becoming transformed into a haunted house. Determined to rid herself of her rival, she takes an axe and, in an episode mingling violence with a sense of pathos, descends the stairs to the basement and demolishes her. However, in destroying the cyborg, Lucille also destroys an aspect of herself. As Brome indicates, in representing a construct of femininity, Albertine signifies Lucille's alter ego and mirror image. Whereas Albertine has been constructed by a male scientist working in the field of cybernetics according to the blueprint that he invented, Lucille is culturally constructed according to the conventions of a phallocentric society and its image of 'woman'.

The name 'Albertine' that Richard assigns to the cyborg he constructs also recalls, of course, the female character Albertine who features in Marcel Proust's *A la Recherche du Temps Perdu*. Proust's narrator becomes emotionally obsessed with Albertine both on account of her personal attractions and because, as he discovers, she has sexual relationships with women, the event giving her a mysterious erotic allure. Richard, in turn, becomes obsessed with her cybernetic double that he has constructed, even telling his fellow scientists that he is in love with her. On learning that Lucille has in fact destroyed her, he is emotionally devastated – as likewise is Proust's narrator when he learns of Albertine's death.

Brome's utilisation of the double and doubling in *Love in the Plague*, as my analysis illustrates, indicates that the two motifs, rather than representing merely intriguing devices that the writer employs to construct a tightly structured plot, contribute to the narrative's thematic and conceptual interests. The numerous incidents of doubling that Brome introduces serve to metaphorically construct a web that enfolds the various characters, indicating the claustrophobic nature of their lives, entrapped as they are in the grip of the different epidemics and the urban contexts they inhabit. The two motifs have, in this respect, socio-political significance in serving to illustrate the destructive effects of the epidemics on society.

In contrast to Brome who utilises motifs of the double and doubling to explore the AIDS crisis of the 1980s and centres his novel on a comparison between the AIDS virus and the bubonic plague, the Canadian Susan Swan, writing in the early 1990s, employs them in *The Wives of Bath* to treat gender and its construction, in particular female to male transsexuality. Reference to doubling occurs frequently in discussions of transsexuality. Prosser, for example, describes the F to M transsexual as being 'haunted'[81] by the thought of the male double that she seeks by means of transitioning to access and embody. Halberstam similarly depicts the transsexual as existing in a state of cross-identification, with his persona failing to match his identity.[82] Both analyses, as we shall see, are relevant to Swan's *The Wives of Bath*.

Swan locates her novel in the Toronto of the early 1960s, focusing on the experiences of the thirteen-year-old Mouse and the sixteen-year-old transsexual Paulie, the friend she makes while studying at Bath Ladies College. As well as exploring topics of gender performance and transsexuality, Swan also constructs a feminist critique of the misogynistic and transphobic attitudes that operated in the pre-feminist society of the period. She utilises the motif of the double, as well as imagery with connotations of the grotesque and monstrous, to represent both the difficulty Mouse initially experiences in understanding Paulie's gender change and the conflict that Paulie herself feels to exist between, to cite the phrase Prosser employs, her 'inner and outer body'.[83]

The novel opens with Mouse, positioned as narrator, explaining how she came to exchange the name 'Mary Beatrice', with which she was christened, for her current unflattering nickname. She describes herself, in addition to having 'slender, fan shaped ears' and 'a long, pointed nose', as being 'humpbacked like a rodent',[84] the deformity, as she explains, resulting from her having contracted polio as an infant. She compares her appearance with the grotesque figure Quasimodo in the film of Victor Hugo's *The Hunchback of Notre Dame*, though cheering herself with the thought that, unlike him, she has no disfiguring zits or protruding teeth. She has secretly named her deformed shoulder 'Alice' after her mother who died shortly after her birth. Although, as she admits, her shoulder is a source of humiliation, it has the advantage of keeping the memory of her mother alive for, as she wryly observes, 'Alice will always be with me' (p. 31).

Having given an account of her maternal history, Mouse proceeds, in an episode reminiscent of Antonia White's *Frost in May* that similarly interrelates fiction of the gynaeceum with Gothic,[85] to describe her arrival at Bath Ladies College. She is sent to the institution against her will on account of the fact that, so she suspects, her stepmother Sal, her father Morley's second wife and her rival in his affections, 'wanted to get rid of me' (p. 15) in order to enjoy his full attention. Mouse hopes that her father, on noticing the College's grim exterior with its barred windows, will change his mind about sending her there and decide to take her home. Instead, he meekly observes, in a remark that Mouse dismisses as an abject attempt to flatter her stepmother, 'Well, Sal, you're a woman. I guess you know best' (p. 17).

The atmosphere of College life turns out in fact to be as rigid and stultifying as Mouse had feared. As she perceives, oppressive gender codes operate there as they do at home, with the pretty girls receiving attention while the plain or argumentative ones tend to be ignored. She also notices that women, whether pretty or plain, are generally treated as inferior to men. The dance she attends at the end of the first term furnishes her with a vivid illustration of this. Noting the contempt with which her date Jack and his male peers, imported for the evening from the boys' school in the area, treat the female residents 'from the teachers who terrorized us with their bells and gatings to the overfed boarders and snobby day girls' (p. 217), she recognises that, from a male viewpoint, 'We were all wives of Bath...for no matter how hard any of us struggled, Bath Ladies College was only a fiefdom in the kingdom of men' (p. 217). Though resenting the boys' low opinion of women, Mouse, on casting a glance at her female fellow pupils, finds herself sneakingly endorsing it. In a comment that recalls Luce Irigaray's representation of phallocentric culture as signifying 'an economy of the same',[86] since it defines women, intellectually and socially, as defective men, she thinks despondently, 'Girls were only mock boys as far as I was concerned' (pp. 14–15).

Like White in *Frost in May*, Swan represents the College as resembling a Gothic castle. It is housed in a private mansion constructed in the nineteenth-century and has ornamental towers and a turreted roof. She portrays Mouse, on first entering the building, being haunted by eerie events and encountering a series of uncanny doubles of herself and her deceased mother in images in pictures, mirrors and dreams. Mouse is assigned to a dormitory in one of the towers and, on struggling up the staircase to reach it, she notices on the wall a portrait of an eccentric-looking woman dressed in Edwardian-style cycling gear. The groundsman Sergeant, who is carrying her suitcase, informs her that this 'holy terror' (p. 26), as he disrespectfully calls the figure, is Viola Higgs, the founder of the College and its first headmistress. After presiding over the institution for a number of years, she committed suicide by hanging herself from a hook in the ceiling of the tower. Mouse is disturbed to see the headmistress's appearance replicated in the image of herself she encounters reflected in the mirror in the dormitory. Catching sight of what she terms 'her sly, wise face' with its 'thin, lopsided mouth', she thinks, with a pang of self-disgust, 'Mouse, you are grotesque!' (p. 31).

These events are re-worked in the dream relating to her maternal genealogy that Mouse experiences during the first night that she spends at the College. The dream scenario opens with her hearing a strange whirring noise resembling 'a delicate mechanical sound like the *flap-flap* of tiny metal wings' (p. 40) that is replaced by the sound of the voice of her deceased mother singing. Her mother then enters, followed by 'the ghostly figure' (p. 41) of Viola Higgs on her tricycle. Mouse watches her mother unbuckle the leather case she is holding and, taking from it an oilcan and a pair of gardening shears, hand them to Miss Higgs. She then seats herself on a bench while Miss Higgs, as Mouse describes, 'tilts the can close to her neck, until a thick, slow stream of oil bled down the front of my mother's frilled blouse' (p. 42). Cutting a hole in her mother's blouse in proximity to her heart, Miss Higgs proceeds to hack off clumps of her hair. Mouse runs to her mother in an effort to protect her but is prevented from doing so by Miss Higgs slamming the door in her face. The dream concludes with Mouse hearing her mother singing the words of the hymn, 'Take my hands and let them move/ At the impulse of Thy love' (p. 42). Interpreted in the context of the assault that Miss Higgs has perpetrated on her, they evoke not Christian self-sacrifice but masochistic self-punishment.

Freud's analysis of the multiple identifications that the dreamer can adopt[87] serves to illuminate the significance of Mouse's dream. Although, identifying as herself, Mouse enacts the role of loving daughter who tries to protect her mother from Miss Higgs's attack, identifying with her mother, she features as its victim. In identifying with Miss Higgs, she appears to enact, on the contrary, the role of her mother's tormenter, possibly articulating the repressed anger she feels toward her for dying and leaving her at the mercy of her stepmother Sal and the College staff.

Swan's description of Mouse being alerted to her mother's presence in the dream by hearing her sing has Gothic connotations since it intertextually echoes the experience of Ellena, the heroine of Ann Radcliffe's *The Italian*. While imprisoned in a convent, Ellena is alerted to the presence of her mother Olivia, whom she had assumed to be dead, by hearing her singing in the chapel choir.[88] The intertextual reference to Radcliffe's novel has the effect of foregrounding Mouse's emotional isolation since her dream encounter with her mother concludes not in a joyful act of reunion, as occurs in Radcliffe's narrative, but, since Mouse's mother is dead, in emphasising her absence.

Another pupil at the College whom Swan portrays suffering from a lack of maternal nurture is Paulie, the sixteen-year-old pupil whom Mouse encounters in her first term there. Paulie is typecast by both pupils and teaching staff as the 'bad girl' of the institution – and she performs the role with evident relish. Rumour relates that her mother is in a mental institution and that the current headmistress Miss Vaughan has rescued her from a home for problem girls where she had been dumped. On hearing Mouse express sympathy for Paulie on account of the fact that she too lacks 'a real mother' (p. 80), Miss Vaughan selects her as Paulie's companion. She suggests that she befriend her and, hinting at Paulie's rebellious reputation, 'keep an eye on her' (p. 81).

Mouse initially makes contact not with Paulie herself but with her twin brother Lewi – or the individual whom everyone at Bath College assumes to be her twin. He occasionally appears at the College at weekends to assist Sergeant with odd jobs around the place and, on accidentally meeting him in the tower, Mouse finds his air of yobbish masculinity distinctly intimidating. She regards the sight of what she vividly describes as 'his full mouth that spread like a hostile ripple across his bony face' (p. 32) unnerving in the extreme.

One evening, while walking with Paulie in the College grounds, Mouse loses sight of her in the encroaching mist and, while searching for her, is startled to see Lewis appear in her place. On perceiving how his 'teeth sparkled and glistened like a werewolf's' (p. 85), she fears that he may be intending to rape or kill her. Reference to sounds of an eerie kind, as Royle observes,[89] can have the effect of enhancing the uncanny nature of an event and, as Swan describes, Mouse's terror is exacerbated by her hearing 'the wind in the ravine trees, mixed with the soft whooshing sound of traffic on the highway bridge to the north' (p. 86). As occurred in the dream of her mother that she experienced on her first night at the College, they incongruously link the natural world with the technological. Insisting he is taking her to meet Paulie, Lewis steers Mouse toward the dark cavity of the coal shed that houses the ancient boiler that heats the building. Hearing the strange mechanical noise emerging from the 'dilapidated machinery' (p. 86), Mouse experiences the disturbing sense, 'That Lewis was not who he said he was, that he'd lied' (p. 86). He unexpectedly grabs hold of her arm and, in a sexually provocative manner, as she describes, 'tilted my head back and stuck his tongue in my ear. He then put his bony face right next to mine and hissed "Bradford, don't you know who I am?"' (p. 86). The words prompt her to recognise his identity. She perceives in astonishment that Paulie and Lewis, rather than being two different people, are one and the same. Lewis is, in fact, not a different individual but Paulie's transsexual double. Confused by the surreal nature of the perception, she wonders, 'Or *was* this person Paulie? Maybe it was a creature that could move with the authority of a man one minute and giggle like a girl the next?' (p. 88).

Paulie's unexpected metamorphosis into Lewis strikes Mouse, as she describes, as 'confusing and interesting – like watching a wizard melt into male and female shapes before your eyes' (p. 88). Her bemused response to her friend's sex change is illuminated by Royle's reference to the way in which 'uncertainties about sexual identity'[90] can evoke a sense of the uncanny, while her remark about the wizard's shape-shifting abilities echoes James Kinkaid's analysis of the way in which experiences of an eerie kind involve perceptions that appear to 'lie outside the realm of the explicable, outside of language'.[91] Prosser's observation, articulated with reference to the transsexual, that 'The body that should be home is foreign, the familiar is felt as *unheimlich* and most strange'[92] also sheds light on Mouse's response.

The unexpected transformation of Paulie into Lewis influences, as Mouse perceives, her own responses and behaviour. She notices that, 'Every change in Paulie provoked a change in me. When she acted like Lewis, I wanted to exhale responsibility for myself like a sigh; when she acted like Paulie, I was myself again. Well, almost myself – as much as a mouse can be' (p. 88). Watching herself succumb to Lewis's erotic charm and domination, she hears the voice of her stepmother Sal ringing ironically in her ears, 'See, Mary Beatrice, you're a girl after all – deferring to a man the way a woman should!' (p. 88).

Gender roles and identities, Butler argues, are not authentic but are constructed by 'the repeated stylization of the body'. They take the form of 'a set of repeated acts within a highly rigid regulatory frame that congeal over time to produce the appearance of substance, of a natural sort of being'.[93] Although the individual cannot entirely control this 'stylization', he can, to a degree, subversively re-cast it. This is the strategy that, as Mouse discovers, Paulie employs. Imitating the body movements and speech of the working-class boys she sees on the Toronto streets, she constructs her identity as Lewis in contrast to the image projected by their upper-class peers. On watching her race through the corridor of the College, she regards her as 'one of the wild boys who live in girls' dreams' (p. 118) and, though she does not admit the fact to her, finds her appearance sexually exciting. On waking one night and glimpsing her standing by the open window in the dormitory contemplatively smoking, she describes how, 'She looks so like Lewis right then that I pulled the covers over my head and did what I often did in my bedroom at home – i.e. masturbate' (p. 97).

On recognising in Mouse a potential pal and side-kick, Lewis – for this is the name that Mouse now privately addresses her by – volunteers to share his skills of male performance with her, enabling her, as he observes, 'to be a boy, like me.' Unconsciously exposing the oppressive nature of 1960s constructs of femininity, he enthusiastically observes, 'It's easier for a girl to become a boy than the other way round... If you act with authority, people will accept that you're a boy. But if you want to be a girl you have to act like a dope, and acting stupid is harder' (p. 119). He adds as a lure, 'You'll look better as a guy', adding, with a perfunctory nod at Alice Hump, 'It'll be easier to cover up – that' (p. 90).

Lewis is true to his word. In addition to lending Mouse a masculine-style jacket and building up the shoulders so that her figure, as he describes, 'looks bulky, not deformed' (p. 120), he teaches her to stand upright and lock her knees while walking in order to enact an imperious male swagger. He also introduces her to the mysterious underground world of the tunnels that lies beneath the College and that he has appropriated as his domain. The College resembles the 'double architecture, one above ground, the other subterranean'[94] that Anthony Vidler describes in *The Architectural Uncanny*, and together the two teenagers explore the uncanny secrets of the submerged location. Mouse's description of the way 'the heating pipes undulated in the gloom like fat, dark worms' (p. 100) recalls the 'maze of stone-shadowed twilight'[95] and the monstrous creatures inhabiting the underground world that H. P. Lovecraft describes in *At The Mountains of Madness* (1936). It also evokes the fantasy world of the unconscious and, while traversing it, the two teenagers appropriately come across Viola Higgs's ancient tricycle that featured in Mouse's dream and a trunk containing the deceased headmistress's cycling gear.

On exiting the underground area near the entrance to the ravine that traverses the city, Lewis emerges with Mouse into the light of the street lamps. Here he engages in a boisterous fist-fight with his arch rivals, the boys from the nearby College, while Mouse, acting as his second-in-command, does her best to protect him. Dropping the persona of a timid rodent that she has enacted all her life, she proudly re-invents herself as 'a troublemaker, a bad girl, a rule-breaker' (p. 103). She also joins Lewis in flirting with the girls from the city who transgressively visit the location at night in search of sex.

Another adventure on which Lewis and Mouse embark together introduces reference to lesbianism, illustrating the punitive measures that the custodians of law and order in the period adopted in an attempt to prevent same-sex female involvements. On stealing a cache of letters written by two members of the College staff who had formed a relationship together, they discover an account of the way in which one of the women had been assaulted by a police officer in a coffee booth in the park when he happened to see her kissing her female partner.

In subsequent weeks Mouse accompanies Lewis on several more expeditions to the ravine. She finds the adoption of a male persona thrillingly liberating, giving scope for the expression of self-assertiveness for which the feminine one, to which she was accustomed, furnished little scope. However, as the weeks pass, she starts to experience doubts. As well as feeling guilty about deceiving the girls with whom she flirts about her gender, on kissing them she finds herself feeling confused about whether she is a girl or a boy. She also dislikes the tests of masculinity that Lewis, inspired by his gorilla idol Kong, whose heroic though scary image stares down from the movie poster on the wall of the boiler room, commands her to perform. Although Mouse succeeds in enduring the severe caning that Lewis, instructed by Kong who appears to endorse the belief, current in the period, in training men to endure pain, inflicts upon her, she finds herself emotionally incapable of caning him in return. The event has the effect of alerting her to the oppressive nature of constructs of masculinity. As she tells her hero President Kennedy in one of the numerous fan letters she sends him, 'I don't like being a man that much, Mr. President. I don't know how you do it' (p.138). By instructing Paulie in male role performance in the early stages of their friendship, Lewis enhanced her self-esteem and confidence and introduced her to a transgressive world of teenage culture she found liberating. However, now that he insists on instructing her in the brutal facets of the male role she understandably questions his tutelage and starts to reject it.

Swan's reference to Kong, and the important role she describes him playing in Lewis's imagination as his personal god and avatar, is one of the most inventive and, in giving an insight into the socio-cultural perspectives of the period, effective features of Swan's narrative. A series of films focusing on the gorilla, the first produced in 1933, celebrated his physical prowess. One in fact appeared in cinemas in 1962, the period in which Swan sets her novel. Both the divine status that Lewis assigns to Kong and his intense emotional investment in him connects the latter intertextually with the eponymous polecat-ferret Sredni Vashtar who features in Saki's scary Gothic tale.[96] Saki portrays the sickly ten-year-old protagonist Conradin keeping the creature in the shed at the end of the garden and treating him as a mixture of idol, alter ego and defender. Saki concludes the story by portraying Conradin employing the creature to get rid of the oppressive female guardian to whose care he has been relegated, the splashes of blood that appear on its fur furnishing gruesome evidence that it has performed the task. The macabre act of murder that Swan portrays Lewis committing in the concluding stages of her novel strikes the reader as more horrific still since Lewis performs it himself rather than using a surrogate, as Conradin does. The performance of it has the effect of moving the narrative from Gothic into the genre of Horror.

While residing at the College Lewis has formed an intimate relationship with Tory,[97] another pupil who studies there, and, feeling confident that he can sustain his male identity and persona, offers to escort her to the end-of-term dance. However, Tory's brother Rick has heard a rumour circulating in the institution that Lewis is not in fact a boy and, when Lewis comes to collect Tory to take her to the dance, obscenely demands that he show him his penis as proof of his masculinity. Lewis refuses and strides indignantly away, while secretly conceiving a crazy, violent plan to fulfil Rick's demand. When Mouse, worried by his absence, goes in search of him on the night of the dance, she finds him crouching in the tunnel beneath the College beside the castrated corpse of the groundsman Sergeant. After killing him with blows from a hockey stick, Lewis has removed his penis with a scalpel and is struggling to glue it on his female body in order to furnish Rick with physical proof of his manhood.

Swan's representation of Lewis's murder of Sergeant and the grotesque strategy she describes him employing to transition to male, invites different interpretations. Although it is possible to read her introduction of the event as indicating that she is condemning transsexuality as unnatural and violent, the sympathetic portrayal she creates of Lewis in other episodes, emphasising his isolation, the macho constructs of masculinity he inherits from society, and the lack of therapeutic and social assistance available to transsexuals in the period, all suggest that this is not the case. The poignant love scene that Mouse witnesses occurring between him and Tory prior to his murder of Sergeant endorses this. Mouse watches him from the window standing with Tory at the base of a military statue on the College lawn, the stone figure with its raised sword symbolising the militaristic ideal of masculinity that furnishes Lewis with his model of manhood. On this occasion, however, Lewis enacts a very different model, one that reflects ideals of male gentleness and protectiveness. Taking Tory's hand in his, he raises it to his lips and tenderly kisses it. Moved by his gesture and by the sense of affection and mutual trust that the two lovers display, Mouse thinks, 'They looked so happy and absorbed' (p. 152) – that is until the sound of the banging on the windows by the other pupils, who have been angrily observing the scene, interrupts the lovers' idyll, alerts Lewis's attention and forces him to flee.

In addition, although Mouse, like society in general, is appalled by Lewis's murder of Sergeant and the bizarre method of 'transitioning' that he employs, she sympathises with his predicament in living in a society that insists on defining masculinity by the body. Alerting attention to the essentialism of this, while looking forward to the performative focus of queer theory, she thinks, 'It did seem unfair that Paulie needed a penis to be a man. John Wayne would still be John Wayne if he had a vagina, wouldn't he?' (p. 213). Her remark, as well as endorsing Butler's concept of gender as performative, illustrates Swan's utilisation of provocative humour as a strategy to jolt the reader into confronting the complexities of sexual politics. Defining her own ambitions in life, Mouse observes, 'I wanted something more grand than a penis. I wanted what my hero, President Kennedy, had: courage, individual style, a life of action, and an intellect.' Then, relapsing into the doubt and self-deprecation that characterised her behaviour before she met Paulie, she timidly adds, 'Was I asking too much for a Mouse?' (p. 116).

The novel concludes on a depressing note with Lewis being incarcerated in a mental institution and Mouse receiving news of both the assassination of President Kennedy and, a catastrophe with significant personal implications, the death of her own father. Both are men in whom, despite her father's emotional neglect of her, she had invested a significant degree of admiration and trust. As for Kong, his image continues to gaze down at her from the silver screen when she visits the cinema, reminding her of her involvement with Paulie. Interrelating the personal with the political, she describes, on the novel's final page, how, 'I still see Kong in late-night movies – and wonder what he'd say if he knew that he'd inspired a two-girl fan club in the days before President Kennedy died' (p. 236).

As this chapter illustrates, the vampire and double, two motifs that feature prominently in Gothic texts, play a versatile role in queer Gothic. Reference to the vampire features prominently in the theoretical writing and fiction produced by members of the lesbian sexual radical movement that emerged in the UK and USA in the 1980s and early 1990s. The recognition by theorists, such as Sue Ellen Case, that the creature, on account of its associations with so-called deviant sexualities and the marginalised life of the outcast, serves as an appropriate metaphor for lesbian and gay existence in homophobic society served to promote its utilisation in fiction and film. Male gay writers such as Richard Dyer also helped to develop the figure of 'the sympathetic vampire'. They portray him acting as narrator and telling his own story in a manner resembling the way that lesbians and gay men, after years of being silenced by heterosexist sociopolitical forces, were similarly striving – often in the context of episodes of homophobic oppression and backlash – to achieve.

As Kingston's novel *Chrystal Heart* illustrates, present-day writers develop the tradition, established in the 1980s and 1990s, of utilising the motif of the vampire to explore issues relating to sexual politics. Interweaving conventions of Gothic, sci-fi, neo-Victorian narrative and steam-punk, Kingston centres her novel on the adventures of Chrystal, a vampire with cyborg connections. Whereas the narrative's playful tone, combined with the interplay of different genres and fictional forms that it constructs, relates it to the lesbian feminist fiction produced in the 1980s and early 1990s, Chrystal does not, in fact, identify as lesbian. Regarding her sexuality as mobile, she affirms her right to have love affairs with men as well as women.

Writing in an earlier period at the start of the 1990s, the American Gary Bowen, though anticipating Kingston in interrelating the vampire's sympathetic image with its traditionally monstrous one, focuses *Diary of a Vampire* on the adventures of the male gay Rafael. Re-working the topic of homosexual legibility that features in nineteenth-century fiction and utilising vampiric identification as a metaphor for homosexual, Bowen illustrates the fears about coming out and legibility that the gay man living in the period experienced. A focus on the vampire's shape-shifting abilities, evoking a sense of Deleuzian pleasure in becoming an animal, also informs the novel, alleviating its focus on prejudice and oppression.

Another motif with Gothic connotations that plays a significant role in queer Gothic, its versatility reflected in the contribution that it makes to the representation of both homosexuality and different forms of transgender, is the double. Twentieth- and twenty-first-century writers employ it in different ways. Juxtaposing in *Love in the Plague* episodes set in London and Massachusetts during the 1980s AIDS crisis with ones located in seventeenth-century London in the era of the bubonic plague, Brome compares the two epidemics and their effects on the different populations.

The proliferation of incidents of doubling that occurs in the narrative illustrates and enacts the sense of entrapment and claustrophobia that the characters are portrayed experiencing as a result of the fears and restrictions that the epidemics create.

Swan, in contrast, setting *The Wives of Bath* in the early 1960s, skilfully pioneers the utilisation of the double and doubling as vehicles to represent transsexuality and different forms of gender performance. As well as employing the motifs to represent the shift that the transsexual Paulie enacts from a female identity and persona to that of her male double Lewis, and her friend Mouse's view of her transformation as uncanny, she utilises them to depict the masculine gender performance with which Paulie encourages Mouse to experiment. Oppressive constructs of masculinity also receive critique. The novel illustrates especially vividly the uses that Gothic motifs play in illuminating transsexuality and the onlooker's and society's view of it.

As is illustrated by the vampire Rafael's transformation into a bloodthirsty cougar in Bowen's *Diary of a Vampire*, Kingston's description in *Chrystal Heart* of Sam's astonishment at glimpsing the 'unlikely combination of flesh and mechanics' (p. 163) that Chrystal's unclothed body reveals, and the depiction of the cyborg Albertine in Brome's *Love in the Plague*, representations of the vampire and the double evoke on occasion connotations of the monstrous and grotesque. This introduces us to the topics of the monster and the shape-shifting abilities associated with it on which the following chapter focuses and the contribution that they make to queer Gothic.

Notes

1. Fred Botting, 'Introduction: Twentieth Century Gothic: Our Monsters, Our Pets', in Botting and Townshend, eds., *Gothic: Critical Concepts in Literary Studies*, vol. 4, pp. 7–8. (Botting 2004).
2. Catherine Spooner, *Contemporary Gothic*, pp. 26–7, 51–2. (Spooner 2006).
3. Greg Herren and J. M. Redmann, *Night Shadows*, p. 3. (Herren and Redmann 2012).
4. Richard Dyer, Kim Newman, Henry Sheehan and Ian Sinclair, 'Dracula and Desire', *Sight and Sound*, 3 (1993), 10. (Dyer et al. 1993).
5. See for example Eric Garber (ed.), *Embracing the Dark* (Garber 1991); Bianca de Moss, *Blood Sisters: Lesbian Vampire Tales* (Moss 2006); Pam Keesey, *Dark Angels: Lesbian Vampire Stories*. (Keesey 2001).
6. Ahmed, *Queer Phenomenology*, p. 107.
7. Halberstam, *Skin Shows*, p. 36.

8. Michael Rowe, 'All the Pretty Boys' in Redman and Herren (eds), *Night Shadows*, pp.114–118. (Rowe 2012).
9. Halberstam, *Skin Shows*, p. 21.
10. Karl Heinrich Ulrichs, 'Manor', translated by Hubert Kennedy, in Eric Garber (ed.), *Embracing the Dark*, p. 107. (Ulrichs 1991).
11. Bram Stoker, *Dracula*, p. 39. (Stoker 1996).
12. Christopher Craft, '"Kiss Me With Those Red Lips": Gender and Inversion in Bram Stoker's *Dracula*', *Representations*, 8 (1984), 109. (Craft 1984).
13. Craft, "Kiss Me with Those Red Lips", p. 109.
14. William Veeder, '"Carmilla": The Arts of Repression', in Botting and Townshend (eds), *Gothic: Critical Concepts*, vol. 3, p. 117 (Veeder 2004).
15. Gina Wisker, 'Devouring Desires: Lesbian Gothic Horror', in Hughes and Smith (eds), *Queering the Gothic*, p. 126. (Wisker 2009).
16. Joan Gordon and Veronica Hollinger (eds), 'Introduction: The Shape of Vampirism', in *Blood Read: The Vampire as Metaphor in Contemporary Culture*, p. 2. (Gordon and Hollinger 1997).
17. Botting, 'Introduction: Twentieth Century Gothic: Our Monsters, Our Pets', in Botting and Townshend, eds., *Gothic: Critical Concepts*, vol. 4, pp. 7–8. (Botting 2004).
18. Spooner, *Contemporary Gothic*, p. 52.
19. Sheridan Le Fanu, 'Carmilla', in Pam Keesey (ed.), *Daughters of Darkness: Lesbian Vampire Stories*, p. 53. (Le Fanu, 1993).
20. Critics who discuss the concept of 'the sympathetic vampire' and the development of the motif include Gordon and Hollinger, 'Introduction', *Blood Read*, p. 2; Botting, 'Introduction: Twentieth Century Gothic: Our Monsters, Our Pets', vol. 4, pp. 7–8 (Botting 2004); and Milly Williamson, 'Let Them All In: The Evolution of the Sympathetic Vampire', in Leon Hunt, Sharon Lockyer and Milly Williamson (eds), *Screening the Undead: Vampires and Zombies in Film and Television*, pp. 71–91. (Williamson 2014). Williamson's essay, though useful, is disappointing since, while referring to a number of relevant films, she does not refer to the contribution that theorists and writers associated with the lesbian and gay liberation movements of the 1980s and early 1990s, especially the lesbian sexual radical movement, made to the development of the vampire motif and the debates that it has provoked.
21. See Williamson, 'Let Them All In', pp. 71–91.
22. Palmer, *Lesbian Gothic*, pp. 99–127.
23. See Emma Healey, *Lesbian Sex Wars*, pp. 89–160. (Healey 1996); and Jagose, *Queer Theory*, pp. 62–70.
24. Jessica Benjamin, 'Master and Slave: The Fantasy of Erotic Domination', in Ann Snitow, Christine Stansell and Sharon Thompson (eds), *Desire: The Politics of Sexuality*, p. 208. (Benjamin 1984).

25. Sue-Ellen Case, 'Tracking the Vampire', *Differences: A Journal of Feminist Cultural Studies*, 3/2 (1991), 1–20. (Case 1991).
26. Barbara Creed, *The Monstrous Feminine: Film, Feminism, Psychoanalysis*, pp. 60–67. (Creed 1993).
27. Richard Dyer, 'Children of the Night: Vampirism as Homosexuality: Homosexuality as Vampirism', in Susannah Radstone (ed.), *Sweet Dreams: Sexuality, Gender and Popular Fiction*, p. 58. (Dyer 1993).
28. Ellis Hanson, 'Undead', in Fuss (ed.), *Inside/Out*, pp. 325–40. (Hanson 1991).
29. Anna Livia, *Minimax*, p. 112. (Livia 191).
30. For reference to steampunk see Gail Ashurst and Anne Powell, 'Under Their Own Steam: Magic, Science and Steampunk', in Justin D. Edwards and Agnieszka Soltysik Monnet (eds), *The Gothic in Contemporary and Popular Culture*, pp. 148–163. (Ashurst and Powell 2012).
31. Meg Kingston, *Chrystal Heart*, p. 36. (Kingston 2013) Subsequent references are to this edition and in the text.
32. Aspasia Stephanou, 'A "Ghastly Operation": Transfusing Blood, Science and the Supernatural in Vampire Texts', *Gothic Studies*, 25/2 (2013), 54. (Stephanou 2013).
33. Jackson, *Fantasy*, p. 119.
34. Donna J. Haraway, 'A Cyborg Manifesto: Science, Technology and Socialist-Feminism in the Late Twentieth-Century', in Haraway (ed.), *Simians, Cyborgs, and Women: The Reinvention of Nature*, p. 176 (Haraway 1991).
35. Linda Williams, 'When the Woman Looks', in Mary Ann Doan, Patricia Mellencamp and Linda Williams (eds), *Re-Visions: Essays in Feminist Film Criticism*, pp. 83–97 (Williams 1984).
36. Sue-Ellen Case, 'Tracking the Vampire' pp. 13–15.
37. Jagose, *Queer Theory*, pp. 69–70.
38. See, for example, Nancy Toder, *Choices* (Toder 1980).
39. Jan Clausen, 'My Interesting Condition', *Out/Look: National Lesbian and Gay Quarterly*, 7 (1990), 19 (Clausen 1990).
40. Spooner, 'Gothic Charm School, or, How the Vampire Learned to Sparkle', in Sam George and Bill Hughes (eds), *Open Graves, Open Minds: Representations of Vampires and the Undead from the Enlightenment to the Present Day*, p. 146. (Spooner 2013).
41. Sedgwick, *Epistemology of the Closet*, p. 80.
42. Fincher, *Queering Gothic in the Romantic Age*, pp. 137–45. (Fincher 2007).
43. Lee Edelman, *Homographesis: Essays in Gay Literary and Cultural Theory*, p. 5. (Edelman 1994).
44. Gary Bowen, *Diary of a Vampire*, p. 121. Subsequent references are to this edition and in the text (Bowen 1995).

45. Le Fanu, *Carmilla*, p. 42.
46. Fincher, *Queering Gothic in the Romantic Age*, p. 45.
47. Oscar Wilde, *The Picture of Dorian Gray*, p. 32. (Wilde 1996).
48. See Melanie R. Anderson, 'Wilde's Dorian Gray as Aesthetic Vampire', *POMP: Publications of the Mississippi Philological Association*, 12/2 (2008), 157–159. (Anderson 2008).
49. Sedgwick, *Epistemology of the Closet*, p. 68.
50. Aldana Reyes, '"Who Ordered the Hamburger with AIDS?": Haematophilic Semiotics in *Tru(e) Blood*', *Gothic Studies*, 15/1 (2013), 56. (Reyes 2013).
51. Elizabeth Grosz, 'Intolerable Ambiguity: Freaks as/at the Limit', in Rosemary Garland Thomson (ed.), *Freakery: Cultural Spectacles of the Extraordinary Body*, p. 182. (Grosz 1996).
52. Robert Azzarello, 'Unnatural Predators: Queer Theory meets Environmental Studies in Bram Stoker's *Dracula*', in Noreen Giffney and Myra J. Hird (eds), *Queering the Non-Human*, pp. 140–8. (Azzarello 2008).
53. Stoker, *Dracula*, p. 34.
54. MacCormack, 'Unnatural Alliances', in Chrsanthi Nigianni and Merl Storr (eds) *Deleuze and Queer Theory*, p. 143. (MacCormack 2009).
55. Trevor Holmes, 'Coming Out of the Coffin: Gay Males and Queer Goths in Contemporary Vampire Fiction', in Joan Gordon and Veronica Hollinger eds., *Blood Read*, p. 181. (Holmes 1997).
56. William Patrick Day, *In the Circles of Fear and Desire: A Study of Gothic Fantasy*, p. 21. (Day 1985).
57. Marshall Brown, *The Gothic Text*, p.128. (Brown 2003).
58. Freud, 'The Uncanny', p. 358.
59. Townshend, '"Love in a Convent": or Gothic and the Perverse Father of Queer Enjoyment', in Hughes and Smith (eds), *Queering the Gothic*, p. 17. (Townshend 2009).
60. David Stuart Davies (ed.), 'Introduction' to Richard Marsh, *The Beetle: A Mystery*, p. ix. (Davies 2007).
61. Eric Daffron, 'Double Trouble: The Self, the Social Order and the Trouble with Sympathy in the Romantic and Postmodern Gothic', *Gothic Studies*, 3:1 (2001), 78 (Daffron 2001). Haggerty similarly describes the creature Frankenstein that constructs as his 'second self' and 'secret (homoerotic) desire' (Haggerty, *Queer Gothic*, p. 52).
62. Haggerty, *Queer Gothic*, pp. 123-5.
63. Elaine Showalter, *Sexual Anarchy: Gender and Culture at the Fin de Siècle*, pp. 105–14. (Showalter 1992).
64. Henry James, *The Turn of the Screw*, p. 38 (James 1976). Eric Savoy discusses the significance of the governess's remark in 'Theory *a Tergo* in *The Turn of the Screw*', in Steven Bruhm and Natasha Hurley (eds),

Curiouser: on the Queerness of Children, p. 268 (Savoy 2004). He also alerts attention to James's reference to the governess thinking that she recognises on her first night at Bly, 'faint and far, the cry of a child' (*The Turn of the Screw*, p. 15).
65. See Butler, *Gender Trouble: Feminism and the Subversion of Identity*, pp. 79–149. (Butler 1990).
66. Julie Anne Peters, *Luna*, p. 17. (Peters 2004).
67. Douglas Crimp, *AIDS: Cultural Analysis/Cultural Activism*, pp. 12–14. (Crimp 1988).
68. See Owen Bowcott, 'Aids: Thatcher Tried to Block Public Health Warnings' *The Guardian*, December 30, 2016, p. 34. (Bowcott 2016).
69. Emmanuel S. Nelson, 'Introduction' in Nelson (ed.) *AIDS: The Literary Response*, pp.1–9. (Nelson 1992).
70. Crimp, *AIDS: Cultural Analysis/Cultural Activism*, p.12.
71. Laurel Brodsley, 'Defoe's *The Journal of the Plague Year*: A Model for Stories of the Plague', in Emmanuel S. Nelson (ed.), *Aids: The Literary Response*, pp. 11–21. (Brodsley 1992).
72. Vincent Brome, *Love in the Plague*, p. 35 (Brome 2001). Subsequent references are to this edition and in the text.
73. John Herdman, *The Double in Nineteenth Century Fiction*, p. 16. (Herdman 1990).
74. Day, *In the Circles of Fear and Desire*, p. 21.
75. For reference to the motif of the Gothic city see Robert Mighall, *A Geography of Victorian London: Mapping History's Nightmares*, pp. 28–45 (Mighall 2003); and Mighall, 'Gothic Cities', in Catherine Spooner and Emma McEvoy (eds), *The Routledge Companion to the Gothic*, pp. 54–62. (Mighall 2007).
76. Day, *In the Circles of Fear and Desire*, pp. 23–27.
77. Dewey, 'Music for a Closing: Responses to AIDS in Three American Novels', in Nelson (ed.), *AIDS*, p. 24.
78. Brodsley, 'Defoe's The Journal of the Plague Year: A Model for Stories of Plagues', in Nelson (ed.) *AIDS*, p. 19.
79. Freud, 'Transformations of Puberty: Three Essays in the Theory of Sexuality', in James Strachey, *Pelican Freud Library*, vol. 7, p. 145.
80. Elisabeth Bronfen, *Over Her Dead Body: Death, Femininity and the Aesthetic*, p. 324. (Bronfen 1992).
81. Jay Prosser, *Second Skins: The Body Narrative of Transsexuality*, p. 178, p.159. (Prosser 1998).
82. Halberstam, *In a Queer Time and Place*, p. 59.
83. Prosser, *Second Skins*, p. 70.
84. Susan Swan, *The Wives of Bath*, p. 6. (Swan 1993). Subsequent page references are to this edition and in the text.

85. See Palmer, 'Antonia White's *Frost in May:* Gothic Mansions, Ghosts and Particular Friendships', in Hughes and Smith (eds), *Queering the Gothic*, pp. 105–122. (Palmer 2009).
86. See Margaret Whitford, *Luce Irigaray: Philosophy in the Feminine*, p. 114. (Whitford 1991).
87. Freud, 'A Child is Being Beaten', in James Strachey and Angela Richards (eds), *The Pelican Freud Library*, pp. 163–93. (Freud 1981).
88. See Diane Hoeveler's discussion of the episode in *Gothic Feminism*, p. 109. (Hoeveler 1998).
89. Royle, *The Uncanny*, p. 46.
90. Royle, *The Uncanny*, p. 43.
91. James Kinkaid, 'Designing Gourmet Children', in Ruth Robbins and Julian Wolfreys (eds.), *Victorian Gothic*, p. 8. (Kinkaid 2000).
92. Prosser, *Second Skins*, p. 178.
93. Butler, *Gender Trouble*, p. 33.
94. Anthony Vidler, *The Architectural Uncanny: Essays in the Modern Unhomely*, p. 132. (Vidler 1999).
95. H. P. Lovecraft, 'At the Mountains of Madness', (1936) in Lovecraft, *Novels of Terror*, p. 60. (Lovecraft 1966).
96. Saki, 'Sredni Vashtar' in *The Chronicles of Clovis* (Saki 1989).
97. Swan's description of Tory's feelings of romantic attraction to the transsexual Paulie interestingly resembles the attraction that women felt for the US transsexual Teena Brandon who was murdered in 1993. Judith Halberstam, seeking to explain to hostile biographers who disparage Brandon as 'a quasi man' the erotic attraction she held for her female partners, suggests that 'Brandon's successful and romantically viable approximation of heterosexual masculinity attracted women precisely because it *was* denaturalized' and represented 'an ideal, improved version of the usual forms of masculinity they came across' (*In A Queer Time and Place*, pp. 65–68). Paulie's performance of romantic masculinity appears to attract Tory for similar reasons. Swan contrasts it with the boorish nature of the actual teenage masculinity of the period as represented by Jack, the boy who escorts Mouse to the school dance.

CHAPTER 4

Tracking the Monster

The Monster and Queer Sexuality

The monster is, of course, a popular motif in Gothic fiction and film. Figures exemplifying it and the grotesque body with which it is associated include the creature that Victor Frankenstein is depicted creating in his 'workshop of filthy creation'[1] in Mary Shelley's novel; Stevenson's portrayal of Dr Jekyll's grotesque doppelganger Hyde; and the goblin men in Christina Rossetti's *Goblin Market* characterised by their cats' faces and tails. US Gothic has also produced inventive representations of the motif. Examples include Edgar Alan Poe's Hop-Frog, represented in terms of his alien race and deformed body; and the residents of the US coastal village who, in H.P. Lovecraft's 'The Shadow over Innsmouth', assume gills and – to the horror of the narrator who discovers himself to be related to them – mutate into aquatic creatures and emigrate to the sea.

The monsters referred to above, though differing in appearance and the date of their creation, share common features. They are depicted as hybrid figures interrelating, as Kelly Hurley describes in *The Gothic Body*, different species and categories such as animal and human.[2] In transgressing conventional boundaries and evoking in the reader an ambivalent response of fascination and horror, they reveal connections with the Kristevan abject and its tendency to 'disturb identity, system, order' by failing to 'respect borders, positions, rules'.[3]

The grotesque appearance that is generally attributed to the monster and, as illustrated by Stoker's vampire Dracula and Marsh's eponymous Beetle, the plasticity of its body and ability to morph into different forms, are portrayed at times as endangering not only the life of the human protagonist of the novel or film in which it features. Its representation, as Jeffrey Jerome Cohen describes, 'as transgressive, too sexual, perversely erotic'[4] indicates another threat it poses – that of infecting the protagonist and reader with its perverse sexuality. The shape-shifting abilities and the mobility that writers frequently assign to it indicate this danger. As Fincher explains, 'The monster is transgressive and unnatural because it blends those categories that should be classified as distinct' and, as a result, 'questions the authenticity and stability of masculinity and femininity'.[5] It resembles, as a result, the representation of the homosexual or trans individual as perversely interrelating male and female attributes, as the individual tends to be portrayed in eighteenth- and nineteenth-century texts. Writers in the period, as Fincher illustrates, frequently describe 'mollies' [eighteenth century effeminate male homosexuals] as monstrous in appearance (p. 68). The monster's association with excess, another concept with which, as Fincher illustrates (p. 70), he is linked, also connects him with homosexuality. As mentioned in the introductory chapter, homosexual lifestyles and sexual practices tend to be regarded by society as excessive to heteronormative.

The association of the image of the monster with sexualities regarded as deviant has received critical attention. Benjamin Scott Grossberg, in examining the lesbian content of *Christabel*, refers to Coleridge's portrayal of the vampiric Geraldine as attempting to contaminate the eponymous heroine with her embraces,[6] while Stevenson's portrayal of Jekyll's doppelganger Hyde is also discussed in the context of queer sexuality. Halberstam describes Hyde, in representing his creator Jekyll's repressed homoerotic aspect, as signifying 'sexuality as perversion and degeneration',[7] while Showalter connects his portrayal with the expressions of homosexual panic that erupted in England in the 1880s and 1890s.[8] Cohen too links the ambiguous attraction that the fictional representation of the monster holds to the sexual prohibitions operating in Victorian England. Interpreting the monster in the context of Foucault's analysis of 'the society of the panopticon',[9] in which the individual's behaviour, including his sexual practices, are controlled by surveillance, he suggests that its grotesque appearance and the threat of contamination that it implies are intended to deter readers from engaging in deviant forms of sex. However, since the fascination that the monster holds stems in part from its ability to arouse forbidden fantasies, we may, on the contrary, find its perverse sexuality alluring.

In constructing the image of the monster, writers and film directors on occasion perpetuate prejudicial stereotypes. The viewpoint they adopt may be racist, as is the case in H.P. Lovecraft's *The Call of Cthulhu*; misogynistic, as exemplified by William Friedkin's film *The Exorcist*; or homophobic, as illustrated by Alasdair Gray's derogatory depiction of a group of lesbians in *Something Leather* and, as Robin Wood argues,[10] by certain of Stephen King's references to homosexuality in his fiction. Alternatively, however, the image may deliberately challenge prejudice. The critic Harry M. Benshoff, in an essay sassily entitled 'Satan spawn and out and proud: Monster queers in the postmodern era' (1997), having admitted that 'The (homo)sexual implications of the monster movie continue to lurk just barely beneath the surface of social awareness' and that some films promote homophobia, concludes his discussion by celebrating the 'valorization of the monster queer as sexual outlaw'[11] that others achieve. Novelists also employ strategies that celebrate, rather than denigrate, the queer subject and his associations with the monstrous. Engaging in a form of counter discourse, they treat the grotesque features that society assigns to him parodically and, as Teresa de Lauretis describes, seek to 're-create the body otherwise: seeing it perhaps as monstrous or grotesque... and certainly also sexual'.[12] Monique Wittig utilises this strategy effectively in *Across the Acheron*. She portrays her lesbian narrator ridiculed by her heterosexual companions, perhaps in a jibe at the way some lesbian feminists refuse to submit to dictates of fashion and remove the hair from their legs and armpits, as 'one of those monsters with hair all over their bodies and scales on their chests'.[13] The narrator, refusing to be intimidated by their tactics of monsterisation, retaliates by dramatically calling their bluff. She metamorphoses into a beast and develops an extended clitoris, the grotesque signifier of the tribade in eighteenth-century sexual discourse.[14] Winterson employs a similar strategy in *The Passion* by assigning to her protagonist Villanelle the grotesque feature of webbed feet. Since it signifies Villanelle's mobility both on land and in water, critics interpret it as metaphorically signifying her sexual mobility.[15] The novels and stories by Peter Ackroyd, Jeanette Winterson, Kathleen Winter and Randall Kenan, discussed in this chapter, employ strategies of a similarly inventive kind in depicting the figure of the monster and illustrating the role he plays in representing queer sexuality and experience.

Making Monsters

The title 'Making Monsters' that I have assigned to this section has, of course, more than one meaning. While denoting the writer's fictional representation of the construction of the monster, as illustrated by Mary Shelley's portrayal of Victor Frankenstein assembling the creature in her famous novel, it can alternatively refer to the re-casting of Shelley's narrative by writers and film directors writing in a later period. The phrase can also signify the figurative transformation of the individual or a group of people into monsters by stigmatising them as abhorrent on account of their sexuality, gender, race or religion. Members of the queer community are, of course, extremely vulnerable to this for, as Cohen observes, '"Deviant" sexuality is susceptible to monsterization'.[16] These different interpretations are relevant to the two novels discussed in this section: Peter Ackroyd's *The Casebook of Victor Frankenstein* and Jeanette Winterson's *The Daylight Gate*.

Ackroyd's re-casting of Shelley's novel introduces interpretations of features of it that are likely to be familiar to students of nineteenth-century Gothic. They include Haggerty's reading of the creature as metaphorically signifying Victor's uncanny double and homoerotic desires,[17] as well as Mair Rigby's reference to Frankenstein's paranoiac response to the creature on account of his terror of queer sexuality.[18] Critical readings such as these have in fact been made partially accessible to the general public in Nick Dear's dramatic adaptation of Shelley's novel entitled *Frankenstein*, directed by Danny Boyle and performed at the London National Theatre in 2011. The production indicates a degree of familiarity with them.

In contrast to Ackroyd, Winterson re-casts not a well-known Gothic novel but an episode from seventeenth-century British history: the events that led up to the trial of a group of women for witchcraft at Lancaster Assizes in 1612. In depicting the women being persecuted both by the local community and officials from London representing King James I, Winterson indicates the socio-political and sexual significance of their oppressive treatment by referring to their outcast status and, in the case of some of them, their deviant sexuality. The two novels, as well as differing in theme and historical context, vary in style and the discursive influences they reflect. Whereas Ackroyd creates a work of historiographic metafiction that interrelates fictional characters with historical personages and radically re-works the geographical locations to which Shelley refers, Winterson's novel is indebted, as is indicated by her utilisation of colloquial language, reference to folklore and introduction of episodes of body horror, to traditions of popular Gothic. The differences the two novels display indicate the range of diverse interpretations that the monster and the topic of monsterisation receive in contemporary fiction, as well as their ability to generate new and intriguing interpretations.

Gothic is well-known for the re-castings that the key texts exemplifying the genre frequently receive, and Mary Shelley's *Frankenstein* has proved to be especially fertile in this respect. Peter Ackroyd's *The Case Book of Victor Frankenstein* is one of the latest in a series of cinematic and literary adaptations that the novel has inspired. Cinematic adaptations include James Whales's *Frankenstein* (1931) and *The Bride of Frankenstein* (1935), Francis Ford Coppola's *Mary Shelley's Frankenstein* (1996), and a number of Hammer cinematic productions. Fictional re-workings are exemplified by Shelley Jackson's *Patchwork Woman* (1995) and Lynn Shepherd's *A Treacherous Likeness* (2013). Versions of Shelley's novel employing reference to queer sexuality and gender have also appeared in print. Christopher Bram, as I illustrate in my analysis of the novel in *The Queer Uncanny*, focuses *Father of Frankenstein* (1995) on the fantasy relationship that the homosexual film director James Whale, having previously re-created the image of the two characters on the silver screen, forms with both Victor Frankenstein and his creature. Richard O'Brien's *The Rocky Horror Show* (1973) and Jim Sharman's *The Rocky Horror Picture Show* (1975) treat in musical comedy format the adventures of a sweet transvestite from Transsexual, Transylvania, while Susan Stryker's poem 'My Words to Frankenstein above the Village of Chamonix'[19] gives a trans interpretation to the creature's complaint about his outcast situation and the social rejection he experiences.

Ackroyd's re-working of Shelley's narrative differs radically from the versions produced by the writers and film directors mentioned above. An important modification he introduces, one suiting his reputation as chronicler of London history, is to transfer to Britain, London in particular, a number of the key events that she describes taking place in Switzerland and Germany. He opens his novel by portraying Frankenstein pursuing a course of study not at Ingoldstadt University but at Oxford. He represents him carrying out his experiments to create new life initially in a barn in Headington and, on moving to London, in a disused pottery in Limehouse. He also represents the creature, on fleeing Victor's company on account of his rejection, receiving his education from a poverty-stricken family living on the marshes bordering the Thames.

Regarded in the context of his interest in London and its history, Ackroyd's transposing of certain key episodes in Shelley's novel to the city and its surroundings is predictable. However, other revisions that he introduces are more unexpected. With the impish wit typifying his writing, he takes concepts and strategies associated with historiographic metafiction to extreme lengths. Although we are familiar with post-modern novelists, in treating history as a construct that is accessed chiefly in textual form, interspersing fictional characters with historical personages, we may be surprised by the extreme lengths to which he takes this strategy. William Godwin, Lord Byron, John Polidori, Percy Shelley and Mary Shelley herself, as well other nineteenth-century personages, all appear in the novel. They are represented from the viewpoint of Victor Frankenstein, the fictional character from Shelley's novel whom Ackroyd employs as narrator.

Ackroyd's portrayal of the creature that Victor Frankenstein constructs in fact agrees in some respects with present-day critical interpretations. Haggerty, like Rigby,[20] describes the creature signifying 'the secret (homoerotic) desire'[21] that Frankenstein, to his cost, refuses to acknowledge. He also argues that it is Frankenstein's harsh rejection of the creature that has the effect of transforming him into a monster by provoking him to react in a 'violent, excessive' (p. 54) manner. This turns him, as a result, from 'sensitive, intelligent, loving and an alter ego, as it were, of whom he could be proud to 'misshapen, scarcely human, and grotesque' (p. 54). Ackroyd, in addition to similarly associating the creature with same-sex desire, illustrates the process of monsterisation that he subsequently undergoes by portraying him, when Victor rejects his offer of love, embarking on a rampage of carnage in which he kills not Justine, as occurs in Mary Shelley's novel, but Percy Shelley's first wife Harriet. He also interestingly represents the creature, though deeply distressed by Victor's initial rejection, on subsequently requesting him to create him a mate, passionately insisting that, if he refuses, then 'I choose you to be my spouse'.[22] He poignantly tells Victor that he looks forward to them becoming 'inseparable, two living things joined together' (p. 185). This is, of course, a prospect that horrifies Victor. He rejects the creature once again, contributing, as a result, to his future acts of violence.

However, whereas several features of Ackroyd's portrayal of the creature agree with contemporary critical readings of Shelley's novel, others, as far as I know, are unprecedented. Interrelating textual and historical categories, as he does throughout his novel, Ackroyd portrays Victor fabricating the creature from the corpse of an individual called Jack Keat – an alias, we discover, for the poet John Keats. He represents Keat working in the field of medicine and dying of tuberculosis, as Keats himself in fact did. And, although he does not portray Keat actually writing poetry, he describes him mentioning his enjoyment in reading it.

Ackroyd portrays Frankenstein first encountering Keat in the dissecting room at St Thomas's Hospital in London. Describing the location as 'not a place for the fearful or the faint of heart', Victor paints a macabre and gory picture of the corpses lying on the dissecting tables with 'six or seven students intent upon rummaging about their bones and entrails' (p. 42). He discovers, from the brief conversation he holds with him in the grim surroundings, that Keat is training to become an apprentice surgeon. While discussing his studies at the Hospital and referring to his love of poetry, Keat breaks into a painful fit of coughing, indicating the weakness of his lungs. The reader assumes that this is the last meeting that will occur between the two characters but Ackroyd unexpectedly portrays Victor encountering Keat – or rather his corpse – again on a later occasion. The resurrectionists whom he employs to furnish him with a corpse to use in his experiments to create new life comment enthusiastically on the beauty of the one they have just obtained, describing it, with mordant humour, as 'as fresh as a peach' (p. 122). On discovering to his astonishment that it belongs to Keat, Victor feels uneasy about employing it in his experiments. However, on remembering Keat's brave words, 'We must take courage in pursuit of our researches' (p. 124), he decides to go ahead. Though describing Keats's body as 'the most beautiful corpse I have ever seen' (p. 130), he is shocked by the speed with which its condition deteriorates. His attempt to revive it to its initial perfect condition is unsuccessful for he perceives with horror that 'in a moment the body in front of me had gone through all the stages of decomposition before being reclaimed and restored to life' (pp. 131–2). The episode evokes Kristeva's description of the corpse as 'the utmost of abjection ... death infecting life'.[23] It also prompts the reader to ask why should Ackroyd choose to utilise the poet Keats, albeit under the pseudonym 'Keat', as furnishing the foundation for the creature that Victor constructs? What possible connection does he envisage existing between Keats and Frankenstein's creature?

One topic that connects the deceased poet with the character that Mary Shelley creates is, of course, death. Whereas the creature, in being fabricated from a corpse, has obvious connections with it, Keats features in literary tradition as the archetype of the writer whose career was tragically blighted by death. Keats also addresses the topic of death memorably in his poetry. As well as portraying himself in 'Ode to a Nightingale' as 'half in love with easeful death' and expressing a desire 'to cease upon on the midnight with no pain',[24] he writes unflinchingly in a later poem about his imminent demise, depicting the physical changes that it will effect with a chilling intensity very different from his romantic reference to death in the Ode. Having described how, 'This living hand, now warm and capable/ of earnest grasping' grows 'cold',[25] he portrays himself 'holding it out towards you [the reader]' in a gesture that uncannily resembles the one that the creature employs in extending his hand to Victor in Mary Shelley's novel.

Another feature, besides his association with death, that the poet Keats shares with Shelley's creature – though this may surprise the reader – is his connection with queer sexuality. Although there is no evidence to suggest that Keats was in fact homosexual, he was nonetheless linked with the topic both during his lifetime and after his death. James Najarian describes in his study *Victorian Keats: Manliness, Sexuality, and Desire* that the beauty of Keats's appearance, typecast as effeminate in a culture obsessed with heterosexual masculinity, combined with the sensuousness and lyricism of his poetry, appear to have generated this myth. Najarian also illustrates how the sensuousness of Keats's verse proved useful to writers who were seeking to articulate homoerotic emotions in their own poetry. He refers to the way in which Alfred Lord Tennyson, in passages referring to Arthur Hallam in *In Memoriam* as well as in other poems, 'uses Keats's language to create spaces of ambivalently directed intimacy'[26] and 'hint at an eroticism that depends on Keats's sexually borderline reputation' (p. 71). He suggests, in addition, that poets who were writing after Tennyson such as John Addington Symonds, who have 'anxieties about sexuality' (p. 6) and whose poetry treats homoerotic topics, adopted Keats's style of writing as a model. It appears likely that it is the myth of Keats's queer sexuality, as well as the beauty of his appearance and association with death, that explains Ackroyd utilising him, under the alias Jack Keat, as a blueprint for Victor's creature.

In addition to re-casting the Gothic motif of the monster and foregrounding his homoerotic associations, Ackroyd, as is indicated by his references to London, constructs his text as a work of regional Gothic. In transposing episodes in Mary Shelley's text from Europe and the snowbound landscape of the Arctic to London locations, he prioritises the River Thames and the sites relating to it. Victor describes the creature, after he has rejected him, fleeing from the workshop to the river bank. He vividly describes how he 'raised his face, as if he had sensed the river close by...and then seemed to look keenly downstream towards the sea' (p. 133); after pausing for a moment, 'He raised his arms above his head in a gesture of celebration or supplication, and plunged into the water' (p. 133). From this moment on, the creature is portrayed living almost entirely in water, even following the boat that Victor and his companions, including Mary and Percy Shelley and John Polidori, take to the continent when they visit Byron in Geneva. Ackroyd's reference to the creature's movement from the land to the water recalls the mutation that Lovecraft describes the inhabitants of the US coastal town experiencing in 'The Shadow over Innsmouth', as well as Winterson's portrayal of Villanelle walking on the water of the canal in *The Passion*. However, he depicts the creature's aquatic interests as relating him not to the abject and subhuman, as Lovecraft does, but as evoking, in a manner that echoes Winterson's portrayal of Villanelle, a sense of wonder.

The monster in Gothic fiction, as well as being represented as a hybrid figure, is frequently credited with powers of transformation and shape-shifting. Ackroyd develops the motif by describing the passers-by who catch sight of the creature in the Thames as unable to agree on his exact appearance and form. Whereas some of them portray him as a fish or an otter, Byron, on catching sight of him, refers to him as a sea monster. The black beach-comber Job, whom Ackroyd describes frequenting the area, as well as depicting the creature as 'a phantom...with eyes of fire' (p. 235), refers to him, with unconscious accuracy, as 'a dead man living...brought to life by magic' who, in consequence, is 'greater than a man' (p. 235). Job, on account of his outcast situation and the abuse that the colour of his skin provokes, in fact has features in common with the creature. As he despondently tells Victor, it is the destiny of his race 'to be harried, cursed and beaten' (p. 235). Ackroyd's introduction of him has the significant effect of extending the treatment of monsterisation to encompass race as well as sexuality. Mary Shelley herself in fact previously achieved this by describing the creature's appearance as displaying features that appear foreign, including flowing black hair and skin with a yellowish tint.

Having encouraged the reader to regard Victor and the creature as autonomous individuals, Ackroyd concludes the novel by unexpectedly pulling the rug from under his feet and revealing that the two characters are, in fact, one and the same. Having referred to the import of homosexuality as a guilty secret, Rigby remarks, in his critical reading of Mary Shelley's novel, that 'The flip side to unspeakability is a powerful inducement to confess'[27] – and Ackroyd portrays Victor experiencing a similarly strong impulse to acknowledge the creature's existence and the role that he himself has played in it. Having selected Byron's physician John Polidori, whom Ackroyd portrays as having given him opiates to enable him to sleep, as his confidant, he invites him to his lodgings to view what he terms his 'handiwork' (p. 295). He is astonished when Polidori, on looking at the chair where he believes the creature to be seated, insists that he can see 'nothing' (p. 295). Accusing Victor of being deluded, Polidori scornfully observes, 'You have dreamed all this. Invented it' (p. 295). He also insultingly suggests that the fantasy of the creature Victor has conceived has been provoked by his envy of Shelley's and Byron's literary abilities and his wish to enjoy 'the sublimity and power' (p. 295) that they have achieved in their writing.

Ackroyd does in fact plant occasional clues in the narrative that he intends the reader to regard the creature as the product of Victor's imagination. The title *The Casebook of Victor Frankenstein* that he uses, with its implications of a psychoanalytic case study focusing on Victor's mental instability, has this effect. And, as well as portraying Victor referring to the creature as 'my double, my shadow... without which I would not exist' (p. 187), he portrays him, in a laudanum-provoked dream that he experiences while sailing on the Thames, feel a hand suddenly grasp his in an attempt, as he describes, 'to pull me down' (p. 231), whether in order to embrace or kill him he is uncertain. Ackroyd's association of the creature with water, of course, suits his portrayal of him as Victor's fantasy doppelganger since the element has mythical associations of narcissistic mirroring.

The interplay between fictional characters and historical personages that is a distinctive feature of Ackroyd's novel raises a number of intriguing questions. How, for instance, should we interpret his references to the attempts that the creature makes to contact Mary Shelley? Does the creature seek to injure her, as she and Percy Shelley fear, or merely communicate with her? Are the attentions that he pays her brutal or benign in intent? Does he seek revenge on her for her assigning to him the abject roles of monster and outcast in her narrative or does he seek to request her, in a manner resembling the characters in Luigi Pirandello's *Six Characters in Search of Author* (1922), to revise her representation of him and make it less grotesque?

While being chiefly of interest for its inventive re-casting of Mary Shelley's novel, Ackroyd's narrative also furnishes the reader with a treasure trove of intertextual references to nineteenth-century Gothic texts. As well as portraying Victor conversing with Polidori on the topic of the golem, he depicts him describing the visit that he makes to a manufacturer of spectacles, an individual resembling the figure Coppola whom E.T.A. Hoffmann portrays in 'The Sandman' and Freud mentions in 'The Uncanny'. In addition, the reference to the unexpected appearance of the creature at Mary Shelley's bedroom window one night in the guise of a phantom recalls Stoker's depiction of Dracula appearing at Lucy's in the form of a bat. Other references to Stoker's novel also occur. In re-casting the famous historical episode of the ghost story competition that took place between Byron and his friends at the Villa Diodati in Geneva, Ackroyd portrays Polidori recite a tale that, though based on 'The Vampyre' that he wrote in 1819, introduces, in its reference to the town of Whitby, a location that Stoker was to employ seventy or so years later in *Dracula*, published in 1897. In the fascinating historiographic-metafictional world that Ackroyd creates, time presents no barrier to the imaginative fecundity of his narrative. Events appropriated from Stoker's text intermingle with ones from Polidori's, increasing the intertextual vitality of Ackroyd's novel.

Like Ackroyd's *The Casebook of Victor Frankenstein*, Jeanette Winterson's *The Daylight Gate* treats topics relating to queer sexuality in the context of themes of monsterisation and the ostracised existence that the social outcast experience. However, whereas Ackroyd, in portraying Frankenstein's feelings of abhorrence toward the creature he constructs, treats the rejection of a male figure, though one who, on account of his homoerotic connotations, can be interpreted as exemplifying an oppressed section of society, Winterson in *The Daylight Gate* centres her narrative on a group of female figures. Her fictional representation of the experiences of the women who were tried for witchcraft at the Lancaster Assizes in 1612 introduces the reader to a cross-section of female Jacobean society, both poor and affluent.

The trial of the so-called 'Pendle Witches' was one of most famous trials of its kind that took place in seventeenth-century England. The trials of witches occurred chiefly as a result of the bigoted opinions of the Protestant James 1 who, having ascended the English throne on the death of Queen Elizabeth in 1603, harboured an obsessive fear of what the characters in Winterson's novel refer to as the twin evils of 'witchery popery'.[28] The majority of the women accused of witchcraft whom Winterson portrays belong to a Lancashire family known locally as 'the Demdike Clan'. While focusing on their social vulnerability and family loyalty, she resists the temptation to idealise them. As well as describing the acts of theft and violence they commit, she emphasises their readiness, stemming from envy of her social status, to betray the upper-class Alice Nutter, despite the fact she attempts to protect them and permits them to live in her property of Malkin Tower in Pendle Forest free of charge. However, while acknowledging the Demdike women's faults, Winterson also illustrates the oppressive treatment and harassment they experience from the local community. She focuses in the opening chapters on an episode representing Sarah Device, known in the area as 'the Demdike witch' (p. 9), being tied up by a group of local men on the river bank. After stripping her to search her body for 'witch-marks', they subject her to sexual assault and threaten to drown her. If Alice had not arrived to rescue her, she would no doubt have died.

Winterson portrays Alice as a widow of independent means. She represents her having achieved her fortune not by inheritance, as was usual for women in the period, but from the invention and sale of a magenta dye that attracted the attention of Queen Elizabeth. The transgressive lifestyle that Alice leads differentiates her, as she herself perceives, from other upper-class women in the Pendle area whom she mockingly describes as 'the milk-and-water well behaved wives of religious husbands with their hidden mistresses' (p. 7). Her lack of respect for convention is illustrated by her refusal to re-marry after her husband's death and her preference for riding astride instead of side-saddle. The latter provokes from the locals accusations of 'unnaturalness' (p. 14), the term also hinting at their suspicions of her unorthodox sex life. In her youth Alice accepted an invitation from the mathematician John Dee to join his scientific circle in London in their search for the elixir. Here she met Elizabeth Southern, another of his assistants, and became her lover. Although, when the novel opens, the relationship with her has long since ended, Alice remembers the year 1582, when she lived with Elizabeth, as the happiest of her life. She nostalgically recalls how, 'I learned life from her and learned love from her as surely as I learned astrology and mathematics from John Dee' (p. 61).

Like the female characters whom Tondeur and Kingston represent in their novels, discussed in Chapters Two and Three, Winterson describes Alice's sexuality as mobile and depicts her in engaging in relationships with men as well as women. She portrays her, after leaving Elizabeth, forming a relationship with the Roman Catholic Christopher Southworth whose religious allegiance brings him into conflict with the Protestant authorities. In 1611, the date at which the narrative opens, Elizabeth has not seen him for some years since he has taken refuge in France on account of his suspected involvement in the Gunpowder Plot. However she encounters him briefly again when, risking his life, he returns to Lancashire in a perilous attempt to rescue his sister who is threatened with execution on the trumped- up charge of holding a Black Mass.

Winterson wrote *The Daylight Gate* as an Arrow publication in association with British Hammer Productions, the latter well-known in the 1950s and 1960s for the production of films with a Gothic or Horror component. As suits this connection, as well as her narrative's rural context, she employs in its construction a form of Gothic that has links with popular culture. As well as writing more colloquially than in her earlier novels, she introduces devices from oral story-telling, whetting the reader's appetite for the uncanny events she recounts with dramatically monosyllabic references to the novel's setting and the animal life associated with it. This is exemplified in the sentences 'Sheep graze. Hares stand like question marks' (p. 1). She also issues grim warnings about the superstitions operating in the Pendle area, reminding the reader, whom she positions on occasion as a seventeenth-century listener to her story, that 'It is not safe to be buried on the north side of the church and the North Door is the way of the Dead' (p. 1).

Another device that Winterson utilises, one with associations of Gothic and horror fiction, is reference to the grotesque body, exemplified by references to incidents of shape-shifting and the anthropomorphising of animals and other creatures. Although she does not portray Alice herself metamorphosing into an animal, she portrays her suspecting her lover Christopher Southworth of doing so. Knowing him to be in the Pendle area, she wonders if, in order to escape his pursuers, he has transformed himself into a hare, a form of shape-shifting associated with Pendle Forest. Winterson also depicts the naïve Jem Device, while in the custody of Constable Hargreaves, seeking advice from a spider – although, as Jem later learns to his cost, the words the arachnid utters, indicating the equivocal nature of magic, are not necessarily trustworthy. Having predicted for him a prosperous future, including the possession of a wife and a home, the spider then reneges on its promise. It advises Jem to escape from custody as quickly as he can, adding with a spark of wit, 'Eight legs could not carry you fast enough away!' (p. 124). The theme of humans metamorphosing into animals and animals developing powers of speech that Winterson employs, illustrated in the above examples, are associated with folk tale. Hans Christian Andersen portrays Gerda conversing with a crow in 'The Snow Queen', while the Brothers Grimm represent a fox, on having his feet and head cut off after his death, unexpectedly metamorphosing into a man in 'The Golden Bird'. However the creatures that Winterson introduces, rather than assisting humans, as is the case with the crow in Andersen's story, tend on the contrary to mislead them, exacerbating the atmosphere of uncertainty and danger that pervades the novel.

In addition to representing incidents of human/animal metamorphosis and conversation, Winterson introduces episodes of 'body horror' representing the body in pain. Examples include the rape of Sarah Device and the acts of torture to which Robert Southwell and Alice are subjected by the socio-political authorities. Episodes of this kind, as Pam Perkins observes,[29] are by no means new to Gothic but, as the novels of Horace Walpole and Matthew Lewis illustrate, have been conventional components of it since its advent in the eighteenth-century. Aldana Reyes defends their introduction in fiction and film, disturbing though they are. He argues that the vividly physical representation of 'corporeality, its transgression, limits and the horror of embodiment',[30] performs a vital role in Gothic. As well as alerting attention to 'the corporeal, somatic and visceral side' (p. 17) of the genre, they encourage the reader or spectator to recognise the vulnerability of the body, perceiving that 'it ages and hurts' (p. 19), and to 'negotiate fears surrounding changes in our bodies or our perception of ourselves' (p. 18). Motifs of this kind with a physical component are, he argues, more effective in this respect than others such as spectrality with its associations of the immaterial and spiritual.

Commenting on the motif of dismembered body parts and the uncanny effect that reference to it can evoke, Freud cites as key examples 'dismembered limbs, a severed head, a hand cut off at the wrist'.[31] All three feature prominently in Winterson's novel. One of the most grotesque examples that she introduces is the representation of the head that, having been amputated from a corpse in the local graveyard and fitted with a mouldering tongue, Elizabeth Device boils in a pot while imprisoned in the dungeon of Lancaster Castle. The magic rite she utilises it to perform resembles the one that the witches in Shakespeare's *Macbeth* enact. Elizabeth performs it in the hope that the spirit that the head embodies will speak and lead her and her family through the prison walls to freedom. Although the head fails to speak to her, illustrating the contradictory nature of magic it addresses Alice Nutter and Jennet Device. As well as endorsing Dr Dee's prophecy that

Alice having 'been born in fire' will 'by fire depart' (p. 133), it advises Jennet to get rid of her brother Tom Peeper who habitually subjects her to sexual abuse. Jennet promptly obeys, entrapping Tom in the cellar of Malkin Tower and leaving him there to starve.

Winterson's references to heads, tongues, hands and other dismembered body parts, as well as alerting the reader's attention to the vulnerability of the body and enhancing the atmosphere of physical horror that pervades the novel, also influence the action. The words of advice that the severed head gives Jennet result in her liberating herself from Tom Peeper's control. Robert Nowell's discovery of the tongue in Alice's bag after she has rescued Sarah Device from rape (Sarah in fact bit the tongue from the mouth of the youth who was sexually abusing her) furnishes him with fake evidence of her involvement in witchcraft. This assists him in achieving her conviction as a witch at Lancaster Assizes, resulting in her death by hanging.

Winterson places the motif of dismembered body parts in a wider context, both literary and political, in the episode in which Alice, accompanied by Thomas Potts, the agent of James 1, visits the estate of Hoghton Tower in order to watch a performance of *The Tempest* that William Shakespeare is also represented attending. When the conversation turns to Shakespeare's play *Macbeth*, Potts, pronouncing an anti-witchcraft message as King James expects of him, describes the play as 'suspicious' on account of it representing 'hags, witches and beldames' (p. 88). Echoing the phrase 'witchery, popery', that features as a refrain throughout the novel, he connects what he calls 'the pilot's thumb that they throw in their infernal pot' (p. 88) with the severed thumb of the Jesuit Edmund Campion recently executed for treason. Potts's reference to *Macbeth*, as well as illustrating the political significance that the literary texts produced in the period could carry, alerts attention to the frequency with which Winterson appropriates themes and imagery from Shakespeare's play.

Winterson's fiction is, in fact, well known for its utilisation of intertextual reference. Whereas her early novel *Oranges Are Not the Only Fruit*, as Tess Cosslett[32] and Heta Pyrhonen[33] illustrate, re-casts themes and narrative structures from Charlotte Brontë's *Jane Eyre* and the Bluebeard story, *The Passion* re-works, with reference to Venice and the feminine erotic economy that Winterson represents the city exemplifying in her novel, episodes from Italo Calvino's *Invisible Cities*.[34] With reference to *The Daylight Gate* and its intertextual references to *Macbeth*, a theme of key importance in the novel is the association of the period of dusk with evil. Whereas Shakespeare portrays the witches agreeing to meet 'ere the set of sun' (p. 4, I, l.5) and Macbeth observes, prior to the murder of Duncan, that 'Light thickens... / Good things of Day begin to droop and drowse,/ Whiles night's black agents to their preys do rouse' (pp. 89, III, iii, l.50–4), Winterson entitles her novel *The Daylight Gate*, the phrase signifying, as she describes, 'the liminal hour' when 'it would soon be dusk' (p. 3). She also portrays certain significant events, such as the pedlar John Law's scary encounter with Sarah Device, taking place in the twilight.

Another theme that links Winterson's novel to *Macbeth* is the unreliable nature of magic. Shakespeare portrays the witches tricking Macbeth into believing himself to be physically invincible, despite Banquo's warning that 'The instruments of darkness tell us with truths;/Win us with honest trifles, to betray's/In deepest consequence'.[35] Winterson similarly describes magic forces or the fantasies of them that her characters create tricking Jem Device into trusting the words spoken by the spider and Alice believing herself to be safe when, as the ghost of John Dee and the herbalist (pp. 121–2) tell her, she is in danger.

However, the most important theme that Winterson appropriates from *Macbeth*, utilising it to inform her novel's structure, is the interrogation of 'the real'. Whereas Macbeth questions whether the dagger that he sees before him is real or 'a false creation,/a dagger of my mind' (p. 49, 2, I, l.38) and Banquo wonders if the witches are figments of his imagination, the pedlar John Law in Winterson's *The Daylight Gate* questions whether the figure walking towards him on Pendle Hill is an actual woman or 'the Devil himself stepping through the Daylight Gate' (p. 4). Jem Device, having described himself dreaming that he was a hare, goes on to depict himself transformed into one, leaving the reader uncertain if the transformation was real or imagined. As suits the important role that the interrogation of 'the real' assumes in her narrative, Winterson assigns to Shakespeare, or the image of him she constructs, the role of alerting attention to the significance of these ambiguities. She portrays him reminding Alice, in a reference to the performance of *The Tempest* that they watch together at Hoghton Tower, that, 'There are many kinds of reality. This is but one kind' (p. 92).

In interrogating the nature of 'the real' and comparing different forms of 'reality', Winterson, as might be expected, introduces the device of magical realism. Elizabeth T. Hayes describes 'doubleness' as 'the hallmark of magic realism'[36] since, in the narratives utilising it, 'the supernatural and the material are equally weighted contraries simultaneously inscribed in the text as experienced reality' (p. 169). Doubleness of this kind is exemplified in *The Daylight Gate* by the interrelation and tension between the material and supernatural that Winterson creates. An event she describes occurring while Alice is visiting Hoghton Tower illustrates its uses. Whereas one moment Alice is resting on her bed at the local inn, the next, as Winterson describes, 'The room was not there. Alice was standing on Pendle Hill ... in the driving rain' (p. 94) talking with the ghost of her lover Elizabeth–or a deceptive spirit that enacts her persona. Instead of clarifying whether the event actually took place or is the product of Alice's fantasy, Winterson teases the reader by appearing to furnish an answer but subsequently refuting it. The fact that Alice, on discovering that she is back at the inn, finds 'Everything as it had been before' (p. 95) prompts us to interpret her meeting with Elizabeth as a fantasy – only to have this contradicted by her recognition that 'She was soaking wet' (p. 95), her sodden clothing furnishing proof of the fact that she had been in 'the driving rain' (p. 94).

As Maggie Ann Bowers observes, 'The oxymoronic "magic realism" reveals that the categories of the magical and the real are brought into question by their juxtaposition'.[37] Winterson interrogates the two different categories in other episodes besides her portrayal of Alice's encounter with Elizabeth on Pendle Hill. They include Jem's conversation with the untrustworthy spider, Alice's questioning if a hare she encounters in her path is, in fact, Robert Southwell or if the thought is superstitious folly, and the conversation she holds with the ghost of John Dee in which he warns her of the dangers besetting her. In addition to interrogating supernatural constructs of the real, Winterson examines socio-political constructs of it. This suits the emphasis she places in the novel on the tyrannical political system operating in Jacobean England and the readiness of the Protestant establishment to employ accusations of both witchcraft and Roman Catholicism to persecute people it regards as troublemakers and dissidents. Reference to socio-political constructs of the real achieves prominence in the words that Shakespeare addresses to Alice at Hoghton Tower. After reminding her that, 'There are many kinds of reality', he cautions her, 'not to be seen to stray too far from the real that is clear to others or you may stand accused of the real that is clear to you' (p. 92). His enigmatically coded words of advice, in hinting at the danger Alice runs in sheltering the Roman Catholic Robert Southwell in her home, as she is currently doing, foregrounds the political dimension that the debates about 'the real' and the ambiguities they assume in the novel. They explain the darkly Gothic treatment she gives her inventive fictional re-casting of an oppressive period of seventeenth-century history.

Shapeshifting and Transformation in the Intersex Novel and the Slave Narrative

Discussing the portrayal of the monster in Victorian fiction, Halberstam alerts attention to the fact that, rather than being assigned a unitary, stable form, it tends to be disturbingly represented in terms of 'the disruption of categories, the destruction of boundaries'.[38] Kathy Hurley similarly describes the monster as characterised by 'its morphic variability continually in danger of becoming other'.[39] As she illustrates, the shape-shifting abilities of the monstrous figures depicted in Victorian Gothic tend to mirror the unsettling Darwinian representation of the species as existing in a state of flux and the ideas of fragmentation and degeneration associated with it. She also remarks on the way that the physical mutations and transformations that the monster assumes serve as indicators of their mobile and frequently deviant sexuality.

Present-day writers of queer Gothic continue to utilise reference to somatic transformation and the theme of shape-shifting to represent and explore alternative genders and sexualities, though they treat them very differently from their Victorian predecessors. Creating a form of counter-discourse and generally writing from the viewpoint of the queer subject, they employ strategies of this kind metaphorically to explore lesbianism and homosexuality or, in the case of the trans individual, to indicate his dissatisfaction with his existing embodiment and desire to transition. Maria, the protagonist of Emma Donoghue's *Stir Fry*, on unexpectedly discovering that her two flatmates are in a lesbian partnership, unconsciously transfers her image of them as weird and grotesque to the portrait of them that she is sketching. On completing it, she sees that it resembles 'a two-headed monster in a fairy-tale ... or a gargoyle, with two tongues for waterspouts'.[40] However, on subsequently recognising and accepting the fact that she too is sexually attracted to women, she finds her view of her flatmates changes – as also does her image of herself. Imagining herself metamorphosing into the transgressive figure of a witch, she pictures herself flying over the city of Dublin at night, 'black air between her legs, the office windows glinting as she skimmed by' (p. 28). Julie Anne

Peters also employs reference to metamorphosis and shapeshifting in *Luna* to portray her teenage transsexual protagonist Liam and his situation. She refers to the anger he feels at being coerced by social prejudice into 'strangling'[41] the female identity Luna that, though invisible to his parents, he regards as his authentic self. He resents being pressured by the transphobic attitudes of society into, as he bitterly describes, 'holding her down, keeping her caged' (p. 20).

Annabel by the Canadian-based Kathleen Winter and 'Let the Dead Bury Their Dead' by the African-American Randall Kenan, the two works of fiction discussed below, also utilise reference to metamorphosis and shape-shifting to explore the situation of the queer subject. Winter employs the motif of uncanny doubling and imagery with spatial associations, both somatic and relating to the natural environment, to represent the journey of self-discovery that her protagonist Annabel makes in understanding and coming to terms with her intersex situation. As well as feeling uncomfortable with her father's efforts to raise her as a boy, when she senses intuitively that she is female, she is shocked by the ridicule she encounters when she embarks on the process of transitioning.

The African-American Kenan in 'Let the Dead Bury Their Dead' employs the shape-shifting abilities associated with the Gothic monster very differently from Winter, emphasising their performative aspect. Locating his story on a plantation in North Carolina owned by the nineteenth-century Owen Cross, he compares the trickery and role-play that the African-American slave Pharaoh employs to achieve racial freedom for himself and his fellows, with the strategy the homosexual Phineas, Cross's son, utilises to win sexual liberation. Cross and his wife, while vilifying Pharaoh as a monster and devil on account what they see as his treachery in instigating a slave rebellion, ridicule Phineas as effeminate due to the interest he evinces in the feminised discipline of botany. Both Winter and Kenan, while creating narratives that are stylistically disparate, employ reference to shape-shifting and metamorphosis to explore topics relating to gender and sexuality.

Intersexuality, the topic of Winter's *Annabel*, is an anatomical and physiological condition that was known in earlier centuries as 'hermaphroditism'. The symptoms relating to it, as Vernon A. Rosario describes,[42] vary considerably. They can range from minor genital abnormalities and defects that have no significant effect on the gender identity of the individual to ones of a more pronounced kind that render it ambiguous. Although, as Rosario observes, intersexuality is not an elective identity but a physiological condition, it can be appropriately discussed in the context of queer politics since, as Susan Stryker argues, 'The ambiguous bodies of the physically intersexed demonstrate in the most palpable sense imaginable that "sex", *any* sex, is a category which "is not one"'.[43] The body of the intersex subject has, in fact, important sexual political implications since it challenges the conventional view, still held by many members of society, that, as Stryker writes, 'Gender is a system for correlating two normative and fixed categories, man and woman' (p. 9).

Cases of pronounced intersex ambiguity involve the medical practitioner, as well as the parents, in making complex decisions regarding the baby's sex and the advisability of corrective surgery, as well as the form that, if considered necessary, it should take. Arguments can arise both about surgical intervention and the date of its performance. Whereas members of the medical profession tend to insist that the individual needs to identify as male or female at an early age in order to function socially, critics argue that surgery should not be performed until the person is old enough to decide on the appropriate sex.[44] References to debates of this kind form the medical and socio-political context of the opening chapters of Winter's novel. The intersex baby, to whom they relate, is born, as Winter describes, with a genetic anomaly: it is discovered at birth to have, in addition to a labia and a vagina, a small penis.

Winter describes the baby's birth as taking place in a rural area of the Canadian region of Alaska in 1968. The doctor who attends it, on perceiving the baby's intersex condition, recommends, as was usual in the 1960s, immediate surgical intervention. Since the baby's penis is long enough to function effectively and the father Treadway passionately desires a son, the surgeon decides to perform a surgical masculinisation involving the closing of the vagina. However, his decision to operate is a source of parental disagreement since it conflicts with the wishes of Jacinta, Treadway's wife and the baby's mother. She regards the baby as a girl and has even chosen a feminine name for it, selecting 'Annabel' in memory of the daughter of her close friend Thomasina who has recently drowned in a canoeing accident. In addition to resenting the fact that the decision whether to operate has been taken by two men, while her own opinion as a woman and mother is sidelined, Jacinta is angered by the view the surgeon expresses – or so she interprets it – that her baby is, in some way, flawed. The conversation she holds with him prior to the operation introduces the first reference in the novel to the motif of the monster, one that re-appears in subsequent chapters. Objecting to his observation that he intends to create for her baby 'a believable masculine anatomy'[45] and thinking that his use of the word 'believable' implies that he sees the baby in its present manifestation as an abhuman monster, she indignantly retorts, 'You think my child – the way he is, the way she is – is unbelievable? Like something in a science fiction horror movie?' She continues with fierce irony, 'And you want to make her "believable". Like a real human?' (p. 50).

On discussing the conversation with Thomasina, Jacinta blames herself for capitulating to the surgeon's and Treadway's persuasion and allowing corrective surgery to take place. Referring to what she sees as the surgeon's disparaging of her baby as in some way monstrous, she protectively states, employing the masculine name that her husband intends to give it, 'If Wayne had two heads I'd get used to that in a few months, and I would wonder why anyone would want to change him' (pp. 66–7).

In addition to conflicting with Treadway about the topic of the baby's sex and the question of surgical intervention, Jacinta differs from him in the approach to temporality she adopts. Treadway is portrayed endorsing the concept of 'linear time' that depicts temporal existence as strictly organised in units of minutes, hours, and months, a view Kristeva describes as typically masculine.[46] He accepts, in consequence, the surgeon's view that a decision has to be made and implemented about the baby's sex at once. Jacinta, on the contrary, accepts a cyclical 'feminine' approach to time that defines temporal structures less rigidly. She would have been happy, had her view not been ignored, to have postponed the operation till a later date, in this way permitting the child's sex to remain ambiguous until further understanding of it emerged. As she tells Thomasina prior to the surgical operation, 'All I need is a little more time, and everything will become clear. The baby will, in some way we have to learn about, be just fine' (p. 24). Winter's narrative, as it subsequently unfolds, in fact endorses Jacinta's view.

Although during the months following the operation Jacinta appears to become reconciled to the baby's masculinisation, both she and Thomasina continue to intuitively regard it as female and think of it as 'Annabel'. When, at the christening ceremony in the local church, Treadway names the baby 'Wayne', Jacinta defiantly whispers under her breath 'Annabel' (p. 62). As Winter, referring to Jacinta's belief in the baby's femininity and employing the eco-critical imagery[47] of the natural world that she frequently utilises in the novel, describes, 'The name Annabel settled on the child as quietly as pollen alongside the one bestowed by Treadway' (p. 62). From this point on in the narrative, as the simile indicates, Wayne is haunted by a female double.

Names, and the lack of them, signify a topic of major importance in Winter's novel. Treadway is a trapper by profession and loves the Alaskan wilderness where he spends the summer months plying his trade. As well as visiting brilliantly colourful rural areas, illuminated by 'brief blasts of summer' where 'pitcher plants and bog sundews burst open' (p. 9), he visits sites that are more mysterious in nature. His favourite location is, in fact, the one known as 'the unnamed lake' (p. 14) that is central to the landscape. The lake, as he admits, does not, in actual fact, lack a name. On the contrary, it has two. Whereas one has been assigned to it by the Canadian mapmakers, the other, 'a different name, a name that remains secret' (p. 14), has been bestowed on it by the natives of Labrador. Treadway's reference to the lake and its ambiguous naming alerts the reader's attention to the ambiguity of Wayne's two names, the masculine one by which he is socially identified and the feminine that remains secret, known only to Jacinta and Thomasina. It also illustrates the political significance of the act of naming. Just as the name given the lake by the official mapmakers has public import and assumes priority over the one bestowed by the native Alaskan inhabitants who, in keeping it secret, indicate a wish to keep it unsullied by imperialist intervention, so the name 'Wayne', that Treadway confers on the baby in the public realm of church, assumes priority to the name 'Annabel' that his mother gives it. However, unlike the name that the local population gives the lake, the name 'Annabel', though secretly conferred on the baby, eventually comes to light. As a result, it makes an entry into public discourse.

Winter constructs *Annabel* as a *bildungsroman* structured in four loosely defined sections. Whereas the first, as indicated above, describes the event of Wayne's birth, his intersex anatomy and the controversy between Jacinta and Treadway about the surgical correction of his sex to male, the second treats his childhood years. It describes Treadway's unsuccessful attempt to rear him to conform to a Labrador model of masculinity – what Treadway, on account of his conservative background, describes as 'a real boy' (p. 105). Wayne, aware of his father's concern for him, dutifully strives to adopt the 'grim, matter-of-fact attitude' (p. 71) to life that his father considers appropriate to the male sex. He makes an effort to take an interest in building fences and repairing snowmobiles, occupations that, since Treadway is a trapper, are vital to his livelihood. However, though trying to comply with his father's wishes, Wayne in fact prefers engaging in pursuits that tend to be typecast as 'feminine', such as art and dance. And, instead of forming friendships with boys, as Treadway assumes he will, he enjoys socialising with girls. Gender conflicts of this kind provoke a further rift between Wayne's parents for, whereas Treadway tries to coerce Wayne into conforming to his expectations of masculinity, Jacinta, increasingly convinced that her view of him as a girl is correct, accepts his artistic interests and choice of female companions. As Winter, hinting at the benevolent natural-cum-supernatural forces that influence her view of him, describes, 'Many times during Wayne's childhood a wind had whipped through Jacinta's mouth. The word had breathed through her and told her that her son was also a daughter' (p. 314).

Whereas Treadway regards Wayne as male and Jacinta as female, Thomasina increasingly envisages him as androgynous. She teaches at the local school and, marvelling at the gender ambiguity that he displays as he moves around the building, thinks, 'When Wayne Blake walked, he floated. He was Wayne, she saw now, and he was Annabel. He was both at the same time, but did not know this' (pp. 171–2).

Winter devotes the second and third section of the novel to representing the crisis, mental as well as physical, that Wayne experiences when he reaches puberty and, at around the age of fifteen, the female and male components of his physiology start significantly to conflict. On experiencing a severe pain in his abdomen, he enters the local hospital and undergoes an operation. The surgeon who performs it confirms what both Jacinta and Thomasina, on perceiving the increasing prominence of Wayne's breasts, suspected. The corrective surgery that he experienced as a baby, combined with the regime of hormone pills and injections that he has since been following, have failed to suppress his female physiology. The pain he suffered prior to the operation was caused by a build-up of menstrual fluid. It is at this point, that his parents and Thomasina, though feeling uneasy about taking the step, feel forced to reveal to Wayne the details of his intersex history.

Up to this point in the novel all three adults have maintained an unspoken pact of secrecy and silence with reference to Wayne's intersex condition. The topic has featured in their lives in the role of 'the phantom',[48] the concept that Abraham employs in his analysis of the phenomenon of transgenerational haunting. As mentioned in relation to Tondeur's *The Water's Edge*, discussed in Chapter Two, Abraham argues that, 'What haunts us are not the dead, but the gaps left within us by the secrets of others' (p. 287). He utilises the concept to describe the phenomenon of the transference of a transgressive secret from the unconscious of one generation to that of the next where, as he describes, 'It works like a ventriloquist, like a stranger within the subject's own mental topography' (p. 290). Abraham's ideas shed light on the mysteries and confusions that Wayne has sensed surrounding him since his infancy. As he tells Jacinta, after she has divulged to him his intersex condition, though puzzled by the facts that Thomasina occasionally referred to him in the past as 'Annabel' and he even dreamed one night that he was a girl, he had no idea, consciously at least, what these events signified. He admits to having felt haunted from early childhood by a female doppelganger, though he was unaware of its import at the time. He remembers how, though generally conforming to the male role, when Treadway was absent from home he experimented secretly with wearing his mother's eye-liner and practised dance steps before the mirror (p. 265). In addition, after watching a performance of synchronised swimming on television and longing to take part, he was depressed to discover that boys are debarred from participating. He even took the step of requesting Jacinta to purchase him a colourful swimming costume and, when she told him that boys don't wear them, logically replied, 'They could, if people would let them' (p. 85).

The information Wayne receives from the surgeon that, though his vagina is masked, he has female anatomical features and has experienced a build-up of menstrual fluid, initially distresses him, causing him to regard himself as a freak. Thomasina, however, who shares Jacinta's belief in the reparative effects of time and the forces of nature, encourages him to accept the somatic changes he is experiencing, disturbing though they appear. Referring to the transformations that occur in the natural world, she reassuringly tells him, 'Everyone is a snake shedding its skin...We are different people all through our lives. You even more so' (p. 207).

While undergoing the operation to drain the menstrual fluid from his body, Wayne remains semi-conscious in 'a state between waking and sleeping' (p. 226). He feels himself to be experiencing a journey of exploration through the mysterious red terrain of his body, one that, though frightening, is simultaneously exhilarating. As he describes,

> The inchoate red world took form: a red trench, a tunnel, a map of the womb inside him and the passageway leading from it, which had all been closed and he had no idea existed. The red world knew everything in him and showed him the map of his own feminine parts, and they were the most vivid, living, seductive red he had known in waking or in dreaming life. (p. 227)

Winter's description of the interior space of Wayne's body, with its reference to the metaphorical tunnels and passageways through which he envisages himself travelling, is complex in import. As well resembling in miniature 'the mystery' (p. 225) of the vast spectacle of the Northern lights, with its flickering expanse of pink and red, that Treadway, as he describes, is currently observing from the edge of the forest, it also recalls the narrative strategies that Radcliffe employs in her novels. Cynthia Griffin Wolff interprets the secret chambers and castle vaults that she portrays her heroines traversing as metaphorically representing the 'inner space'[49] of the female body, as well as the mysteries and conflicts relating to sexuality that both the heroine of the novel and the eighteenth-century female reader experience. The heroine's encounter with this hidden world hopefully results, as Wolff describes, 'not in a rejection of her sexuality but an embracing of it' (p. 215). Winter represents Wayne's journey of somatic self-discovery as eventually having a similarly positive outcome.

In depicting Wayne's experience of coming to terms with what he refers to as 'his feminine parts' (p. 226), Winter utilises motifs of doubling. The surgeon, on explaining his current situation, tells him that if he ceases taking hormone pills and injections, his physiology will become increasingly female since, 'You're already a girl inside' (p. 236). Wayne finds the phrase that the surgeon employs disconcerting. He wonders, 'How could he be a girl inside? What did that mean?' (p. 237). He envisages his female avatar taking the form of his school friend Wally Michelin and pictures Wally 'smaller than her real self, lying quietly in the red world inside him, hiding' (p. 337). Earlier, when he had assumed himself to be a boy, Wayne had felt himself to be in love with Wally, though sensing that, at the same time, also he identified with her. As Winter writes, 'He had felt so in love that he wished he could become her... He would have transformed himself into his father's lure [the bait that Treadway uses to catch fish], slipped under Wally Michelin's divinely freckled skin and lived inside her, looking through her eyes' (p. 99). The interrelation and tension between desire and identification is a topic of debate in queer studies. In contrast to Freud who maintains that the two are separate, the theorist Alan Sinfield argues that 'the confounding of the distinction between the desire-to-be and the-desire-for is endemic in same-sex passion'.[50] Winter's treatment of the topic with reference to the intersex Wayne/Annabel endorses Sinfield's view.

Although initially having felt exhilarated by the news of his intersex condition and the explanation it furnished for his former confusion about his sex, during the months that follow the operation he experienced

Wayne feels increasingly isolated and depressed. He is forced to admit to himself the fact that he is 'not the son your dad wanted. Not a Labrador trapper, strong mettled, well read, solitary but knowing how to lead a pack' (p. 333) but, on the contrary, 'ambiguous, feminine, undecided' (p. 333). Around the age of eighteen he takes the decision, though recognising it may prove difficult, to cease the regime of hormone tablets and injections that he has been following in order to maintain his masculinity and, instead, transition to female. With the aim of making a fresh start, free from the prying eyes of neighbours and the gossip pervading the rural community, he leaves home and moves to the city of St John's. Here, with the emotional and financial support of Treadway who is still struggling to come to terms with the fact that the son he deeply desired has turned out queerly to be a daughter, he commences the process of transitioning physically to 'Annabel'.

As well as utilising the motifs of the double and doubling to represent and clarify Wayne's intersex experience, Winter also employs it with reference to Treadway. Though having made every effort to rear Wayne as a socially gregarious male, Treadway himself, we discover, is ironically something of a loner. Instead of enjoying socialising with other men, he looks forward to the summer months that he spends alone in the wilderness, enjoying the solitude and proximity to nature. He also tends to share any personal problems he may experience not with his wife Jacinta or a male friend but with the creature that he regards as his own personal avatar: the boreal owl, native to the Alaskan forests. Winter humorously describes Treadway and the owl sharing physical and temperamental affinities. Both, as she describes, in addition to being 'quiet and modest', have 'a compact, rounded shape, efficient and not outwardly graceful' (p. 214). Feeling worried about Wayne and the process of transitioning that he is currently undergoing in the city, Treadway seeks out the owl and confides his anxieties to it for, as Winter describes, 'He thought of it, really, as himself' (p. 216). By assigning to Treadway a feathered double from the Alaskan countryside, to which he is emotionally attached, Winter increases the complexity of his characterisation. She also employs his acquisition of the owl as a doppelganger to parodically comment on, in a gently humorous way, the gender doubling that the intersex Wayne experiences.

Even in the context of the relative anonymity of urban life in St John's Wayne finds the experience of transitioning to female by no means easy. He is shocked to find himself treated as a weirdo not only by members of the urban population in general but also by representatives of the medical profession. When he visits the hospital in order to obtain medical advice, he has the impression that some of the staff regard him as a grotesque 'exhibit' (p. 369). His ambiguous gender appearance also makes him prey to the bully Derek Warford and his gang, whose members he encounters while wandering the city streets. Derek and his mates, pleased to find a target for their abuse, on discovering the fact that Wayne has had a sex operation and adopted the name 'Annabel', subject him to ridicule and treat him as a freak. 'What's he got down there?' Derek asks mockingly, pointing to his genitals, 'A cunt or what?'(p. 379). He concludes his mockery by assaulting Wayne with a broken beer bottle, cutting his eye and 'treating him', as the latter angrily describes while recovering from the attack, 'like a piece of garbage they wanted to use and discard' (p. 402). The fact that the name 'Annabel', after remaining secret for many years, has entered public discourse, is, as Wayne recognises, positive since he regards it as signifying his true identity. However, it simultaneously has the adverse effect of making him prey to attack by transphobes and bullies.

On learning from Wayne that he is being persecuted, Treadway decides to pay him a visit in St John's, though he dislikes the prospect of entering an urban environment. He ingeniously plans to try to protect Wayne from suffering abuse by setting a snare for Derek, resembling the kind he formerly constructed in in the wilderness to entrap lynx. However, a conversation that he holds with an erudite hawk that he encounters on Signal Hill prompts him to reject the scheme. On being reminded by the hawk of the biblical words 'Vengeance is Mine, I will repay, saith the Lord' (p. 444), he has second thoughts about it and decides to dismantle the trap he has set. His offer to help Wayne, however, has served a useful function since it has demonstrated his readiness to help and protect him.

Winter's portrayal of Treadway planning to set a snare in which to entrap the street bullies of St John's, as well as being relevant to his relationship with Wayne, contributes to the novel's structure and thematic focus by comparing the topics of danger and survival in the rural environment of the wilderness with their urban counterpart. Like the creatures inhabiting the Alaskan wilderness, Annabel has to learn the tactics of coping with city life and avoiding the threats and dangers that it poses.

Unlike Winter, who explores in *Annabel* the changes in embodiment that her eponymous intersex protagonist undergoes and the abusive treatment she suffers while in the process of transitioning, Randall Kenan in 'Let the Dead Bury Their Dead' explores topics of racial persecution and homophobia and the different strategies that the individuals who experience them employ in an attempt to combat or elude them. Kenan centres the story on two characters, the black slave Pharaoh who features in the narrative from the start and Phineas, the white homosexual son of the owner of the plantation in North Carolina where Pharaoh is bound, who enters it at a later stage. Although Phineas differs from Pharaoh in race, age, class and sexual orientation, his ability to liberate himself from his oppressive family background and embark on a homosexual lifestyle, as well as the encounter he experiences with Pharaoh in the final stages of the story, forge a connection between the two men. By describing the different strategies they utilise to liberate themselves from their oppressive circumstances, Kenan, in addition to exploring their different lifestyles and experiences, focuses attention on the thirst to achieve freedom that connects them.

Although the forms of oppression that non-white and queer people experience differ in form and socio-political context, they nonetheless share, as Donald Hall argues, common features. Both originate, he argues, from society's impulse 'to assign values to identities' and irrationally assume that 'to be "of color" is to be a lesser version of being "white" and to be homosexual is to be a lesser version of heterosexual'.[51] Kenan's decision to treat themes of homosexual prejudice and racial oppression in a single work of fiction is not unusual, as is illustrated by the way in which Ackroyd in *The Casebook of Victor Frankenstein* implicitly compares the rejection that the creature experiences from Victor Frankenstein with the persecution and harassment that the black beachcomber Job suffers. Victorian writers also connect the two, interrelating them on occasion in the portrayal of a single figure. The physical features that Mary Shelley assigns to the creature that Frankenstein constructs resemble those that, as David A. Hedrich Hirsch describes, 'are commonly encountered in colonial depictions of Asian, Indian and African "savages"',[52] while Halberstam refers to the way in which Shelley's association of the creature with both queer sexuality and racial difference 'props up the analogy between mixed blood and inherent [sexual] perversity'[53] inherent in nineteenth-century culture. Stevenson in *Jekyll and Hyde* likewise interrelates Hyde's homoerotic associations with features signalling his mixed race. As well as representing Jekyll's friends suspecting him of being a 'rough trade' sexual acquaintance from his youth,[54] he describes his physical appearance as hirsute and dark. The linking of queer sexuality and race reflected in Shelley's and Stevenson's portrayal of the two characters gives an insight into the different attributes that the image of the monster can be utilised to represent. As Halberstam observes, 'Monsters are meaning machines' and can be utilised to treat a range of different topics including 'gender, race, nationality, class and sexuality'.[55]

Kenan's 'Let the Dead Bury Their Dead' is a complex, multifaceted work of fiction that interweaves a number of different themes and genres. The quotation from Mikhail Bakhtin's *The Dialogic Imagination* with which he prefaces it, with its reference to the '*realistic fantastic*' and the interplay that it creates between folklore and fantasy and the 'real, here-and-now material world',[56] alerts attention to his own treatment of the form. The American slave narrative, to which his story is also indebted, is, as Justin Edwards illustrates,[57] a similarly hybrid kind of writing that frequently introduces reference to Gothic. In creating a post-modern version of the slave narrative in the style of 'the realistic fantastic', Kenan develops its Gothic dimension. As well as introducing reference to sorcery and spectral visitation, he refers to the homely/unhomely house and the American *topos* of the wilderness with its connotations of mystery and fear. He also exploits the stylistic versatility of Gothic by punctuating episodes of pathos or horror with ones that introduce quirky and macabre humour. Although Gothic fiction is generally associated with an atmosphere of fear, it can also create comic effects. Vijay Mishra describes certain works of eighteenth- and nineteenth-century Gothic reflecting 'a discourse of instability' that, 'like "laughter" and the "carnivalesque", is always on the verge of madness',[58] while Royle too refers to the uncanny effect that laughter can produce.[59]

Kenan locates his story, as he frequently does his fiction, in the context of Tims Creek, a fictional town in North Carolina, tracing its development from a maroon commune, allegedly established by a group of run-away slaves in the nineteenth-century, and referring to the lives of both its African-American and white residents. At the centre of his narrative is the black slave Pharaoh, an exotic and imposing-looking individual who reputedly enjoys magic powers. Kenan describes how in the year 1856 Pharaoh successfully instigated a slave revolt on the plantation owned by the white Owen Cross. After killing Cross's eldest son in the skirmish that ensued, he escaped with his fellow slaves into the forest where they established a commune, surviving by growing and harvesting crops.

Illustrating the slippery nature of historical research and the reconstruction of the past that it involves, Kenan opens the story with a dramatic dialogue that he represents taking place in the late-nineteenth century between two self-appointed authorities on the history of Tims Creek: Ezekiel Thomas Cross, a member of the black line of the Cross family, and his wife Ruth. In an attempt to ascertain the role that the slave Pharaoh played in the founding of the settlement, the couple engage in a heated argument about his identity and origins, topics rendered problematic by lack of reliable evidence. The phrase 'Let the Dead Bury Their Dead' that Kenan utilises as the title of his story is relevant here. He appropriates it from a passage in 'The Eighteenth Brumaire of Louis Bonaparte' in which Karl Marx discusses the way in which people living in the present, in an attempt to bring about political change, 'anxiously summon up the spirits of the past to their aid'.[60] The summoning up of such 'spirits', in which Cross and his wife engage, creates a parodic version of the kind to which Marx refers. Utilising the couple's attempted reconstruction of the history of Tims Creek as a frame for his narrative, Kenan creates a humorous work of historiographic metafiction illustrating the difficulties that the attempted recovery of the past can involve. Fiction of this kind, as Linda Hutcheon observes, though it 'does not in any way deny the existence of the past real, focuses attention on the act of imposing order on that past, of encoding strategies of meaning-making through representation'.[61]

The efforts that Ezekiel and his wife make to recover the history of Tims Creek are marked from the start by controversy – and, in representing their dialogue, Kenan moves from passages of humour that render the events that they recount absurd to flights of lofty, biblical-style rhetoric that serve to elevate them. The dialogue opens with Ezekiel's reference to the instigator of the slave rebellion on Cross's estate as 'Old slave name of Pharaoh' (p. 287) being fiercely contradicted by Ruth's riposte, 'No such man ever existed!' (p. 287). The couple's account of the rebellion is further complicated by the fact that it has been edited after their death by one of their descendants, the Reverend James Malichai Greene, Baptist Minister of Tims Creek. The substantial footnotes that Greene has added, though inserted with the aim of clarifying it, have in fact the reverse effect. Instead of illuminating Pharaoh's identity, they increase the difficulty of ascertaining it by citing a list of other exotic names with different racial associations, including 'Menes, Sultan, King, Prince, Alexander, Caesar and Montezuma' (p. 287), by which he was allegedly known. The title and origin of the book of magic spells that he is said to have possessed is also uncertain. Ezekiel, his imagination running riot, cites as possibilities, 'A book in Carthaginian stolen from the library in Timbuku, a text dating back to Zoroastrianism and containing creation myths...as well as the [Egyptian] Book of Life, the Book of the Dead' (p. 287).

Having struggled, despite his wife's interruptions, to ascertain Pharaoh's race and identity, Ezekiel moves on to reconstructing the role that he played in instigating the slave rebellion on Cross's estate. As well as referring to Pharaoh's knowledge of magic, he portrays him as a skilful tactician and trickster. He describes how the white estate owner Cross, after being presented with him as a gift on his election to the Senate or, according to Ruth's more racy account, having 'won him fair and square in a card game' (p. 299), sends him to work in the fields. However, as Ezekiel describes, to the annoyance of 'the light-skinned niggers' (p. 300) who regard indoor work as their prerogative, Cross, impressed by Pharaoh's apparent loyalty, promotes him to the role of house slave. In fact so attached to Pharaoh does Cross become that the affection he displays for him prompts his wife Rebecca to question his sexual preferences. As she candidly writes in her diary, 'If I did not know My Husband's long History of more Conventional Fleshly Perversions & Shameful Self-Indulgences, I might think He had taken this Pharaoh into Horrible Abomination' (p. 308).

Whatever the nature of the affection that Cross feels for Pharaoh he makes the unwise move of giving him access to the plantation house. Once ensconced there, as Ezekiel admiringly describes, 'Ole Pharaoh played the good slave. Tomming it up, you know...he witched the sucker [Cross] good-fashioned, they tell me...keeping the juju on him but all the time plotting and plotting behind his back' (pp. 299–300). Here Ezekiel portrays Pharaoh enacting a version of what Homi K. Bhabha describes as 'colonial mimicry',[62] transforming his humble position as slave into a performative role in order to outwit his master. By utilising these tactics, Pharaoh successfully transforms Cross's homely house into an unhomely site of conspiracy and rebellion. As Bhabha describes, 'The recesses of the domestic space become sites for history's most intricate invasions' since 'in that displacement, the borders between home and world become confused' (p. 13). In consequence, as he continues, 'Uncannily, the private and public become part of each other, forcing upon us a vision that is as divided as it is disorientating' (p. 13). The acts of deception and trickery that Ezekiel attributes to Pharaoh interestingly resemble the strategies that actual nineteenth-century slaves, such as William Wells Brown and Nat Turner, utilised in order to instigate rebellions on the plantations where they were bound.[63]

The African-American and white residents of Tims Creek, as one might expect, respond in markedly different ways to the role that Pharaoh played in initiating a slave rebellion on Cross's estate and the tactics of cunning and violence that he employed. Whereas Cross and his wife portray Pharaoh as 'the Devil himself', an agent of 'Satan' and 'a monster' (p. 311) in wreaking havoc on their home and killing their eldest son, Pharaoh's fellow slaves and Ezekiel and his wife celebrate him as a hero. Ezekiel portrays him in fact as an instrument of divine retribution. In the rhythmically poetic speech that Kenan assigns to him, he dramatically describes how, in initiating the rebellion, 'Pharaoh bideth his time, learnt and learnt. And one day, by and by, like the Angel of Death coming, he up and went' (p. 301).

The roles of devil and monster that Cross and his wife assign to Pharaoh serve to connect him with the motif of 'the black monster', with its Gothic connotations, that achieved prominence in the discourses of slavery that flourished in nineteenth-century North America and Britain. Elizabeth Young describes in *Black Frankenstein: The Making of an American Metaphor* how nineteenth-century opponents of the abolition of slavery, influenced by Mary Shelley's representation of the murders that the creature in *Frankenstein* commits and the connections his portrayal displays with the image of the African American slave, introduced the motif of 'the black monster'[64] in their propaganda. Writers and artists, as Young illustrates, refer in speeches, stories and cartoons to the danger they regard the black man posing to white communities. Ambrose Bierce's *Moxton's Master* (1898) exemplifies this trend. However, members of the movement for the abolition of slavery challenged these racist representations. They argued that, if black men do on occasion behave violently, it is on account of the oppressive treatment that they receive from white society. Dick Gregory, an African-American stage performer and Civil Rights supporter champions this view,[65] while James Baldwin, whose fiction has influenced Kenan's, describes in his essay 'Stranger in the Village' how the residents of an isolated Swiss village that he visited, unused to seeing a black man, reacted to him as if he were a monster and a freak.[66]

Having completed – as far as his wife permits him – his account of the rebellion that Pharaoh initiated on Cross's estate, Ezekiel, rejecting realism and moving unashamedly into the realm of fantasy, goes on to portray Pharaoh returning from the dead in order to combat an evil white preacher who was oppressing the Tims Creek community. Creating a comic version of the ghost story, he describes how the preacher attempted to steal Pharaoh's book of magic spells that he believed to be buried with him in the churchyard. Here, as Ezekiel describes, with 'owls beginned to hoot' and 'bats come out flapping' (p. 289), the preacher came one night accompanied by the group of townsfolk he had commandeered to assist him. However the efforts they make to recover the book conclude in chaos. 'Ole Mose' (p. 292), who had been buried in the churchyard the previous week, terrifies them by unexpectedly appearing in spectral form. Ezekiel describes how Zaceus, the bravest of the company, 'held the lantern up to Mose's face and said: "Nigger, you ain't who they think you is, is you? We buried Mose Pickett last week". Whereupon Mose winked at him, "Yep, you sure did"' (p. 292). On hearing the spectral Mose speak, Zaceus drops the lantern and, tripping over it in the dark, falls into the open grave, while his companions scuttle away in terror into the woods.

Ezekiel follows this comically supernatural anecdote with one that is even more far-fetched. Moving from farce to horror, he describes how the white preacher, in an effort to maintain control of the community of Tims Creek, created an army of zombies to perform his bidding. Whereupon Pharaoh, perceiving the threat that he poses to the townsfolk, returned from the dead in order to destroy him. Emphasising the drama of Pharaoh's entry into the settlement, Ezekiel portrays him 'riding in on a great black bull with a shiny gold ring through its nose, snorting flames' (p. 331). Introducing a note of horror, he exuberantly continues, 'Some said he had a big sword in one hand and his book in another. Said he rode right up to that Preacher and lopped off his head in one whack!' (p. 331).

Kenan concludes his unconventional account of the history of Tims Creek by commenting on the family life of the plantation owner Cross. He describes how Cross's remaining son Phineas, fascinated as a teenager by the exotic blooms that he sees growing in the forest bordering the plantation, many of which he discovers to be unclassified, embarks on the study of botany. His parents, however, rather than welcoming his new interest in flowers and botanical specimens, ridicule it as sissy and unmasculine. Tired of seeing him, as Rebecca complains in her diary, 'sitting in his little Room to dawdle [with] his little Plants' (p. 309), they decide to send him to England in the hope that 'the Lord will', as she hopefully writes, 'Reach into His Frivolous Brain 1 Day and Shrink it to Normal Size and Deliver him from this UN-seemly Madness' (p. 313).

On arriving in England, Phineas, instead of engaging in bouts of drinking and gambling as his father, to judge from his wife's unflattering diary entries, would have done, takes the step of enrolling at London University. On graduating, he succeeds in obtaining, as a result of the essays on the exotic flora in the Carolina region that he has published, a research post at Oxford and, while studying there, forms a relationship with British youth called Nigel. While paying a brief visit to his parents in North Carolina, he enters the forest surrounding the estate in search of the botanical specimen Venus flytrap. On wandering further into the interior than he intended, he encounters instead the escaped slave Pharaoh.

Kenan describes the meeting between the two men in a letter dated 1859 that Phineas addresses to his lover Nigel in Oxford. Romantically addressing Nigel as 'My Siegfried of the Isis', Phineas commences it by expressing pity for the remaining slaves on his father's estate, describing how 'they are treated as animals... and their humanity is denied them' (p. 321). He celebrates, in contrast, the 'untrammelled beauty' of the wilderness that he describes as having been 'made by God to manifest... His grand wonder' (p. 323). Having explained that he entered the site in search of the flower 'Dionaea muscipula [Venus flytrap]' (p. 321), he moves from botanical discourse to erotic fantasy, amorously telling Nigel, 'I could see us among... the lustrous and luxuriant Magnolia grandiflora, intoxicated by its perfume, buggering like mad' (p. 327). He then proceeds to depict his unexpected encounter with Pharaoh, attempting to impress on his lover both the terror and the wonder of the event. He describes how, on seeing a figure whom he recognised from his stature to be the escaped slave approaching through the trees, he firmly stood his ground, though regarding him as the 'most awesome of Negroes I have ever beheld' (p. 324). When he reminds Pharaoh that, since the forest belongs to his father, he is committing an act of trespass, Pharaoh, true to his democratic principles, pointedly replies, 'Only God owns land' (p. 324). Raising his hand majestically, he tells Phineas that, although he would have killed any other man he encountered near the commune, remembering the kindness that, in contrast to his brother, he showed to him when he was a slave, he intends to spare his life. He then disappears into the trees as mysteriously as he came.

Kenan's account of the meeting between white homosexual botanist and escaped black slave effectively interrelates fantasy with wit. On entering the forest, Phineas discovers not the Venus Flytrap bloom that he is seeking but the black Pharaoh who metaphorically resembles it since he too is represented as 'beguiling, beautiful, most deadly' (p. 321). Having tricked the plantation owner Cross into trusting him by means of his apparent loyalty and achieved access to the plantation house, he unexpectedly sprung a trap on him by inciting a rebellion and luring away his slaves.

The forest where the Venus flytrap flower grows and Phineas and Pharaoh encounter one another by chance also acquires symbolic significance. White American writers of Gothic, as Allan Lloyd Smith describes, generally represent the wilderness as a sinister and scary location, depicting it as the haunt of witches or 'a correlative for some uncanny aspects of the deeper self'.[67] Kenan, on the contrary, influenced by African-American and environmentalist perspectives, inverts this image by representing it positively. Whereas Pharaoh regards the wilderness as a place of freedom where liberated slaves can establish communities and plant crops, Phineas values it as the location where the exotic plants he studies grow and a pastoral 'green world'[68] that, as novels such as Isabel Miller's *Patience and Sarah* and E.M. Forster's *Maurice* illustrate, furnishes same-sex lovers with a refuge from homophobia and a context for homoerotic fantasy. As Kenan illustrates, the two men, though appreciating the location for different reasons, both agree on its value.

Contemporary writers of queer Gothic, as this chapter illustrates, respond in different ways to the association of the queer subject with monstrosity and the grotesque. Ackroyd in *The Casebook of Victor Frankenstein* creates a metafictional text that, in re-working Mary Shelley's *Frankenstein*, develops the creature's connections with queer sexuality, an interpretation previously developed by critics such as Haggerty and Rigby. In addition to substituting areas associated with London for the German and Swiss locations that Shelley employs, Ackroyd unexpectedly associates the creature with the poet John Keats and the myth of homosexuality that, on account of his beauty and the sensuous lyricism of his verse, as Najarian describes, evolved around him.

Winterson's *The Daylight Gate*, in contrast, in constructing a fictional re-working of the events that preceded the Lancaster witch-trials in 1612, treats the monsterisation of a group of women living in the seventeenth-century. As well as illustrating the harassment and abuse to which the Demdike clan is subjected by the local community on account of its poverty and outcast status, she portrays the persecution that the upper-class Alice Nutter suffers as a result of her unorthodox sexuality and interest in magic. Employing conventions of popular Gothic, Winterson makes effective use of devices from oral storytelling and themes with folk-tale associations. As suits her introduction of Shakespeare in her cast of characters, she structures her narrative around intertextual allusions to *Macbeth*.

In addition to exploring the vilification of the queer subject and his association with the unnatural and the grotesque, writers of queer Gothic also re-work in their texts the shape-shifting powers and transformational abilities to which the monster is traditionally portrayed as having access. The Canadian-based Winter employs imagery of uncanny doubling and spatial exploration, both somatic and geographical, in *Annabel* to represent her protagonist's discovery of her intersex condition, while the African-American Kenan constructs 'Let the Dead Bury Their Dead' on an innovative interplay between historiographic metafiction, the slave narrative and different forms of Gothic. The unexpected encounter between the escaped black slave Pharaoh and Phineas, the homosexual son of the white plantation owner, with which the novel concludes, foregrounds the thirst for freedom that, despite their differences in race, age and social status, the two men share and the inventive strategies and ruses they employ to achieve it.

The four novels discussed here, while differing thematically and in terms of structure, all contain memorable representations of geographical locations, both urban and rural. Urban examples include Ackroyd's description of the disused warehouse in Limehouse where Victor Frankenstein carries out his experiments to create new life and the ghoulish site of the dissecting room in St Thomas's Hospital where he encounters Jack Keat. Rural sites are exemplified by Winterson's uncanny description of Pendle Forest centring on the mysterious Malkin Tower and Kenan's reference to the forest in North Carolina known for its exotic flora. Further illustrations of the contribution that reference to geographical environment makes to queer Gothic, both in texts produced in earlier periods and today, and the important roles they have played in the development of lesbian and male gay lifestyles and community structures occur in the following chapter.

Notes

1. Mary Shelley, *Frankenstein or the Modern Prometheus*, p. 55. (Shelley 1969).
2. Hurley, *The Gothic Body*, pp. 23–31, 55–64. (Hurley 1996).
3. Kristeva, *Powers of Horror*, p. 4. (Kristeva 1982).
4. Cohen, 'A Monster Culture: Seven Theses', in Cohen (ed.), *Monster Theory*, p. 16. (Cohen 1996).
5. Fincher, *Queering Gothic in the Romantic Age*, p. 68. (Fincher 2007).
6. Benjamin Scott Grossberg, 'Making Christabel: Sexual Transgression and its Implications in Coleridge's *Christabel*', *Journal of Homosexuality*, 41/2 (2001), 145–65. (Grossberg 2001).

7. Halberstam, *Skin Shows*, p. 69. (Halberstam 1995).
8. Showalter, *Sexual Anarchy*, pp. 106–7, 10 (Showalter 1992); Cohen, 'Monster Culture: Seven Theses', p. 14. (Cohen 1996).
9. Cohen, 'Monster Culture: Seven Theses', p. 14.
10. Robin Wood, 'Cat and Dog: Lewis Teague's Stephen King's Movies', in Glenwood Irons (ed.), *Gender, Language and Myth: Essays on Popular Culture*, pp. 302–17. (Wood 1992).
11. Harry M. Benshoff, *Monsters in the Closet: Homosexuality and the Horror Film*, pp. 236–8. (Benshoff 1997).
12. Teresa de Lauretis, 'Sexual Indifference and Lesbian Representation', *Theatre Journal*, 40/2 (1988), 167. (Lauretis 1988).
13. Wittig, *Across the Acheron*, trans. D. Le Vay with M. Crossland, pp. 15–16. (Wittig 1989).
14. See Creed, 'Lesbian Bodies', in Elizabeth Grosz and Elspeth Probyn (eds), *Sexy Bodies*, pp. 91–2. (Creed 1993).
15. See Sonya Andermahr, *Jeanette Winterson*, p. 63. (Andermahr 2009).
16. Cohen, 'A Monster Culture: Seven Theses', p. 9.
17. Haggerty, *Queer Gothic*, pp. 51–60.
18. Mair Rigby, '"Do You Share My Madness?": *Frankenstein's* Queer Gothic', in Hughes and Smith (eds), *Queering the Gothic*, pp. 42–3. (Rigby 2009).
19. Susan Stryker, 'My Words to Victor Frankenstein above the Village of Chamonix: Performing Transgender Rage', in Stryker and Stephen Whittle (eds), *The Transgender Studies Reader*, pp. 244–55. (Stryker 2006).
20. Rigby, '"Do You Share My Madness?"', in Hughes and Smith (eds), *Queering the Gothic*, pp. 38–41. (Rigby 2009).
21. Haggerty, *Queer Gothic*, p. 54.
22. Ackroyd, *The Casebook of Victor Frankenstein*, p. 185. (Ackroyd 2008).
23. Kristeva, *Powers of Horror*, p. 14.
24. John Keats, 'Ode to a Nightingale', *The Poems of John Keats*, p. 208. (Keats 1969).
25. Keats, 'This Living Hand', *The Poems of John Keats*, p. 438. (Keats 1969).
26. James Najarian, *Victorian Keats: Manliness, Sexuality, and Desire*, p. 54. (Najarian 2002).
27. Rigby, '"Do You Share My Madness?"', in Hughes and Smith (eds), *Frankenstein's Queer Gothic*, p. 43. (Rigby 2009).
28. Winterson, *The Daylight Gate*, p. 19. Subsequent page references are to this edition and in the text. (Winterson 2012).
29. For reference to the representation of acts of brutality and violence in eighteenth-century Gothic, see Pam Perkins, 'John Moore, Anne Radcliffe and the Gothic Vision of Italy', *Gothic Studies*, 8/1 (2006), 37–45. (Perkins 2006).
30. Reyes, *Body Gothic*, p. 17.

31. Freud, 'The Uncanny', p. 366.
32. Tess Cosslett, 'Intertextuality in *Oranges are Not the Only Fruit*: The Bible, Malory and *Jane Eyre*', in Helena Grice and Tim Woods (eds), *I'm Telling You Stories: Jeanette Winterson and the Politics of Reading*, pp. 24–5. (Cosslett 1998).
33. Heta Pyrhonen, 'On Finding the Balance between Earth and Sky: Jeanette Winterson, Charlotte Bronte and the Bluebeard Tale', *Contemporary Women's Writing*, 2/1 (2008), 50–1. (Pyrhonen 2008).
34. Palmer, '*The Passion:* Storytelling, Fantasy, Desire', in Helena Grice and Tim Woods (eds), *Jeanette Winterson and the Politics of Reading*, pp. 112–15. (Palmer 1998).
35. William Shakespeare, *Macbeth*, ed. Kenneth Muir, p. 20, I, iii, lines 123–6. (Shakespeare 1953).
36. Elizabeth T. Hayes, '"Commitment to Doubleness": Literary Magic Realism and the Postmodern', in Jeffrey Weinstock (ed.), *Spectral America: Phantoms and the National Imagination*, p. 169. (Hayes 2004).
37. Bowers, *Magic(al) Realism*, p. 67. (Bowers 2004).
38. Halberstam, *Skin Shows*, p. 27.
39. Hurley, *The Gothic Body*, p. 13.
40. Emma Donoghue, *Stir Fry*, pp. 125–6. (Donoghue 1994).
41. Peters, *Luna*, p. 20. (Peters 2005).
42. Vernon A. Rosario, 'The History of Aphallia and the Intersexual Challenge to Sex/Gender', in Molly Mc Gary and George E. Haggerty (eds), *A Companion to Lesbian, Gay, Bisexual Studies and Queer Studies*, pp. 263–9 (Rosario 2007). See also Harold Garfinkel, 'Passing and the Managed Achievement of Sex Status in an "Intersexed" Person', in Susan Stryker and Stephen Whittle (eds), *The Transgender Studies Reader*, pp. 58–92. (Garfinkel 2006).
43. Stryker, '(De)Subjugated Knowledges: An Introduction to Transgender Studies', in Stryker and Whittle (eds), *The Transgender Studies Reader*, p. 9. (Stryker 2006).
44. For reference to the debate see Patricia Elliot and Katrina Roon, 'Transgenderism and the Question of Embodiment: Promising Queer Politics?', *GLQ: A Journal of Lesbian and Gay Studies*, 4/2 (1988), 241–2. (Roon 1988).
45. Kathleen Winter, *Annabel*, p. 48 (Winter 2010). Subsequent references are to this edition and in the text.
46. Julia Kristeva, 'Women's Time', trans. Lisa Jardine and Harry Black, *Signs*: 7/1 (1981), 18. (Kristeva 1981).
47. For reference to ecocriticism see Michael P. Cohen, 'Blues in Green: Ecocriticism under Critique', *Environmental History* 9/1 (2004), 9–36 (Cohen 2004); and Laurence Coupe (ed.), *The Green Studies Reader: From Romanticism to Ecocriticism*. (Coupe 2000).

48. Abraham, 'Notes on the Phantom: a Complement to Freud's Metapsychology, *Critical Inquiry*, 13/2 (1987), 287 (Abraham 1987). See also Abraham and Torok, *The Shell and the Kernel*, pp. 174–5.
49. Cynthia Griffin Wolff, 'The Radcliffean Gothic Model: A Form for Feminine Sexuality', in Juliann Fleenor (ed.), *The Female Gothic*, p. 210. (Wolff 1993).
50. Alan Sinfield, *On Sexuality and Power*, p. 40. (Sinfield 2004).
51. Hall, *Queer Theories*, p. 13. (Hall 2003).
52. David A. Hedrich Hirsch, 'Liberty, Equality, Monstrosity: Revolutionizing the Family', in Cohen (ed.), *Monster Theory*, p. 118. (Hirsch 1996).
53. Halberstam, *Skin Shows*, pp. 44.
54. Showalter, *Sexual Anarchy*, p. 111.
55. Halberstam, *Skin Shows*, p. 21.
56. Randall Kenan, 'Let the Dead Bury Their Dead', in Kenan, *Let The Dead Bury Their Dead and Other Stories*, p. 274–5 (Kenan 1992). Subsequent references are to this edition and in the text. For reference to the concept of 'the realistic fantastic' see Mikhail Bakhtin, *The Dialogic Imagination*, pp. 150–3. (Bakhtin 1981).
57. Justin D. Edwards, *Gothic Passages: Racial Ambiguity and the American Gothic*, pp. 35–43. (Edwards 2003).
58. Vijay Mishra, *The Gothic Sublime*, p. 55. (Mishra 1994).
59. Royle, *The Uncanny*, p. 50, n. 26.
60. Karl Marx, 'The Eighteenth Brumaire of Louis Bonaparte', in Eugene Kamenka (ed.), *The Portable Karl Marx*, p. 288. (Marx 1983).
61. Linda Hutcheon, *The Politics of Postmodernism*, pp. 66–7. (Hutcheon 1989).
62. Homi K. Bhabha, *The Location of Culture*, p. 122. (Bhabha 1994).
63. Edwards, *Gothic Passages*, pp. 34–5. (Edwards 2003).
64. Elizabeth Young, *Black Frankenstein: The Making of an American Metaphor*, pp. 4–16. (Young 2008).
65. See Young, *Black Frankenstein*, p. 217.
66. James Baldwin, 'Stranger in the Village', in John Gross (ed.), *The Oxford Book of Essays*, pp. 621–33. (Baldwin 2008).
67. Allan Gardner Lloyd Smith, *Uncanny American Fiction: Medusa's Face*, p. 151. (Smith 1989).
68. For reference to the motif of the 'the green world' and the refuge from homophobia that it is represented as furnishing, see Bonnie Zimmerman, *The Safe Sea of Women: Lesbian Fiction 1969–1989*, pp. 79–86 (Zimmerman 1992); and Jeff Bush, '"I'd rather be dirty": The Queering of the Greenwood in E.M. Forster's Maurice', *Dandelion*, 4/1 (2013), 1–13. (Bush 2013).

CHAPTER 5

Regional Gothic: Uncanny Cities and Rural Areas

Geographical Locations and Queer Existence

A feature of the Gothic genre that helps to explain the vivid atmospheric effects that fictional texts exemplifying it create and the attraction that they hold for readers is the representation of geographical locations, both urban and rural, they introduce. Eerie features of the metropolis such as 'the devious mazes of London streets...whereof the mystery was known but to a chosen few',[1] represented by Dickens in *Martin Chuzzlewit*, and the wintry Glasgow lanes obscured by 'dense freezing fog'[2] depicted in Alasdair Gray's *Lanark*, contrast with the forests where evil lurks in the fiction of Nathaniel Hawthorne and 'the Fells...where the sky hung heavy and black over the white earth'[3] described in Elizabeth Gaskell's 'The Old Nurse's Story'. Both urban and rural areas can pose dangers for the protagonist or narrator of the novel or story. The city features typically in Gothic fiction, as Emily Alder describes, as 'a dark, claustrophobic and labyrinthine space, haunted by doubles, secrets and traces of the past'[4] that threatens the individual with fragmentation of identity and moral disintegration. A rural location, on the contrary, may confront him with the fear of isolation and, as illustrated by Grimsley's *Winter Birds*, discussed in Chapter Two, a collapse into depression and entropy.

Writers of Gothic sometimes utilise as the context for their narratives both urban and rural environments, exploiting the differences they display. Stoker, as well as portraying Count Dracula feeling at home among the 'great frowning rocks'[5] and 'rising wind' (p. 12) of the Transylvanian countryside, associates him with the 'lurid lights and inky shadows' (p. 116) of London where he purchases a tract of land. Anne Rice, re-working in *Interview with a Vampire* the difference between countryside and city that Stoker evoked in representing the vampire and his habitat, contrasts the landscape of Eastern Europe, described by the vampire Lestat as 'Lonely, dark, as rural country is always dark',[6] with the urban location of New Orleans with its 'savage and primitive' (p. 219) atmosphere.

Geographical location, urban in particular, on account of the important role that it plays in the lives of queer people, influencing their access to social life and ability to locate friends and partners, also plays an important role in queer studies. Reference to it features prominently in queer sociological studies and the sexual-political discourses that inform them. The historians Alan Bray[7] and Jeffrey Weeks,[8] though disagreeing on the date that the concept of a homosexual identity emerged, agree on the important role that the metropolis, by furnishing the male gay individual with opportunities for social networking and an element of anonymity, performed in its development. The growth of a lesbian identification and lifestyle are also associated with the city, as Shari Benstock illustrates in her reference to nineteenth-century Paris and London 'promising women artistic and sexual freedom from the boundaries of family constraints and enforced domesticity'.[9] According to Didier Eribon, the attraction that urban centres exerted on queer people was so strong that they continued to migrate there even in periods noted for their homophobia such as the 1940s and 1950s, the era of Senator McCarthy's witch hunts in the USA. As well as discussing the attractions that metropolitan life holds for queer individuals, Eribon examines how 'the mythology of the city has developed within gay culture, within the homosexual and lesbian imaginary',[10] influencing the themes that writers treat and the locations in which they choose to set their fiction. The post-Stonewall period has produced numerous novels and stories focusing on male gay and lesbian urban experience. Examples include John Rechy's *City of Night* set in Los Angeles and San Francisco; Jane De Lynn's story collection *Don Juan in the Village* located in New York; and Sarah Waters's *Fingersmith* and *The Night Watch* depicting lesbian life in London in the 1870s and 1940s. Novels treating topics of transsexuality and intersex also refer to the attractions that urban or metropolitan life holds for the protagonist. Winter, as illustrated in Chapter Four, portrays the intersex Annabel/Wayne moving to the city to transition to female, although she is shocked and distressed by the ridicule and physical abuse she encounters in the urban environment. Stella Duffy in her thriller *Beneath the Blonde*, which I discuss in *The Queer Uncanny*, also depicts the transsexual migrating to the city.

In contrast to the numerous sociological and historical studies of queer city life that have appeared in print, the lives of queer people living in rural areas have aroused notably less interest. As Halberstam, accounting for this neglect, observes, 'Most theories of homosexuality within the twentieth-century assume that a gay culture is rooted in cities, that it has a special relationship to urban life', while representing 'rural and small-town queer life as sad and lonely.'[11] Challenging this idea, she alerts attention to the way in which the countryside, rather than necessarily proving inhospitable, fosters on occasion thriving queer communities. As Colin R. Johnson argues in his recently published *Just Queer Folks: Gender and Sexuality in Rural America*, a study that seeks to redress the apparent lack of interest in queer rural and provincial life, the fact that urban locations have promoted the emergence of gay, lesbian and trans communities 'in no way precludes the possibility that same-sexual behaviour and gender nonconformity took place outside of urban contexts'.[12] However, the assumption that it is somehow obligatory for the queer individual to leave the provincial or rural area where he lives and move to the city continues to dominate opinion – or it did so until recently. I remember how a fellow marcher at a Gay Pride event in London, on learning that I lived in the provinces, asked me when I intended to move. When I told her I had no wish to do so as I was a member of several thriving socio-political groups and organisations in my home town, including the lesbian phone-line collective, she looked incredulous.

The topic of queer rural life, however, though having received less attention in sociological and theoretical writing than its urban counterpart, plays an important role in lesbian and male gay fiction, with writers treating it from different perspectives. Several contemporary lesbian novels, such Caia March's *Between the Worlds*, inverting the usual motif of the queer migration to the city, portray lesbians moving from a metropolitan to a rural context in search of a less hectic lifestyle or to join the feminist commune movement. Nicky Edwards's *Mud* focuses on the feminist community of Greenham Common and the protest against nuclear weapons in the 1980s and 1990s associated with it, while E.M. Forster's *Maurice*, written in an earlier period, represents the countryside offering same-sex lovers, as Bonnie Zimmerman describes, 'a refuge from a hostile and violent world'.[13] Grimsley's *Dream Boy*, set in North Carolina, associates rural locations, on the contrary, with a climate of virulent homophobia.

Representations of urban and rural locations in contemporary queer Gothic texts, as some of the novels discussed above illustrate, evoke, as might be expected, a bleak or uncanny atmosphere. Urban sites of this kind include Bowen's depiction of the cemetery in Budapest in *Diary of a Vampire*, where Rafael is accused of being a member of the undead and escapes death only by reciting Psalm 23, and Waters's description of the fog-bound London streets in *Affinity*, their spectral appearance suiting the novel's focus on spiritualism. Rural locations are exemplified by the white expanse of snow, at which young Danny gazes mesmerised, feeling his subjectivity dissolving into it, in Grimsley's *Winter Birds*. Other locations described, reflecting the marginalised situation of the queer subject, are borderline in nature, mediating between different locations. They include the strip of beach connecting the hotel to the sea in Tondeur's *The Water's Edge*, where the ghosts congregate prior to being carried down to Hades; and the underground tunnel linking the rigidly structured environment of Bath Ladies College with the ravine and its associations of transgressive sexuality in Swan's *The Wives of Bath*.

Alan Hollinghurst's *The Folding Star* and Michelle Paver's *Dark Matter*, the two novels that I have selected for detailed analysis in this chapter, also treat a motif that has featured previously. They enable the reader to re-visit the motif of spectrality, to the fore in the novels discussed in Chapter Two, and gain an insight into the roles it plays in fiction with a regional emphasis.

Hollinghurst, focusing his novel on the months that his narrator Edward Manners spends in an unnamed town in Flanders as tutor to the teenage Luc, re-casts in a present-day context a traditional Gothic theme. This is the tension between the opportunities for pleasure and self-enhancement that an urban environment offers the gay man and its contrary significance as a labyrinthine space where he loses his way emotionally and morally.[14] In addition to employing spectrality to treat topics of sexual fantasy and voyeurism, he utilises the motif to represent the haunting of the urban location in which he sets his narrative by the violent events that occurred in the past.

In contrast to Hollinghurst, who represents the Flemish town that Edward visits as signifying metaphorically, in personal and socio-political terms, a haunted location, Paver in *Dark Matter* structures her novel on an actual spectral event. She portrays her narrator Jack, while visiting the Arctic on a scientific expedition, experiencing an encounter with a ghost – or what, influenced by uncanny events that he witnesses while staying there and the tumult of unfamiliar emotions he experiences as a result of falling in love with a male colleague, he interprets in this way. Like Hollinghurst, Paver describes the Arctic location where she portrays Jack spending the winter as haunted by acts of violence from a previous era. However, both the form they take and the sources from which they stem differ radically, as we shall see, from those that Hollinghurst describes. The two novels illustrate, in this respect, the different uses that spectrality and the figure of the ghost can assume in queer Gothic fiction focusing on urban and rural areas.

CITIES, RURAL SITES AND QUEER SPECTRALITY

David Alderson, in discussing Alan Hollinghurst's fiction, remarks on the fact that critics discussing his novels generally appear to assume that his representation of the post-Stonewall male gay culture of the 1960s and early 1970s, for which his fiction is well known, is predominantly affirmative in viewpoint and to regard him as uncritically celebrating its hedonistic aspect. Alderson queries this interpretation by illustrating the frequency with which Hollinghurst's representation of gay sexual and social encounters is undermined by reference to the feelings of disillusion and anomie that he portrays the narrator experiencing.[15] Reference to the Gothic dimension of Hollinghurst's fiction, a feature of it that up to now has received little attention from critics, in fact supports Alderson's view. *The Folding Star*, like Hollinghurst's earlier novel *The Swimming Pool Library*, is of interest here. By introducing motifs with Gothic associations such as spectrality, uncanny doubling and the experience that Day describes as 'enthrallment',[16] in which the individual surrenders to a morbid sense of interpenetration between internal and external reality, Hollinghurst creates a web of reference that, far from being wholly celebratory, foregrounds a mood of depression and an emphasis on psychological fragmentation. This is illustrated in *The Folding Star* both by Hollinghurst's portrayal of his thirty-three year-old narrator Edward Manners's capitulation to the meretricious aspects of urban gay life, as well as by the sudden infatuation that he experiences with the attractive seventeen-year-old Luc whom he is employed to tutor. It is also signalled in the novel's opening pages in which Hollinghurst undermines Edward's sense of elation at the prospect of the enjoyments the city offers the gay man by introducing spectral references that indicate their insubstantiality.

Hollinghurst portrays Edward, on first arriving in the Flemish city where he has accepted the post of tutor and riding through the city centre at night in a tram, eagerly anticipating the companionship and sexual pleasures that, as he knows from experience, an urban location can offer the gay man. He looks forward to what he evocatively describes as 'the evening routines which will soon be mine, the tug of an unknown suburb, or a bar, or a lover'.[17] However, Hollinghurst's reference to the 'the ghost-throng of arrivals' (p. 4) on the steps of the hotel that Edward enters in search of a drink and companionship, with its echoes of T.S. Eliot's allusion to the ghostly residents of London in *The Wasteland*,[18] has the effect of problematizing Edward's optimism. As well as referring to the anonymity of the visitors to the city, it hints at the shallowness of the enjoyments they seek.

The hopes Edward has of making social and sexual contacts are initially fulfilled. He picks up the Moroccan Cherif at a local bar and rapidly embarks on an affair with him. However, although Cherif becomes strongly attached to Edward, his failure to match up to Edward's stringent ideals of physical beauty results in the latter abruptly dumping him in exchange for the sexy but, as he later suspects, untrustworthy Matt. However, after a few weeks have elapsed, Edward suddenly loses sexual interest in both men. He becomes sexually infatuated with Luc, one of the pupils whom he tutors in English, though aware that the teenage social culture that Luc inhabits makes it unlikely that he will ever have the opportunity to enjoy him sexually. Edward recognises the intensity of the passion he feels not on his first encounter with Luc when he meets him at his parents' home but on a subsequent occasion when he accidentally catches sight of him in the city centre. Narcissistically savouring his own emotional and aesthetic response to the event, as he tends to do, he thinks romantically, 'It was a turning-point in my life, this second-sighting of Luc. I knew at once how the shape of him lingered in me, like a bright image gleaming and floating on the sleepy retina' (p. 43). Alderson, analysing the episode in the context of Hollinghurst's interest in the difference and tension between 'queer' and 'identity categories', interestingly interprets Edward's intense infatuation with the teenage Luc and his sexual pursuit of him as unconsciously reflecting his desire to return to the period of his own youth when his sexual responses were still mobile and unformed.[19]

Edward's obsession with Luc's youth and beauty, to which he speedily capitulates, connects him with certain protagonists of eighteenth- and nineteenth-century Gothic novels. Referring to Lewis's *The Monk*, Stevenson's *Jekyll and Hyde* and other novels of the period, Day describes how, although the passions that the protagonists experience initially appear to promise 'possibilities of self-creation and gratification',[20] they generally prove in the long term delusive and self-destructive. The passion Edward feels for Luc follows a similar trajectory. The attraction that Luc's beauty arouses in him, combining as it does an intensely sexual response with one of emotional idealism, is in fact encouraged by his friend Matt. Hollinghurst positions the latter, in a manner resembling the temptress Matilda in Matthew Lewis's *The Monk* and Jekyll's alter ego Hyde in Stevenson's novel, in the role of sinister tempter. In a satirical dig at the culture of pornography and its merchandising of erotic day-dreams, he portrays Matt working in the gay male porn industry and enthusiastically promoting 'the fantasies it serviced' (p. 127). Matt, as we subsequently discover, also plays an instrumental role in aiding and abetting Edward's fantasies – with unhappy consequences.

On learning of Edward's feelings of attraction for Luc and having discovered that Luc and his school friends Patrick and Sibylle are planning to take a summer-break in Ostend, Matt mischievously proposes that they follow them and likewise holiday there. He suggests to Edward that they rent accommodation in the area of the teenagers' house with the aim of keeping them in their sights and discovering their interests. On arriving at the resort, Edward wanders round the garden of the house he and Matt are renting, weaving romantic fantasies around the three teenagers. Romantically transforming them, in imagery recalling the conventions of medieval courtly love, into the 'holy trinity' (p. 105) that forms the centre of the summer environment, he atmospherically describes the scene as 'very still, with the lull and whisper of the sea nearby but out of view, and hot sunshine that was a miracle in which the Three uncannily took part' (p. 105). When Matt, on returning from a stroll on the beach, discloses to him the fact that he has made contact with Luc and his two companions and engaged in conversation with them, Edward experiences a predictable pang of jealousy. It acts as a prelude to the voyeuristic fantasies that he subsequently creates. Matt has deliberately selected their accommodation next to the villa where three teenagers are staying. Gazing at the building at night, Edward ponders their relationships, wondering whether it is female Sibylle or the male Patrick whom Luc fancies. Succumbing to the process that Freud terms the 'doubling, dividing and interchanging of the self'[21] and the 'animated spectrality and blurring of boundaries between what is "I" and not "I"' that Butler describes as typifying 'the kind of enthrallment with what is other'[22] that we experience when we fall in love, he imagines himself penetrating in spectral form the bedroom where the three teenagers are sleeping. He pictures himself proceeding to 'ghost through it and hover over each sleeping face, him with her or him' (p. 109). Here he metaphorically transforms the teenagers' bedroom into a haunted house that he visits with the aim of discovering their sleeping arrangements and partnerships. The episode illustrates the complex psychological uses that, as Butler indicates, the motif of spectrality can perform in relation to queer sexuality. The process of metaphorical 'haunting' that Hollinghurst describes is, of course, mutual. Whereas Edward is haunted by thoughts of Luc and his passion for him, he in turn haunts Luc by obsessively thinking about him, focusing his fantasy life on him, and seeking to pry into his relationships.

Themes of voyeurism and the divided self are again to the fore in Hollinghurst's portrayal of Edward sitting semi-dressed in the window the following morning, with Matt manually bringing him to orgasm, while gazing through binoculars at Luc who is sunbathing in the garden next door. Commenting humorously on his own situation and the division it reflects, Edward thinks, 'I was rather tied up, head and hands in one place, heart and mind out there where my pupil lay and day-dreamed' (p. 116). Though experiencing a pang of self-disgust at the fact that he is enjoying Matt's sexual attentions while fantasising having sex with Luc, he pragmatically admits that, 'half the time I saw it suited me' since 'with Matt I did the dozen things I couldn't do with Luc'(p. 97).

Referring to the figure of the voyeur and his representation in Gothic, Day explains that his 'power and pleasure are potentially infinite, as long as distance from the innermost desires of the self can be maintained'. Alerting attention to the risks that the voyeur runs, he continues, 'Once that distance is lost, however, he becomes a participant in the spectacle, the event resulting in the fragmentation and destruction of the self'.[23] On account of the intensity of his passion for Luc, Edward is unable to maintain this distance and becomes, in consequence, increasingly emotionally involved with him. He also begins to distrust Matt and question his loyalty. On returning to the city and entering the public baths, he is surprised to encounter him there chatting casually with Luc and Patrick as if the two were close friends. The event leads him to suspect that Luke Matt may be more familiar with the teenagers than he had admitted and, in cultivating their company, is pursuing his own sexual agenda.

The theme of the fantasy production of doubles, exemplified by the episode of Edward's sexual fantasising in Ostend and the experience of narcissistic doubling and self-division to which it gave rise, is also exemplified by Hollinghurst's reference to mirror images. He portrays Edward in an earlier episode, while making love with Cherif, admitting to feeling 'confused for a moment by my own reflection in the glass... ghostly features caught in the very silvering of the mirror' (p. 11). He also depicts Edward asking Matt whether he believes in 'the narcissist theory of gay attraction' (p. 156) – only to discover that the school that Luc currently attends is named St Narcissus!

Hollinghurst interrupts his account of male gay life in an urban location by referring to its rural counterpart in the episode in which he portrays Edward returning to his family home in Surrey to attend the funeral of his previous lover Dawn who has died of AIDS. The weeks that Edward spends there in the company of his widowed mother and former school friend Edie arouse in him mixed memories of his teenage years. He compares the periods of loneliness that the gay individual can experience in a rural environment with gay urban life where some form of social or sexual contact is generally available – provided that he is young and attractive. He also recognises uncomfortably that his rejection of Cherif for failing to live up to his ideal of beauty echoes his previous rejection of Dawn whom he dumped for much the same reason.

A topic with Gothic associations that understandably dominates Edward's visit to Surrey is that of death. It occupies his thoughts not only on account of Dawn's funeral but also in relation to his memories of his father's terminal illness and demise. Here Hollinghurst employs the motif of spectrality very differently from the way he utilises in the earlier episodes set in Ostend. The 'great roll of pearly fog' (p. 256) that Edward watches envelop the local common on the night of Dawn's funeral assumes ghostly implications that suit both the occasion and his own melancholic mood. He watches spellbound as, 'The fog circled the hills, and lay thick away to the east – the Flats were submerged and, beyond them only the leafless crowns of the tallest trees showed vaguely in its surface' (p. 256). The description of the fog and its movement, in addition to increasing the mysterious atmosphere of the scene, has psychological connotations evoking the interplay between conscious and unconscious areas of the psyche, and the submerged and accessible drives and emotions that structure them. It also reminds the reader of Edward's personal failures of vision – his inability to perceive that Matt, rather than being trustworthy, may have been exploiting his friendship.

Hollinghurst concludes his account of Edward's visit to Surrey by portraying him experiencing an event relevant to the topic of the accessibility of gay companionship and sex in a rural area. While gazing at the fog-bound meadows, he glimpses through the mist the indistinct silhouette of a figure seated on a bench. It too has a spectral aspect for, as Edward admits, it 'gave me a moment's gooseflesh, as if the person sitting there alone had abruptly materialised' (p. 257). He discovers him to be, as he describes, 'a black kid...perhaps in his early twenties' (p. 257), and, after chatting in a typically British manner about the eerie weather effects, the two engage in a brief sexual encounter. Edward represents the event in terms of gentle humour. He describes how he and his unknown companion, after touching each other's freezing fingers and engaging in a preliminary embrace,' kissed sulkily, with a minor clash of spectacles' (p. 257).

As well as employing the motif of spectrality to represent the sexual fantasising in which Edward engages and depicting the appearance of the fog in the Surrey countryside, Hollinghurst develops the motif of the double. He portrays Edward, while tutoring Luc, forming a friendship with Paul Echevin, the curator of the museum that houses the work of the deceased symbolist artist Edgard Orst who produced much of his work while living in the city. Paul tells Edward the story of the how Orst, after his lover Jane Byron, whom he deeply loved, died, continued obsessively to paint her portrait. Orst also unexpectedly embarked, after her death, on a love affair with an uneducated laundrywoman who, though differing from Jane in character and class, resembled her physically. Edward is disconcerted to discover that some of the photographs and prints that he had previously assumed to depict Jane portray not her but 'the second Jane' (p. 303), the laundrywoman whom Orst regarded as her reincarnation. The obsessive passion that Edward continues to feel for Luc enables him to gain an insight into Orst's obsessions. As he discovered from having sex with Matt while fantasising making love with Luc during the visit he paid to Ostend, bodies can be interchangeable, with one substituting for another in the lover's imagination. Like Orst, who can be accused of betraying his love for Jane after her death by engaging in a love affair with a laundry worker who resembled her physically and even immortalising her in his work, so Edward, as he himself recognises, is guilty of betraying his love for Luc by having sex with the morally flawed Matt.

Hollinghurst, in addition to utilising spectrality with reference to Edward's fantasy life and the natural environment, also employs it to represent the haunting of the Belgian town by incursions of violence. On inspecting some of what he depicts as 'the eerie lithographs' that Orst produced, Edward describes them as evoking 'a sense of dying life, life hidden, haunted and winter slow' (p. 295). The atmosphere they evoke reminds him of that which he associates with the historic buildings in the old quarter of the city. Paul alerts his attention to its palimpsestic significance. As he tells Edward, a number of the fifteenth- and sixteenth-century houses for which he has expressed admiration were commandeered by members of the Nazi army when they invaded the town in the 1940s. He describes how the elderly Orst, in an attempt to avoid arrest, lived 'a kind of ghost existence' (p. 296), spending his final years as 'a premature ghost' (p. 296). On discovering that Edward is, in fact, gay, Paul confides to him the love affair in which, as a teenager, he himself secretly engaged with a German soldier who was stationed in the city. The topic of betrayal, introduced previously with reference to both Edward's suspicions of Matt's lack of trust and Orst's relationship with the laundry-woman Jane, recurs in Paul's guilty admission that he fears it may have been the information about Orst's whereabouts that he inadvertently gave his German lover that eventually led to the arrest of the elderly artist.

Hollinghurst connects the sexual experiences of Edward and Paul, separated though they are in time, by associating them both with the same location: the heterotopic site of the Hermitage. It is Matt who first mentions it to Edward, referring to it unromantically as 'some old gardens on the edge of the town' (p. 51). As Edward discovers, the gardens, previously formal in style though now returning to nature, mark the site of a sixteenth-century convent that has been converted into a public park. While providing a recreation area for the townspeople during the day, they serve illicitly at night as a gay cruising ground. As Paul confides to Edward, he and his German lover used the location for their surreptitious romantic trysts during the war. Intrigued by the thought of the novel experience of anonymous sex, Edward determines to visit the place. He pictures it in his imagination, in an image evoking his own complicated love life, as 'almost a maze' (p. 54).

The heterotopia has both Gothic and queer associations, linking it, as a result, to two different discourses, the literary and the sexual. Commenting on the Gothic associations of the motif, Botting refers to its traditionally labyrinthine structure. He introduces, as literary examples, the secret vault in the catacombs, described by Matthew Lewis in *The Monk*, where Ambrosio makes a pact with the Devil in order to fulfil his incestuous desires for his sister Antonia, and the crypt in which he later imprisons her.[24] Heterotopic locations portrayed in contemporary Gothic fiction include the Overlook Hotel in King's *The Shining* and the Theatre de Vampires in Rice's *Interview with a Vampire*. Foucault, clarifying the homosexual connotations of the motif, describes how heterotopic locations can serve as 'counter-sites'[25] where queer people congregate illicitly in search of social and sexual contact. In describing Edward's visit to the Hermitage, Hollinghurst brings together the motif's literary associations with its queer, while also interrelating themes of secrecy, spectrality and confused perception. They evoke the transgressive associations of the site, as well as Edward's ambivalent response to the anonymous sexual encounter he experiences there.

On climbing the gates into the park, he is struck by the interrelation of heterosexual and gay cultures that the gardens reveal. Whereas the moon-lit outline of the climbing frame in the children's playground reminds him that 'Families came here all the year round' (p. 53), the sound of 'drunken laughter' and 'giggles and whispering' (p. 55) emerging from the bushes alerts attention to the location's sexual significance. With the night mist giving the scene a ghostly appearance and blurring his vision, Edward finds himself confusing art with nature. He momentarily mistakes statues of classical gods and goddesses for living people and feels his 'heart catching sometimes at a waiting figure that was only a lichened Pomona or Apollo' (p. 54). He is also conscious of the farcical aspect of the location and sexual experiences associated with it and finds himself worrying that, since 'each yew-niche was a place of available secrecy' (p. 55), he might in the dark happen to encounter Matt and accidentally end up fucking him. In a passage that, while acknowledging the attraction that cruising and anonymous sex offers, questions if they are necessarily liberating, he thinks:

> You never knew what to expect. You never knew what they expected. You hadn't the advantage of being at college together, or persuading yourself you fancied him over drinks, or knowing each other's name, or anything. The absolute black ignorance was the beauty of it, and the bore.... (p. 56)

The experience of anonymous sex that Edward is seeking, when eventually he experiences it, turns out to be brief and emotionally unilluminating. It concludes in the way in which his sexual liaisons generally do since he

5 REGIONAL GOTHIC: UNCANNY CITIES AND RURAL AREAS   163

has arrived in Belgium, with him fantasising making love with Luc. He feels that, 'It was Luc standing behind me, his spent dick stiffening already between my legs. Luc's strong young hand firmly, almost over-fiercely, jerking me off, set on giving me pleasure, thrilled to do so' (p. 57).

Very different from the fantasy sexual encounter with Luc that Edward imagines taking place in the Hermitage, in which he pictures him eagerly reciprocating his passion, is the actual sexual encounter that he experiences with him towards the end of the novel. It is, in fact, Luc who appears to initiate the event by suggesting that Edward invite him to visit him at his apartment, a gesture perhaps indicating that he is not as sexually inexperienced as he at times appears to be. This view of him is endorsed by the fact that, as his mother previously intimated to Edward, though avoiding disclosing the misdemeanour he allegedly committed, he was expelled from one of the schools that he attended in the past.

Having welcomed Luc to his apartment and seeing him actually standing in his bedroom, as he has often fantasied in the past, Edward is overcome by an attack of nerves and feels too timid to approach him sexually – with the result that it is Luc who makes the first move. When the two eventually make love, Edward has the disconcerting impression that the sexual ardour that Luc shows may not in fact be directed at him but signifies 'some stored-up passion intended for someone else, but brimming and spilling' (p. 335). Edward senses that, 'Somewhere out there was the person Luc loved, a boy or a girl, but for now he was making do' or 'maybe he liked the switch of power in seducing an older man' (p. 335). And when Luc refers vaguely to a 'bet' (p. 338) that he made with a friend, Edward has the humiliating suspicion that his decision to have sex with him may have been merely a response to a teenage dare. Spectral imagery features again in this episode, utilised in different ways. On seeing Luc standing naked before him, Edward describes himself, scared of disappointing him sexually, 'as haunted by potential [sexual] moves' (p. 331). As well as describing how, 'I saw a phantom me, in jerky, melting moves of a time-lapse film, going over to him, hugging and kissing him', he apprehensively pictures Luc's alternative responses to his overtures of love: 'I saw him turning with a raised hand, it could have been to hit... or to caress' (p. 331)

Edward's panic-stricken feeling that Luc is somehow vanishing from his orbit is in fact proved correct when, shortly after his sexual encounter with him, Luc disappears. Is he running away from home, from Patrick or from Sybille who also admits to being in love with him? Is Edward himself in some mysterious way responsible for his disappearance? He wonders in horror if his unspoken fear that the intensity of his passion might give rise to violent consequences has somehow materialised and 'he had murdered Luc and then wiped all memory of it' (p. 396)?

Hollinghurst concludes the novel on a bleakly desolate note by portraying Edward standing in the 'non-place'[26] of the quay at Ostend, in the company of a few late holidaymakers, gazing forlornly at the damaged photo of Luc's face among the mugshots of other missing teenagers. In fact the face in the photo no longer bears much resemblance to Luc's and the image of ideal beauty that it previously projected. In being reduced to merely one more derelict of urban life, Luc has now become, as the emotionally devastated Edward perceives, merely 'a victim, to be stared at and pitied' (p. 422). Edward of course has lost all hope of contacting him. His narrative of erotic enthrallment and passion, like that experienced by the protagonists of other Gothic novels produced in earlier periods, terminates predictably in disappointment and loss.

Michelle Paver's *Dark Matter* introduces the reader to a very different kind of queer regional Gothic from that which Hollinghurst creates in the *Folding Star*. Whereas Hollinghurst employs as his setting a Flemish city, Paver locates her novel on the Arctic island of Gruhuken that she portrays her narrator, the twenty-eight-year-old Jack Manners, visiting in 1937 in the course of a scientific expedition. In addition the two writers, though both introducing motifs of spectrality and haunting, utilise them very differently. Whereas Hollingurst employs them to explore the sexual fantasies that his narrator Edward constructs and his voyeuristic tendencies, Paver creates a ghost story, utilising the spectral figure she introduces to represent, in certain respects, Jack's uncanny double. The isolated rural site she selects as the context for the appearance of the ghost relates her narrative to earlier Gothic texts with a spectral dimension that employ rural locations. British novels of this kind include Emily Brontë's *Wuthering Heights*, set on the west Yorkshire moors, and stories by M.R. James such as 'Oh, Whistle and I'll Come to you, my Lad', the narrative positioned on the windswept east coast. Shirley Jackson's *The Haunting of Hill House*, located in the countryside of New England, exemplifies a US example.

In addition to referring to spectrality, Paver's and Hollinghurst's novels also reveal other connections. The first hinges on the cast of characters that the two writers employ. Hollinghurst, though briefly introducing some female figures, including Edward's friend Edie and Luc's friend

Sibylle, focuses chiefly on events that take place, to cite Kosofsky Sedgwick's famous phrase, 'between men'.[27] Paver prioritises male characters and relationships even more rigorously since she employs an all-male cast.

Another feature that connects Paver's and Hollinghurst's novels is that both writers represent the locations they treat, different though they are, as exemplifying sites of foreign invasion and occupation. Whether the acts of territorial appropriation they depict are situated in the past, as is the case with the Nazi occupation of the Flemish city to which Hollinghurst refers, or are described as continuing into the present, as is the possession of the island of Gruhuken firstly by a group of local miners and secondly by the trio of British scientists that Paver describes as visiting it, both have disturbing resonances. They signify, to cite the evocative phrase that Wolfreys employs to describe the haunting of a Gothic narrative by events that occurred previously or by intertextual references to earlier fiction, the 'manifestation or persistence of the past in the present'.[28]

Paver's novel takes the form of the journal that the narrator Jack wrote while wintering alone on Gruhuken recording the uncanny events that he witnessed there. He opens his account of these events by describing his meeting in a London pub with the four men, all previously unknown to him, in charge of organising the expedition. On encountering them, he is struck by their difference from him in terms of class, wealth and academic opportunity. Whereas he, as he describes, is 'a grammar-school boy with a London degree',[29] the four men who are interviewing him, as he perceives from their accents and conversation, have all received a public school/Oxbridge education. Although the meeting appears to go well, concluding with them inviting him to join the expedition and contribute to the meteorological survey it will involve as 'their communications man' (p. 9), he interprets it very differently. Annoyed by the patronising way in which, with the exception of the Honourable Augustus Balfour, familiarly known as 'Gus', the men treat him, he decides to reject their offer. On leaving the pub, he thinks angrily, 'Tomorrow I'll write and tell them where to put their sodding expedition!' (p. 5). It is only when, while travelling back to his shabby digs in the London suburbs, he happens to see the police in the act of retrieving the corpse of a suicide from the Thames that he changes his mind. Recognising that the expedition represents the only opportunity he may ever have to escape the tedium of his present life and that, if he rejects it, he may end up with the corpses in the river, he decides, despite his dislike for the majority of the organisers, to join it.

On embarking on the trip, Jack is relieved to discover that the two men whom he regards as the most arrogant and obnoxious have dropped out, leaving him in the company of Algie and Gus. Though disliking Algie's enjoyment in shooting birds and the pleasure that he obviously takes in butchering a seal, he warms emotionally to Gus, his affection for him increasing the more he sees of him. As well as appreciating Gus's sympathetic response to his expressions of disappointment at being unable to continue his study of physics on account of lack of funds, Jack is attracted by his appearance – by his 'golden hair' and the 'chiselled purity' (p. 59) of his features. They cause him to resemble, or so Jack idealistically thinks, a hero from Greek mythology. The image of Gus that Jack creates echoes Rider Haggard's reference to Leo Vincey's resemblance to a 'Greek god' [30] in *She*, while the sexual attraction he feels toward him recalls the homoerotic bond that develops, as Ardel Haefele-Thomas describes,[31] between Leo and his fellow adventurer Horace Holly. Jack also shares Gus's interest in astronomy and together they discuss the concept of the hypothetical substance of 'dark matter', in the early stages of analysis, which Jack has read about in about in a journal. The term, as Paver's utilisation of it for the title of her novel indicates, assumes, as the narrative unfolds, diverse meanings.

The initial stages of the three men's visit to the Arctic proceed according to plan. The island of Gruhuken, when eventually they reach it, turns out, as they expected, to be a wilderness with few signs of animal life. However, indications of the habitation of the island by earlier visitors are visible. Mr Eriksson, the skipper of the boat that transports them there who is familiar with the site and its history, describes them as 'Trappers first, miners later' (p. 55). Remnants of their presence include a partially buried pile of rusty knives, a hut and a wooden post set in a cairn of stones. Algie, familiar with hunting routines, identifies the latter as 'a bear post' (p. 64) erected with the aim of luring bears to the hunter's gun. Jack, disliking being reminded of the fact 'that others were here before' (p. 66), insists on destroying the hut and constructing a new one, ignoring Mr Eriksson's objections to the act. He is puzzled both by the latter's negative response to the destruction of the hut and the look of alarm that appears on his face when he himself refers to the island, in its present apparently uninhabited state, as a form of 'No-man's-land' (p. 30).

Jack and his two companions spend their first weeks in their new surroundings busying themselves with improving their living accommodation and checking the meteorological instruments. The location's spectral associations are indicated, however, in the episode in which Jack, on hearing a flock of kittiwakes calling, is reminded by Gus that 'the Vikings believed that their cries were the wails of lost souls' (p. 40). Even more ominous is Mr Eriksson's observation, voiced in response to the discovery of a collection of 'huge arching whale ribs, many decades old' on the shore, that 'We're so far north that "dead things" last for years' (p. 40).

After Mr Eriksson has left, although everything goes well for some weeks, events unexpectedly take a turn for the worse. Gus develops appendicitis and has to be removed from the island by boat in the care of Algie. Jack, remembering Gus's insistence that the expedition should go ahead despite his absence and eager not to let him down, rejects the idea of accompanying his companions. He reluctantly decides, despite his anxiety about the approach of the cold weather and other less tangible fears he keeps to himself, to spend the winter months alone on the island.

Jack's fears of doing so are provoked not only by his doubts about his ability to endure the physical hardship and isolation that the experience will involve but also by the uncanny events he has witnessed. When, shortly after arriving, he caught sight of a figure standing by the bear post, he initially assumed it to be a member of Eriksson's crew. However when he sees it a second time, crouching on the rocks by the sea, he responds very differently. He notes with incredulity that, though it 'was streaming wet and had just hauled itself out of the sea, the stillness was absolute. No sound of droplets pattering on the snow. No creak of waterproofs as it rose' (p. 106). He thinks with horror, 'It's real. I saw it', adding with grim conviction, 'It isn't alive' (p. 107).

Further sightings of the figure that Jack experiences subsequently exacerbate his response of fear. They convince him that, rather than being merely 'an echo' resembling 'a footprint or a shadow' (p. 122) cast by an earlier event, the ghost that haunts the island – for so he now thinks of it – is 'an angry spirit' (p. 196) that seeks to injure him. On remembering the story he heard of a trapper who set up home there and was murdered by a group of miners who appropriated what he regarded as his territory, he recognises what he assumes at this point to be the ghost's objective: 'It wants Gruhuken. And I am in the way' (p. 205).

Jack's residence on the island comes to an abrupt end when events dramatically escalate. Convinced that the spectral trapper is pursuing him, he barricades himself inside the cabin he has built. However, on glimpsing the trapper standing outside the window and recognising the danger he signifies, Jack perceives that he can no long cope with the situation alone and summons assistance by radio. However, his decision to leave Gruhuken comes too late, resulting in tragedy. Although Gus and Algie, on receiving his message, rapidly charter a boat and come to his assistance, while they are leaving the island Gus falls overboard into the sea and, despite the efforts they and the crew members make to rescue him, drowns. Jack is privately convinced that his death is not an accident but that the ghostly trapper deliberately engineered it by pulling him overboard. He remembers noticing that, instead of the appropriate six men in the boat, there were in fact seven, with 'next to Gus – a wet round head' (p. 242). Reliving the scene in his imagination, he remembers, 'I'm shouting, clutching him, trying to drag Gus away from that thing.... The boat's rocking wildly. I can't hold him. He's overboard' (p. 242). He himself leaps into the sea in an attempt to rescue Gus but, on taking his hand, feels it pulled from his grasp by 'a body' that mysteriously intervenes. On gripping it, he 'clutches something soft as mouldy leather' (p. 242) that he perceives 'isn't Gus' (p. 242). The final event he remembers on leaving the island is glimpsing 'a black figure watching from the shore' (p. 242). Mr Eriksson, who participated in the rescue expedition, confirms his account, incredible though it seems. He tells Jack, 'The thing in the boat. I saw it also' (p. 245). Paver describes Jack, on returning with Algie to London, spending a year in a psychiatric institution in an attempt to recover from the traumatic events he has experienced. He subsequently purchases a small house where he lives alone, once a year making a pilgrimage to a beach on the British north coast where he attempts to communicate with Gus's spirit.

The events that Paver describes Jack experiencing on Gruhuken raise intriguing questions, their solution involving reference to Gothic texts produced earlier. Is the ghostly trapper's pursuit of Jack across the island prompted by a desire to get revenge on him for appropriating his island home and destroying his hut or does it reflect an additional motive? And, if Jack's and Mr Eriksson's interpretation of the episode in the boat is correct, what is his objective in dragging Gus into the sea? Regarded in terms of literary influences, *Dark Matter* most obviously appears to resemble, in terms of its male emphasis and treatment of spectral events in a Northern context, the stories of the American Jack London. London's 'In a Far Country' appears especially relevant. The story, set in rural Alaska, portrays two prospectors, mentally unhinged by the physical hardships and claustrophobia they have suffered, becoming convinced that ghosts are invading the cabin where they are wintering. However, London's story, though resembling Paver's in both its Nordic setting and treatment of the motif of spectrality, makes no reference to two male figures pursing one another across the snow or, as Jack and his attraction to Gus illustrates, to homoerotic attraction. In order to find a precedent for these topics, we need to turn to a well-known nineteenth-century Gothic novel that introduces episodes set in the Arctic and reference to which has occurred in the analysis of certain of the other works of contemporary queer Gothic discussed above. This is Mary Shelley's *Frankenstein*.

Sedgwick, commenting on Victor Frankenstein's pursuit of the creature he has constructed across the Arctic landscape in Shelley's novel, intriguingly observes, in a comment that appears relevant to both the spectral trapper's pursuit of Jack and his apparent attempt to gain possession of Gus by dragging him into the sea, that 'in the tableau of two men chasing one another across a landscape, it is importantly undecidable in this tableau, as in many others like it in Gothic novels, whether the two men represent two consciousnesses or only one... and whether their bond is murderous or amorous'.[32] Though in general portraying the trapper as an autonomous figure, Paver represents him on one occasion as signifying Jack's spectral double. She describes him illuminating Jack's subjectivity and emotions in a similar way to that in which, as Haggerty argues, the creature sheds light on Frankenstein's by representing his double and 'second self'.[33] Like the Arctic landscape where Jack resides, the psyche, as Kristeva describes, takes the form of 'a strange land of borders and otherness'.[34] This becomes evident in the dream that Jack experiences while wintering alone on Gruhuken after Gus and Algie have left. In keeping with Freud's theory that the dreamer can assume different identifications,[35] Jack assumes in the dream two identities: his own and that of the trapper. Paver commences the dream scenario by representing Jack as the victim of the trapper's attack. She portrays him, on feeling the trapper grasp his body, clutch hold of a knife and strive to saw off his fingers in an attempt to liberate himself. She then depicts him switching identifications and assuming instead the identity of the trapper being tortured by the miners who have invaded his location. Jack senses with horror, 'I'm tied to the bear post. Now I'm afraid. I can't see. I smell paraffin. I hear the crackle of flames. I hear the clink of metal dragged over the rocks' (p. 223). On waking from sleep, he recognises that the clink of metal he heard in the dream was the sound of the 'big rusty knives' (p. 224) used for killing seals that the miners employed to torture and kill the trapper – and that he and his companions discovered on the beach on arriving at Gruhuken. His perception that 'the terror I had felt [in the dream] had not been my own' prompts him to recognise the fact that, though regarding the spectral trapper as his enemy, he also identifies with him. In addition to being, like the trapper, a loner, Jack resembles him in holding a grudge against the people whom he regards as having usurped his rightful inheritance. Whereas the trapper hates the miners for appropriating his home, Jack resents the way in which the British upper-classes, exemplified by the Oxford-educated organisers of the expedition, have appropriated, by means of their education and wealth, the scientific education and career that he regards as his. The term 'angry spirit' (p. 96) he applies to the trapper is, as the dream reveals, also applicable to himself.

Jack also has another point of connection with the trapper. Paver intimates that the trapper, as well as mirroring Jack's emotions of anger and envy, may also reflect and share his feelings of homoerotic attraction to Gus, in a manner similar to that in which Frankenstein's creature mirrors and duplicates, as Haggerty argues, Frankenstein's 'unspeakable [homoerotic] longings'.[36] Interpreted in this context, the trapper's dragging Gus into the sea in the episode in the boat, rather than being performed merely in a spirit of revenge to punish Jack for appropriating his home, may reflect his desire to keep Gus with him on the island. Like the ghosts and mermen who are represented in folk tales and songs falling in love with mortals and attempting to lure them to their underwater home, the trapper appears intent on achieving possession of Gus. Jack, it seems, may not be the only individual on the island who is attracted to Gus's 'golden hair' (p. 59) and the 'chiselled purity' (p. 59) of his features.

Paver's representation of a ghost who, angered by an intruder appropriating both his home and the object of his erotic interest, returns from the dead to reclaim them, also echoes another well-known work of nineteenth-century Gothic fiction: Henry James's *The Turn of the Screw*. James portrays the spectral Peter Quint who, when alive, was inappropriately permitted by the master of Bly to enjoy the freedom of the estate and cultivate the company of the boy Miles, returning in spectral guise with the aim of reclaiming them from the possession of the governess whom he regards as usurping his role. The narrative strategies that Paver utilises in depicting the trapper pursuing Jack across the island to the hut where he is sheltering resemble those that James employs in representing the spectral Quint pursuing the governess across the estate of Bly. Like the governess who, on first perceiving Quint standing in the distance on one of the towers flanking the house, assumes him to be to be a living visitor to the estate, Jack, on initially glimpsing the ghostly trapper by the bear post, assumes him to be a member of Mr Ericksson's crew. In addition, like Quint, whom James portrays drawing step by step nearer to the house where the governess and her two charges reside, Paver represents the trapper encroaching step by step on the hut where Jack lives. Whereas James uses as markers of Quint's progress the garden, the window and the staircase, features typifying a Victorian country mansion, Paver employs as markers indicating the trapper's movement across the island the features of the rocks, the bear post and the cabin window.

Another question that *Dark Matter* raises is how do Jack's feelings of homoerotic attraction to Gus, that emerge during his visit to Gruhuken, relate to the Arctic environment that Paver employs as the setting for her story? Deterred from acknowledging them by the repressive conventions of 1930s masculinity, it takes some time for Jack to admit, even to himself, the fact that he loves Gus. Only in the concluding stages of residence on the island, when he is standing terrified in the hut with the spectral trapper lurking outside, does he summon up the courage to admit, 'I'm going to be brave and say it now, fearlessly, out loud. Gus, I love you' (p. 235). Why is it here, in this unfamiliar terrain, that Paver portrays him encountering his first and apparently only experience of same-sex love? Her description of the island furnishes a clue. Jack's initial response to Gruhuken, when first he arrives there in summer months, far from being one of fear, reflects a sense of wonder resembling the kind provoked by an encounter with the sublime. The sight of 'the sun blazing in a sky of astonishing blue' and 'the dazzling snow-capped mountains enclosing a wide bay dotted with icebergs' (p. 19) moves him, as he vividly describes, 'like a blow to the heart' (p. 55). Echoing the words previously uttered by Mr Ericksson, he thinks, 'Here I'll be able to see clearly for the first time in years. Right to the heart of things' (p. 41). It is understandable that it is here, in this realm of geographical and visual excess and apparent clarity of vision, that he should experience his first stirrings of same-sex desire, since it too signifies, from a hetero-normative viewpoint, as Lisabeth During and Terri Fealy argue, a form of transgressive excess.[37]

In addition to those exemplified by the Arctic landscape and queer sexuality, Paver also refers in the novel to a third form of 'excess'. This is spectrality, with its connotations of death as the ultimate mystery and a realm transcending mortal experience. Paver concludes the novel by portraying Jack, distressed and perturbed by the 'dark matter' of Gus's death, asking him on one of the visits he makes to the Nordic beach to commune with him the metaphysical questions, 'Are you there in the black water? Do you walk on the shore in the dead grey stillness among the bones? Or were you snuffed out like a spark, all traces extinguished?' (p. 252). Appalled by the thought of Gus being doomed to inhabit the bleak Arctic world in spectral form forever, with the ghostly trapper as his only companion, he grimly concludes, 'Oh, I hope so. I can't bear to think of you still there.'

Notes

1. Dickens, *Martin Chuzzlewit*, p. 185. (Dickens 1843/1968).
2. Alasdair Gray, *Lanark: A Life in Four Books*, p. 37. (Gray 1985).
3. Elizabeth Gaskell, 'The Old Nurse's Story', in Richard Dalby (ed.), *The Virago Book of Best Ghost Stories*, pp. 13–14. (Gaskell 2006).
4. Emily Alder, 'Urban Gothic', in William Hughes, David Punter, Andrew Smith (eds), *The Encyclopedia of Gothic*, p. 703. (Alder 2013).
5. Stoker, *Dracula*, p. 12. (Stoker 2006).
6. Rice, *Interview with the Vampire*, p. 184. (Rice 1976).
7. Alan Bray, *Homosexuality in Renaissance England*, pp. 81–114. (Bray 1992).
8. Jeffrey Weeks, 'Discourse, Desire and Sexual Deviance: Some Problems in a History of Homosexuality', in Richard Parker and Peter Aggleton (eds), *Culture, Society and Sexuality: A Reader*, pp. 125–149. (Weeks 1999).
9. Shari Benstock, 'Paris, Lesbianism and the Politics of Reaction, 1900–1940', in Martin Bauml Duberman, Martha Vicinus and George Chauncey Jr. (eds), *Hidden from History: Reclaiming the Gay and Lesbian Past*, p. 334. (Benstock 1989).
10. Didier Eribon, *Insult and the Making of the Gay Self*, trans. by Michael Lucey, p. 20. (Eribon 2002).
11. Halberstam, *In a Queer Time and Place: Transgender Bodies, Subcultural Lives*, p. 36. (Halberstam 2005).
12. Colin R. Johnson, *Just Queer Folks: Gender and Sexuality in Rural America*, p. 5. (Johnson 2013).
13. See Zimmerman, *The Safe Sea of Women: Lesbian Fiction 1969–89*, pp. 79–86 (Zimmerman 1984); and Bram Dikstra, *Idols of Perversity: Fantasies of Feminine Evil in Fin de Siècle Culture*, p. 154. (Dikstra 1986).
14. See for example the trajectory of Dorian in Oscar Wilde's *The Picture of Dorian Gray*.
15. David Alderson, 'Desire as Nostalgia: The Novels of Alan Hollinghurst' in Alderson and Linda Anderson (eds), *Territories of Desire in Queer Culture: Refiguring Contemporary Boundaries*, pp. 29–48. (Alderson 2000).
16. Day, *In the Circles of Fear and Desire*, pp. 23–27. (Day 1985).
17. Alan Hollinghurst, *The Folding Star* (London: Vintage, 1998), p. 3. (Hollinghurst 1998). Subsequent references are to this edition and in the text.

18. T.S. Eliot, *The Wasteland* in T.S. Eliot, *Selected Poems*, p. 53. (Eliot 1958).
19. Alderson, 'Desire as Nostalgia', pp. 40–1. (Alderson 2000).
20. Day, *In the Circles of Fear and Desire*, pp. 40–1. (Day 1985).
21. Freud, 'The Uncanny', p. 356. (Freud 1985).
22. Jordan Rosenberg, '"Serious Innovation": A Conversation with Judith Butler', in George E. Haggerty and Molly McGarry (eds), *A Companion to Lesbian, Gay, Bisexual, Transgender and Queer Studies*, pp. 382–3. (Rosenberg 2007).
23. Day, *In the Circles of Fear and Desire*, p. 66.
24. Botting, 'Power in Darkness: Heterotopias, Literature and Gothic Labyrinths', in Botting and Dale Townshend (eds), *Gothic: Critical Concepts in Literary and Cultural Studies*, vol. 2, pp. 243–268. (Botting 2004).
25. Michel Foucault, 'Of Other Spaces', *Diacritics*, 16: 1 (1986), 24. (Foucault 1986).
26. For reference to the concept of a 'non-place', see Sears, *Stephen King's Gothic*, pp. 175–6. (Sears 2011).
27. Sedgwick, *Between Men: English Literature and Homosexual Desire*, p. 4. (Sedgwick 1985).
28. Wolfreys, *Victorian Hauntings: Spectrality, Gothic, The Uncanny and Literature*, p. 113. (Wolfreys 2002).
29. Michelle Paver, *Dark Matter: A Ghost Story*, p. 113. (Paver 2011).
30. Haggard, Henry Rider, "She", in *Three Adventure Novels of H. Rider Haggard*, pp. 17–18. (Haggard 1951).
31. Haefele-Thomas, Ardel, *Queer Others in Victorian Gothic: Transgressing Monstrosity* (Cardiff: University of Wales, 2012), p. 88. (Haefele-Thomas 2012).
32. Sedgwick, *The Coherence of Gothic Conventions* (London: Methuen, 1980), ix. (Sedgwick 1980).
33. Haggerty, *Queer Gothic*, p. 52.
34. Kristeva, *Strangers to Ourselves*, p. 191. (Kristeva 1991).
35. Freud, 'A child is being beaten' (1919), in James Strachey and Angela Richards (ed.), *The Pelican Freud Library*, vol. 10, pp. 163–93. (Freud 1985).
36. Haggerty, *Queer Gothic*, p. 52.
37. Lisabeth During and Terri Fealy, 'Philosophy', in Andy Medhurst and Sally Munt (eds), *Lesbian and Gay Studies: A Critical Introduction*, p. 127. (During and Fealy 1997).

CHAPTER 6

Conclusion

My discussion of Hollinghurst's *The Folding Star* and Paver's *Dark Matter* in Chapter Five concludes this study of contemporary queer Gothic. As well as illustrating the contribution that representations of geographical locations make to fiction of this kind, the two novels furnish us, along with some of the other works of fiction discussed above, with an opportunity to review some of the roles that Gothic motifs and narrative structures play in contributing to the representation of queer sexualities and genders.

The utilisation of spectrality in the novels of Hollinghurst and Paver is of especial interest in this respect since it illustrates the numerous different uses that the motif performs in fiction and the varied forms it takes. Hollinghurst in *The Folding Star*, in representing his narrator Edward's sexual infatuation with the teenage Luc, employs the motif with reference to uncanny doubling in order to explore themes of sexual fantasy and voyeurism. Paver, in contrast, locating *Dark Matter* in the Arctic, utilises the ghost story to depict the pursuit of her protagonist Jack by the figure of the spectral trapper. Though keeping the trapper's significance, as suits his mysterious appearance on the island, to a degree ambiguous, she signals the different roles he performs. As well as signifying an 'angry spirit' (p. 196) who resents Jack's appropriation of his island home and appears to regard him as his rival in love, the trapper exemplifies, despite his difference in nationality and lifestyle, Jack's uncanny double, illuminating the grudge he bears society for not allowing him to follow the academic career he wished to pursue.

Reference to spectrality and the figure of the ghost, as the novels discussed in Chapter Two illustrate, also perform other uses in queer Gothic. By portraying the narrator encountering the phantom of an individual from an earlier period or conversing with an older friend with knowledge of the past, writers explore events from queer history and examine the import they hold for the present. Berman portrays his unnamed teenage narrator in *Vintage: A Ghost Story*, by engaging in a relationship with a ghost from the 1950s and learning of his unhappy history, developing a sense of compassion for him, while Edward Manners in Hollinghurst's *The Folding Star*, by conversing with Paul Echevin, discovers secrets with homosexual significance relating to the Nazi occupation of the Flemish town where he lives. Tondeur, in contrast, employs spectrality to represent the ghostly presences from earlier generations that frequent The Water's Edge Hotel, as well as the metaphorical haunting of the hotel by the secrets of the people who currently live there. Instead of, as the reader might expect, contrasting the publicly acknowledged nature of heterosexual relationships with the closeted nature of their lesbian and bisexual counterparts, Tondeur avoids this conventional approach. She illustrates that it is not only queer people who form relationships that society regards as scandalous and, as a result, attempt to conceal them. Heterosexuals also do. Esther, who currently manages the hotel, harbours secrets of both a hetero and a lesbian kind since, as well as having married and given birth to a daughter, she has formed a sexual relationship with her friend Meredith. As a result, as is the case with many people today, she leads a life complicated and enriched by both hetero and queer involvements. Grimsley's *Winter Birds* shares with Tondeur's novel the representation of the family home as a haunted site. Although the series of derelict houses in North Carolina that the Crell family rent are not haunted by the incursion of an actual ghost, Grimsley portrays them, from the viewpoint of the eight-year-old Danny disturbed by his tyrannical father Bobjay and his rages, as such. The ambiguously portrayed figure of the River Man whom Danny conjures up, though compensating to a degree for his father's neglect and brutality, ominously evokes connotations of suicide and death by drowning.

Several of the novels analysed in this study, in referring to 'the haunting relation between past and present',[1] that, as Haggerty describes, the historian Freccero foregrounds, reveal connections with queer historiography, illustrating the interplay between fiction and history that writers of queer Gothic on occasion explore. Others, such as Waters's *Affinity*, in treating a particular episode of queer history, evoke the concept of the 'historical moment'[2] discussed by the historiographer Traub. Centring her narrative on the spiritualist movement that flourished in the 1870s and 1880s, Waters explores the contribution that women made to it and the role that the séance surreptitiously played as a vehicle for expressing lesbian desire. She also employs spectrality metaphorically to illustrate the marginalisation and social invisibility of certain categories of Victorian womanhood. They include the spinster, the housemaid and—of key importance to the socio-sexual focus of her novel—the lesbian.

Another motif that features prominently in queer Gothic, the sexual-political potential of which, as illustrated by the novels referred to in Chapter Three, lesbian feminist and male gay writers writing in the 1980s and 1990s significantly helped to develop, is the 'sympathetic vampire'.[3] The fanged creature, having succeeded, as a result of its representation by writers working in the era such as Anna Livia and Jodi Scott in achieving a voice and distinctive personality, now acts as narrator or protagonist in numerous queer novels, stories and films. Bowen, writing in the early 1990s in the era of the AIDS crisis and re-working the motif of homosexual legibility that features in nineteenth-century literature, utilises his vampiric narrator Rafael in *Diary of a Vampire* to articulate the anxieties about coming out that gay men and lesbians experience especially in homophobic eras. Kingston, writing at the later date of 2013, and influenced by queer and post-modern approaches to sexuality, creates in *Chrystal Heart* a very different form of vampire narrative. Focusing on the cyborg-vampire Chrystal and advertising the artifice of the novel's construction by interweaving conventions of steam punk, Gothic and sci-fi, she creates a protagonist who, instead of identifying as lesbian, as the reader initially assumes, endorses the mobility of sexuality, a view promoted by queer approaches to sexuality and their psychoanalytic emphasis, by engaging in sexual relations with men as well as women.[4] Winterson's *The Daylight Gate* and Tondeur's *The Water's Edge* employ protagonists or key characters of a similar kind. Winter also refers in *Annabel* to another form of psycho-sexual mobility by portraying her eponymous intersex protagonist identifying with her school friend Wally Michelin while also feeling erotically attracted to her.

As Brome's AIDS narrative *Love in the Plague*, discussed in Chapter Three, illustrates, another motif that plays a significant role in contemporary queer Gothic fiction is the double. Portraying his protagonist Lucille acquiring a double in the seventeenth-century, Brome utilises her experiences to compare the effects of the AIDS epidemic on queer communities in 1980s London and New York with those of the bubonic plague in seventeenth-century London. Brome's portrayal of Lucille acquiring an alter ego in the earlier period is illuminated by comments voiced by queer historiographers. The historian Heather Love describes how she herself and her colleagues sometimes feel, 'unsettled by our identification with the figures from the past'[5] whom they research, and the uncanny sense of doubling they encounter. An interesting feature of Brome's novel is the interplay of different genres and fictional forms that it creates. In addition to interrelating the AIDS novel with historical fiction, it re-casts, like Hollinghurst's *The Folding Star*, the narrative of the haunted city.

The monster, with whom the vampire displays connections on account of his grotesque appearance and shape-shifting abilities, also furnishes a vehicle for representing queer experience. Contemporary writers, as illustrated in Chapter Four, employ his hybrid construction and its mobile associations, regarded in the nineteenth-century as posing a threat to the stability of sexuality and gender, as vehicles to represent society's homophobic responses to the queer subject. Whereas Ackroyd's *The Casebook of Victor Frankenstein* and Winterson's *The Daylight Gate* utilise the topic of monsterisation to represent the persecution and harassment of people with a queer sexuality and their relegation to the role of social outcast, Swan's *The Wives of Bath* employs the monster's shape-shifting powers as a strategy to represent the bemused response that the transsexual can evoke from the spectator. The fourteen-year-old Mouse, as Swan describes, regards the transformation that her friend Paulie achieves by means of gender performance into the male Lewis as uncanny—'like watching a wizard melt into male and female shapes before your eyes' (p. 88). Shape-shifting and transformation of a different kind are the focus of Kenan's innovative slave narrative 'Let the Dead Bury their Dead', its construction displaying connections with historiographic metafiction and Gothic. The story focuses primarily on the different strategies that the African-American slave Pharaoh and the white Phineas, the son of the owner of the plantation where Pharaoh is bound, utilise to achieve racial and sexual freedom.

Creating an atmospheric context for the utilisation of the themes and narrative structures referred to above are the different geographical locations, both rural and urban, that writers utilise as their location. Sites especially memorable in this respect include the river bank in Grimsley's *Winter Birds*, where the eight-year-old Danny hears his father's voice echoing threateningly across the fields, and Winterson's description of the wild tract of Pendle Forest in *The Daylight Gate*. The heterotopic location, constructed on the site of a former convent, that Hollinghurst portrays his narrator Edward in *The Folding Star* visiting in search of anonymous sex, contributes to the depiction of the hedonistic gay culture of the period, as well as indicating the darker element of pessimism and disillusion that Hollinghurst suggests can underlie it. Winter's reference to the mysterious 'unnamed' lake in the Alaskan wilderness in her intersex novel *Annabel* also foregrounds the themes that the narrative treats, alerting attention, as it does, to the importance of 'naming'.

The novels and stories discussed in this study, as well as illustrating some of the topics and narrative strategies that writers of contemporary queer Gothic employ, also raise questions pertinent to its development. Will writers continue to interrelate identity categories, such as 'lesbian' and 'gay', with reference to the queer view of identity as provisional and contingent and an emphasis on sexual mobility and the performative dimension of gender? Will the topic of queer history continue to achieve prominence in fiction, with the motif of spectrality contributing to its representation and writers foregrounding the connection between queer narrative and historiography? Though the answers to these questions are perforce obscure, queer fiction and the narrative strategies that writers employ to construct it will hopefully continue to flourish and diversify, contributing new topics and debates to the texts produced in the future.

NOTES

1. Haggerty, 'The History of Homosexuality Reconsidered', in Chris Mounsey (ed.), *Developments in the History of Sexualities*, p. 5. (Haggerty 2013).
2. Traub, 'The Present Future of Lesbian Historiography', in Haggerty and McGary (eds), *The Blackwell Companion to Lesbian Gay, Bisexual, Transgender, and Queer Studies,* p. 126. (Traub 2007).
3. See Chapter Three, note 21.
4. Another contemporary writer who refers to the topic of female bisexuality and sexual mobility in her fiction is Ali Smith. See especially her novels *The Accidental* and *How to be Both*.
5. Heather Love, *Feeling Backward: Loss and the Politics of Queer History*, p. 9. (Love 2007).

BIBLIOGRAPHY

FICTION

Ackroyd, Peter. 2008. *The Casebook of Victor Frankenstein*. London: Chatto and Windus.
Berman, Steve. 2007. *Vintage: A Ghost Story*. Maple Shade, New Jersey: Lethe Press.
Bowen, Elizabeth. 1999. *Collected Stories*. London: Vintage.
Bowen, Gary. 1995. *Diary of a Vampire*. New York: Masquerade Books.
Brome, Vincent. 2001. *Love in the Plague*. London: House of Stratus.
Brown, Rebecca. 2007. *The Haunted House*. New York: City Lights Books.
Buck, Rebecca S. 2011. *Ghosts of Winter*. New York: Bold Strokes Books.
Coe, Jonathan. 2014. *What a Carve Up*. Harmondsworth: Penguin.
Collins, Wilkie. 2008. *The Haunted Hotel: A Mystery of Modern Venice*. London: Nonsuch Classics.
Currier, Jameson. 2009. The Country House. In *The Haunted Heart and Other Tales*, ed. Currier, 40–55. New Jersey: Lethe Press.
Dear, Nick. 2011. *Frankenstein: Based on the Novel by Mary Shelley*. London: Faber and Faber.
Dickens, Charles. 1843/1968. *Martin Chuzzlewit*. London: Penguin.
Dickens, Charles. 1853/1996. *Bleak House*. Oxford: Oxford University Press.
Donoghue, Emma. 1994. *Stir Fry*. London: Hamish Hamilton.
Du Maurier, Daphne. 1992. *Rebecca*. London: Arrow Books.
Edwards, Nicky. 1992. *Tough at the Top*. Only Women Press.
Forster, E.M. 1971. *Maurice*. London: Hodder Arnold.
Garber, Eric, ed. 1991. *Embracing the Dark*. Boston, US: Alyson Publications.

Gaskell, Elizabeth. 2006. 'The Old Nurse's Story'. In *The Virago Book of Best Ghost Stories*, ed. Richard Dalby, 5–27. London: Virago.
Gray, Alasdair. 1985. *Lanark: A Life in Four Books*. Edinburgh: Canongate.
Gray, Alasdair. 1990. *Something Leather*. London: Picador.
Grimsley, Jim. 1997. *Winter Birds*. London: Black Swan.
Haggard, Henry Rider. 1951. *She*. In *Three Adventure Novels of H. Rider Haggard*. New York: Dover.
Herren, Greg and J.M. Redmann, eds. 2012. *Night Shadows*. New York: Bold Stroke Books.
Hoffman, Alice. 1988. *At Risk*. Berkley.
Hoffmann, E.T.A. 1982. 'The Sandman'. In *Tales of Hoffmann*, translated by R.J. Hollingdale, 85–125. Harmondsworth: Penguin.
Hollinghurst, Alan. 1998. *The Folding Star*. London: Vintage.
James, Henry. 1988. *The Turn of the Screw*. London: Dent.
James, M.R. 2011. *Collected Ghost Stories*. Oxford: Oxford University Press.
Keats, John. 1969. *Poems*. Oxford: Oxford University Press.
Kenan, Randall. 1992. 'Let the Dead Bury Their Dead'. In *Let The Dead Bury Their Dead and Other Stories*, ed. Kenan, 283–334. New York: Harcourt and Brace.
King, Stephen. 1983. *Pet Sematary*. London: Hodder and Stoughton.
King, Stephen. 1987. *The Shining*. New York: Doubleday.
Kingston, Meg. 2013. *Chrystal Heart*. London: Jay Walker Writing.
Le Fanu, J. Sheridan. 1993. *'Carmilla'* (1871). In *Daughters of Darkness: Lesbian Vampire Stories*, ed. Pam Keesey, 27–86. Pittsburgh: Cleis Press.
Livia, Anna. 1991. *Minimax*. Portland, OR: Eighth Mountain Press.
London, Jack. 1993. 'In a Far country'. In *The Complete Stories of Jack London*, ed. Earle Labor, Robert C. Leitz and Milo Shepard, 209–223. Stanford, CA: Stanford University Press.
Love, Heather. 2007. *Feeling Backward: Loss and the Politics of Queer History*. Cambridge, MA: Harvard University Press.
Lovecraft, H.P. 1966. 'At the Mountains of Madness'. In *Novels of Terror*, ed. Lovecraft, 11–112. London: Panther.
Lundoff, Catherine. 2008. *Haunted Hearths and Sapphic Shades: Lesbian Ghost Stories*. New Jersey: Lethe Press.
Mains, Geoff. 1989. *Gentle Warriors*. Stanford, CT: Knights Press.
Marsh, Richard. 2007. *The Beetle: A Mystery*. London: Wordsworth Editions Ltd.
Miller, Isabel. 1979. *Patience and Sarah*. London: The Women's Press.
Paver, Michelle. 2011. *Dark Matter: A Ghost Story*. London: Orion Books.
Peters, Julie Anne. 2005. *Luna*. New York: Little, Brown and Company.
Polidori, John. 1997. *The Vampyre*. In ed. Robert Morrison and Christ Baldick. Oxford: Oxford University Press, 1–24.
Radcliffe, Anne. 1797. *The Italian*. In ed. Robert Miles, 2000. London: Penguin.
Rechy, John. 1963. *City of Night*. New York: Grove Press.

Rice, Ann. 1976. *Interview with the Vampire*. London: Raven Books.
Rowe, Michael. 2012. 'All the Pretty Boys'. In *Night Shadows*, ed. Redman and Herren, 118–128. New York: Bold Stroke Books.
Saki (Hector Hugh Munro). 1989. 'Sredni Vashtar'. In *The Chronicles of Clovis*, ed. Saki, 51–57. Harmondsworth: Penguin Classics.
Scott, Jody. 1984. *I, Vampire*. New York: Ace Science Fiction Books.
Shakespeare, William. 1953. *Macbeth*. Ed. Kenneth Muir. London: Methuen.
Shelley, Mary. 1969. *Frankenstein or the Modern Prometheus*. Oxford: Oxford University Press.
Stevenson, Robert Louis. 2007. *The Strange Case of Dr Jekyll and Mr Hyde* [1886]. Oxford: Oxford University Press.
Stoker, Bram. 1996. *Dracula*. Oxford: Oxford University Press.
Stryker, Susan. 2006. 'My Words to Victor Frankenstein above the Village of Chamonix: Performing Transgender Rage'. In *The Transgender Studies Reader*, ed. Stryker and Stephen Whittle, 244–256. New York: Routledge.
Swan, Susan. 1993. *The Wives of Bath*. London: Granta.
Toder, Nancy. 1995. *Choices*. Watertown, MA: Alyson Publications.
Tondeur, Louise. 2003. *The Water's Edge*. London: Headline.
Ulrichs, Karl Heinrich. 1991. 'Manor'. Trans. Hubert Kennedy. In *Embracing the Dark*, ed. Eric Garber, 98–108. Boston: Alyson Publications.
Waters, Sarah. 1999. *Affinity*. London: Virago.
White, Edmund. 1988. 'An Oracle'. In *A Darker Proof: Stories from a Crisis*, ed. Adam Mars-Jones and Edmund White, 207–250. London: Faber and Faber.
Wilde, Oscar. 1996. *The Picture of Dorian Gray*. Harmondsworth: Penguin.
Winter, Kathleen. 2010. *Annabel*. New York: Black Cat.
Winterson, Jeanette. 1987. *The Passion*. London: Bloomsbury.
Winterson, Jeanette. 2012. *The Daylight Gate*. London: Arrow Books in Association with Hammer.
Wittig, Monique. 1989. *Across the Acheron*. Trans. D. Le Vay with M. Crossland. London: The Women's Press.

THEORETICAL AND CRITICAL WORKS

Abraham, Nicolas. 1987. 'Notes on the Phantom: A Complement to Freud's metapsychology'. *Critical Inquiry* 13/2:287.
Abraham, Nicolas, and Maria Torok. 1994. *The Shell and the Kernel: Renewals of Psychoanalysis*. Trans. Nicholas T. Rand. Chicago: University of Chicago Press.
Ahmed, Sara. 2006. *Queer Phenomenology: Orientation, Objects, Others*. Durham, NC: Duke University Press.
Alder, Emily. 2013. 'Urban Gothic'. In *The Encyclopedia of Gothic*, ed. William Hughes, David Punter and Andrew Smith, vol. 2, 703–705. Oxford: Wiley Blackwell.

Alderson, David. 2000. 'Desire as Nostalgia: The Novels of Alan Hollinghurst'. In *Territories of Desire in Queer Culture: Refiguring Contemporary Boundaries*, ed. Alderson and Linda Anderson, 29–48. Manchester: Manchester University Press.

Andermahr, Sonya. 2009. *Jeanette Winterson*. Basingstoke: Palgrave Macmillan.

Anderson, Melanie R. 2008. 'Wilde's Dorian Gray as Aesthetic Vampire'. In *POMP: Publications of the Mississippi Philological Association* 12/2:157 –159.

Armitt, Lucie. 2009. *Twentieth Century Gothic*. Cardiff: University of Wales Press.

Ashurst, Gail, and Anna Powell. 2012. 'Under Their Own Steam: Magic, Science and Steampunk'. In *The Gothic in Contemporary and Popular Culture*, ed. Justin D. Edwards and Agnieszka Soltysik Monnet, 148–164. London: Routledge.

Azzarello, Robert. 2008. 'Unnatural Predators: Queer Theory Meets Environmental Studies in Bram Stoker's *Dracula*'. In *Queering the Non-Human*, ed. Noreen Giffney and Myra J. Hird, 137–158. London: Ashgate.

Bakhtin, Mikhail. 1981. *The Dialogic Imagination*. Austin: University of Texas Press.

Baldwin, James. 2008. 'Stranger in the Village'. In *The Oxford Book of Essays*, ed. John Gross, 621–633. Oxford: Oxford University Press.

Bataille, Georges. 1986. *Eroticism, Death and Sensuality*. Trans. Mary Dalwood. San Francisco: City Light Books.

Benjamin, Jessica. 1993. 'Master and Slave: The Fantasy of Erotic Domination'. In *Powers of Desire*, ed. Ann Snitow, 30–55. New York: Columbia University Press.

Benshoff, Harry M. 1997. *Monsters in the Closet: Homosexuality and the Horror Film*. Manchester: Manchester University Press.

Benstock, Shari. 1989. 'Paris, Lesbianism and the Politics of Reaction, 1900–1940'. In *Hidden from History: Reclaiming the Gay and Lesbian Past*, ed. Martin Duberman, Martha Vicinus and George Chauncey Jr., 332–346. London: Penguin.

Bhabha, Homi K. 1994. *The Location of Culture*. London: Routledge.

Bornstein, Kate. 1994. *Gender Outlaw: On Men, Women, and the Rest of Us*. New York: Routledge.

Botting, Fred. 1999. 'The Gothic Production of the Unconscious'. In *Spectral Readings: Towards a Gothic Geography*, ed. Glennis Byron and David Punter. London: Macmillan.

Botting, Fred. 2004. 'Power in Darkness: Heterotopias, Literature and Gothic Labyrinths'. In *Gothic: Crtitical Concepts in Literary and Cultural Studies*, ed. Fred Botting and Dale Townshend, vol. 2, 243–268. London: Routledge.

Botting, Fred. 2004. 'Introduction: Twentieth Century Gothic: Our Monsters, Our Pets'. In *Gothic: Critical Concepts in Literary and Cultural Studies*, ed. Fred Botting and Dale Townshend, vol. 3. London: Routledge.

Botting, Fred, and Dale Townshend. eds. 2004. *Gothic: Critical Concepts in Literary and Cultural Studies*. London: Routledge, Vol 3, pages 1–11.

Bowcott, Owen. 2016. 'Aids: Thatcher Tried to Block Public Health Warnings'. *The Guardian*, December 30, p. 34.
Bowers, Maggie Ann. 2004. *Magic(al) Realism*. London: Routledge.
Bray, Alan. 1992. *Homosexuality in Renaissance England*. London: Gay Men's Press.
Brewer, William D. 2004. 'Transgendering in Matthew Lewis's The Monk'. *Gothic Studies* 6/2:192–207.
Brodsley, Laurel. 1992. 'Defoe's the Journal of the Plague Year: A Model for Stories of the Plague'. In *Aids: The Literary Response*, ed. Emmanuel S. Nelson, 1–22. New York: Twayne.
Bronfen, Elisabeth. 1992. *Over Her Dead Body: Death, Femininity and the Aesthetic*. Manchester: Manchester University Press.
Bronte, Charlotte. 1940. *Jane Eyre*. London: J.M. Dent and Sons Ltd.
Brookes, Les. 2009. *Gay Male Fiction Since Stonewall: Ideology, Conflict and Aesthetics*. London: Routledge.
Brown, Judith C. 1989. 'Lesbian Sexuality in Medieval and Early Modern Europe'. In *Hidden from History: Reclaiming the Gay and Lesbian Past*, ed. Martin Duberman, Martha Vicinus, George Chauncey, 67–75. London: Penguin.
Brown, Marshall. 2003. *The Gothic Text*. Stanford: Stanford University Press.
Browne, John. 2014. *The Glass Closet: Why Coming Out is Good in Business*. New York: Harper Business.
Bruhm, Steven. 2002. 'The Contemporary Gothic: Why We Need It'. In *The Cambridge Companion to Gothic Fiction*, ed. Jerrold E. Hogle, 259–275. Cambridge: Cambridge University Press.
Buse, Peter, and Andrew Stott. 1999. *Ghosts, Deconstruction, Psychoanalysis, History*. London: Macmillan.
Bush, Jeff. 2013. "I'd rather be dirty': The Queering of the Greenwood in E.M. Forster's Maurice'. *Dandelion*, 4/1:1–13.
Butler, Judith. 1990. *Gender Trouble: Feminism and the Subversion of Identity*. New York: Routledge.
Butler, Judith. 1993. *Bodies that Matter: On the Discursive Limits of Sex*. London: Routledge.
Carroll, Rachel. 2006. 'Rethinking Generational History: Queer Histories of Sexuality in Neo-Victorian Feminist Fiction'. *Studies in the Literary Imagination* 39/2:135–147.
Case, Sue-Ellen. 1991. 'Tracking the Vampire'. *Difference: A Journal of Feminist Cultural Studies* 3/2: 1–20.
Castle, Terry. 1993. *The Apparitional Lesbian: Female Homosexuality in Modern Culture*. New York: Columbia University Press.
Cixous, Helene. 1986. 'Exchange'. In *The Newly Born Woman*, ed. Helene Cixous and Catherine Clement. Trans. Betsy Wing, 152. Manchester: Manchester University Press.

Cixous, Helene, and Catherine Clement. 1986. *The Newly Born Woman*. Trans. Betsy Wing. Manchester: Manchester University Press.

Clausen, Jan. 1990. 'My Interesting Condition'. *Out /Look: National Lesbian and Gay Quarterly* 7:11–21.

Cohen, Jeffrey Jerome. 1996. 'Monster Culture: Seven Theses'. In *Monster Theory: Reading Culture*, ed. Cohen, 3–25. Minneapolis: University of Minnesota Press.

Cohen, Michael P. 2004. 'Blues in Green: Ecocriticism under Critique'. *Environmental History* 9/1:9–36.

Copjec, Jean. 2004. 'Vampires, Breast Feeding and Anxiety'. In *Gothic: Critical Concepts in Literature and Cultural Studies*, ed. Fred Botting and Dale Townshend, vol. 4, 12–29. London: Routledge.

Cosslett, Tess. 1998. 'Intertextuality in Oranges Are Not the Only Fruit: The Bible, Malory and Jane Eyre'. In *I'm Telling You Stories: Jeanette Winterson and the Politics of Reading*, ed. Helena Grice and Tim Woods, 15–28. Amsterdam-Atlanta: Rodopi.

Cox, Liz. January 2008. *Gothic Narratives of Lesbian Identity and Desire in British Women's Fiction 1840–1890*. Doctor of Philosophy thesis, Warwick University.

Coupe Laurence. ed. 2000. *The Green Studies Reader: From Romanticism to Ecocriticism*. London: Routledge.

Craft, Christopher. 1984. '"Kiss Me with Those Red Lips": Gender and Inversion in Bram Stoker's *Dracula*'. *Representations* 8:107–133.

Creed, Barbara. 1993. 'Lesbian Bodies: Tribades, Tomboys and Tarts'. In *Sexy Bodies: The Strange Carnalities of Feminism*, ed. Elizabeth Grosz and Elspyth Probyn, 86–103. London: Routledge.

Creed, Barbara. 1993. *The Monstrous Feminine: Film, Feminism, Psychoanalysis*. London: Routledge.

Crimp, Douglas. 1998. *AIDS: Cultural Analysis: Cultural Activism*. Cambridge, MA: MIT Press.

Daffron, Eric. 2001. 'Double Trouble: The Self, the Social Order and the Trouble with Sympathy in the Romantic and Postmodern Gothic'. *Gothic Studies* 3/1:75–83.

Davies, David Stuart. 2007. 'Introduction'. In *The Beetle: A Mystery*, ed. Davies and Richard Marsh. Ware: Wordsworth Editions, pp. refs.

Day, William Patrick. 1985. *In the Circles of Fear and Desire: A Study of Gothic Fantasy*. Chicago: University of Chicago Press.

De Lauretis, Teresa. 1988. Sexual Indifference and Lesbian Representation. *Theatre Journal* 40/2:155–177.

de Moss, Bianca. 2006. *Blood Sisters: Lesbian Vampire Tales*. New York: Alyson Books.

Derrida, Jacques. 1986. *Memoires for Paul de Man*. Trans. Cecile Lindsay, Jonathan Culler and Eduardo Cadava. New York: Columbia University Press.

Derrida, Jacques. 1992. 'Passions: "An Oblique Offering"'. In *Derrida: A Critical Reader*, ed. David Wood, 21. Oxford: Blackwell.

Dewey, Joseph. 1992. 'Music for a Closing: Responses to AIDS in Three American Novels'. In *Aids: The Literary Response*, ed. Emmanuel S. Nelson, 23–38. New York: Twayne.

Dinshaw, Carolyn. 1999. *Getting Medieval: Sexualities and Communities, Pre and Postmodern*. Durham, NC: Duke University Press.

Dollimore, Jonathan. 1995. 'Sex and Death'. *Textual Practice* 9/1:27–63.

During, Lisabeth, and Terri Fealy. 1997. 'Philosophy'. In *Lesbian and Gay Studies: A Critical Introduction*, ed. Andy Medhurst and Sally Munt, 127. London: Cassell.

Dyer, Richard. 1993. 'Children of the Night: Vampirism as Homosexuality: Homosexuality as Vampirism'. In *Sweet Dreams: Sexuality, Gender and Popular Fiction*, ed. Susannah Radstone, 47–72. London: Lawrence and Wishart.

Dyer, Richard, Kim Newman, Henry Sheehan, and Ian Sinclair. 1993. 'Dracula and Desire'. *Sight and Sound* 3:8–15.

Edel, Leon. ed. 1948. *The Ghostly Tales of Henry James*. New Jersey: Rutgers University Press.

Edelman, Lee. 1994. *Homographesis: Essays in Gay Literary and Cultural Theory*. New York: Routledge.

Edelman, Lee. 2004. *No Future: Queer Theory and the Death Drive*. Durham, NC: Duke University Press.

Edwards, Justin D. 2003. *Gothic Passages: Racial Ambiguity and the American Gothic*. Iowa City: University of Iowa Press.

Elliot, Patricia, and Katrina Roon. 1988. 'Transgenderism and the Question of Embodiment: Promising Queer Politics?'. *GLQ: A Journal of Lesbian and Gay Studies* 4/2:241–268.

Eliot, T. S. 1958. 'The Wasteland' in T.S. Eliot, *Selected Poems*. London: Faber.

Eribon, Didier. 2002. *Insult and the Making of the Gay Self*. Trans. Michael Lucey. Durham, NC: Duke University Press.

Fincher, Max. 2007. *Queering Gothic in the Romantic Age: The Penetrating Eye*. Basingstoke: Palgrave Macmillan.

Flannery, Denis. 2007. *On Sibling Love, Queer Attachment and American Writing*. London: Ashgate.

Fletcher, John. 2000. 'The Haunted Closet: Henry James's Queer Spectrality'. *Textual Practice* 14/1:53–60.

Foucault, Michel. 1986. Of Other Spaces. *Diacritics* 16/1:22–27.

Freccero, Carla. 2006. *Queer, Early, Modern*. Durham, NC: Duke University Press.

Freeman, Elizabeth. 2007. 'Queer Belongings: Kinship Theory and Queer Theory'. In *A Companion to Lesbian, Gay, Bisexual, Transgender and Queer Studies*, ed. George E. Haggerty and Molly Mc Garry, 295–314. Oxford: Blackwell.

Freeman, Elizabeth. 2011. 'Still After'. In *After Sex*, ed. Janet Hallam and Andrew Parker, 32. Durham, US: Duke University Press.

Freud, Sigmund. 1985. 'The Uncanny'. In *The Pelican Freud Library*, ed. Angela Richards and James Strachey, vol. 14, 345. Harmondsworth: Penguin.

Freud, Sigmund. 1985. 'A Child is Being Beaten' (1919), In *The Pelican Freud library*, ed. Angela Richards and James Strachey, vol. 14, 163–94. Harmondsworth: Penguin.

Freud, Sigmund. 1985. 'Transformations of Puberty: Three Essays in the Theory of Sexuality'. In *The Pelican Freud Library*, ed. Angela Richards and James Strachey, vol. 14, 345. Harmondsworth: Penguin.

Freud, Sigmund. 1998. *The Pelican Freud Library*, ed. Angela Richards and James Strachey. Harmondsworth: Penguin.

Furneaux, Holly. 2009. *Queer Dickens: Erotics, Families, Masculinities*. Oxford: Oxford University Press.

Gallop, Jane. 1982. *The Daughter's Seduction: Feminism and Psychoanalysis*. London: Macmillan.

Garfinkel, Harold. 2006. 'Passing and the Managed Achievement of Sex Status in an "Intersexed Person"'. In *The Transgender Studies Reader*, ed. Susan Stryker and Stephen Whittle, 58–93. New York: Routledge.

Garrett, Peter K. 2003. *Gothic Reflections: Narrative Force in Nineteenth-Century Fiction*. Ithaca and London: Cornell University Press.

Gelder, Ken. 2014. 'The Postcolonial Gothic'. In *The Cambridge Companion to the Modern Gothic*, ed. Jerrold E. Hogle, 198–207. Cambridge: Cambridge University Press.

Georgieva, Margarita. 2013. *The Gothic Child*. Houndsmill: Basingstoke, Palgrave Macmillan.

Germana, Monica. 2010. *Scottish Women's Gothic and Fantastic Writing*. Edinburgh: Edinburgh University Press.

Gordon, Joan and Veronica Hollinger. 1996. 'Introduction'. In *Blood Red: The Vampire as Metaphor in Contemporary Culture*, ed. Gordon and Hollinger, 1–7. Philadelphia: University of Philadelphia.

Griffin, Gabrielle. 1993. *Heavenly Love? Lesbian Images in Twentieth-Century Women's Writing*. Manchester: Manchester University Press.

Grimes, Hilary. 2011. *The Late Victorian Gothic: Mental Science, the Uncanny and Scenes of Writing*. Farnham: Ashgate.

Grossberg, Benjamin Scott. 2001. 'Making Christabel: Sexual Transgression and its Implications in Coleridge's "Christabel"'. *Journal of Homosexuality* 41/2:145–165.

Grosz, Elizabeth. 1996. 'Intolerable Ambiguity: Freaks as/at the Limit'. In *Freakery: Cultural Spectacles of the Extraordinary Body*, ed. Rosemary Garland Thomson, 55–66. New York: New York University Press.

Haefele-Thomas, Ardel. 2012. *Queer Others in Victorian Gothic*. Cardiff: University of Wales.

Haggerty, George E. 2006. *Queer Gothic*. Illinois: University of Illinois Press.

Haggerty, George E. 2013. 'The History of Homosexuality Reconsidered'. In *Developments in the History of Sexualities*, ed. Chris Mounsey, 1–15. Lewisburg: Bucknell University Press.
Haggerty, George and Molly McGary. eds. 2007. *A Companion to Lesbian, Gay, Bisexual, Transgender and Queer Studies*. Oxford: Blackwell.
Halberstam, Judith. 1995. *Skin Shows: Gothic Horror and the Technology of Monsters*. Duke University Press.
Halberstam, Judith. 2005. *In a Queer Time and Place: Transgender Bodies, Subcultural Lives*. New York: New York University Press.
Halperin, David M. 2007. 'Deviant Teaching'. In *A Companion to Lesbian, Gay, Bisexual, Transgender and Queer Studies*, ed. George E. Haggerty and Molly McGarry, 146–167. Oxford: Blackwell.
Hall, Donald. 2003. *Queer Theories*. Basingstoke: Palgrave Macmillan.
Haefele-Thomas, Ardel. 2012. *Queer Others in Victorian Fiction: Transgressing Monstrosity*. Cardiff: Wales University Press.
Hanson, Ellis. 1991. 'Undead'. In *Inside/Out*, ed. Diana Fuss, 324–340. New York: Routledge.
Haraway, Donna J. 1991. 'A Cyborg Manifesto: Science, Technology and Socialist-Feminism in the Late Twentieth Century'. In *Simians, Cyborgs, and Women: The Reinvention of Nature*, ed. Haraway, 149–181. London: Free Association Books Ltd.
Hay, Simon. 2011. *A History of the British Ghost Story* Basingstoke: Palgrave.
Hayes, Elizabeth T. 2004. '"Commitment to Doubleness": Literary Magic Realism and the Postmodern'. In *Spectral America: Phantoms and the National Imagination*, ed. Jeffrey Weinstock, 169. Wisconsin: University of Wisconsin Press.
Healey, Emma. 1996. *Lesbian Sex Wars*. London: Virago Press.
Herdman, John. 1990. *The Double in Nineteenth Century Fiction*. London: Macmillan.
Hirsch, David A. Hedrich. 1996. 'Liberty, Equality, Monstrosity: Revolutionizing the Family'. In *Monster Theory: Reading Culture*, ed. Jeffrey Jerome Cohen, 115–142. Minneapolis: University of Minnesota Press.
Hoeveler, Diane. 1998. *Gothic Feminism*. Liverpool: Liverpool University Press.
Hogle, Jerrold. ed. 2002. *The Cambridge Companion to Gothic Fiction*. Cambridge: Cambridge University Press.
Hogle, Jerrold E. ed. 2014. *The Cambridge Companion to the Modern Gothic*. Cambridge: Cambridge University Press.
Holland, Norman and Leona F. Sherman. 1977. 'Gothic Possibilities'. in *New Literary History* 8/2:279–294.
Holmes, Trevor. 1997. 'Coming Out of the Coffin: Gay Males and Queer Goths in Contemporary Vampire Fiction'. In *Blood Read: The Vampire Metaphor in*

Contemporary Culture, ed. Joan Gordon and Veronica Hollinger, 169–188. Philadelphia: University of Pennsylvania Press

Hughes, William, David Punter, and Andrew Smith. eds. 2016. *The Encyclopedia of the Gothic*. Oxford: Blackwell and Wiley.

Hughes, William, and Andrew Smith. eds. 2009. *Queering the Gothic*. Manchester: Manchester University Press.

Hunt, Sharon Lockyer, and Milly Williamson. ed. 2014. *Screening the Undead: Vampires and Zombies in Film and Television*. New York: I.B. Taurus, 91, 23.

Hurley, Kelly. 1996. *The Gothic Body: Sexuality, Materialism and Degeneration at the Fin de Siecle*. Cambridge: Cambridge University Press.

Hurley, Kelly. 2004. '"The Inner Chamber of All Nameless Sin": *The Beetle*: Gothic Female Sexuality and Oriental Barbarism'. In *Gothic: Critical Concepts in Literary and Cultural Concepts,* ed. Fred Botting and Dale Townshend, vol. 3, 241–258. London: Routledge, 2004.

Hutcheon, Linda. 1989. *The Politics of Postmodernism*. New York: Routledge.

Jackson, Rosemary. 1981. *Fantasy: The Literature of Subversion*. London: Methuen.

Jackson, Shirley. 1987. *The Haunting of Hill House*. London: Robinson Publishing.

Jagose, Ann Marie. 1996. *Queer Theory*. Melbourne: Melbourne University Press.

James, Henry. 1976. *The Turn of the Screw*. London: Everyman.

Johnson, Colin R. 2013. *Just Queer Folks: Gender and Sexuality in Rural Areas*. Philadelphia: Temple University Press.

Kahane, Claire. 1985. 'The Gothic Mirror'. In *The [M]other Tongue*, ed. Shirley Nelson Gardner, Claire Kahane, Madelon Sprengnether, 335–351. Ithaca, NY: Cornell University Press.

Keesey, Pam. 2001. *Dark Angels: Lesbian Vampire Stories*. Berkley, CA: Cleis Press.

Kinkaid, James. 2000. 'Designing Gourmet Children'. In *Victorian Gothic: Literary and Cultural Manifestations in the Nineteenth-Century*, ed. Ruth Robbins and Julian Wolfreys, 1–11. Basingstoke: Macmillan.

Kontou, Tatiana. 2000. *Spiritualism and Women's Writing: From the Fin de Siecle to the Neo-Victorian*. Basingstoke: Palgrave Macmillan.

Kristeva, Julia. 1981. 'Women's Time'. Trans. Lisa Jardine and Harry Black, *Signs* 7/1:15–27.

Kristeva, Julia. 1982. *Powers of Horror: An Essay on Abjection*. Trans. Leon S. Roudiez. New York: Columbia University Press.

Kristeva, Julia. 1991. *Strangers to Ourselves*. Trans. Leon S. Roudiez. London: Harvester Wheatsheaf, p. 19.

Lansbury, Coral. 1975. *Elizabeth Gaskell: The Novel of Sexual Crisis*. London: Paul Elek.

Lloyd-Smith, Allan Gardner. 1989. *Uncanny American Fiction: Medusa's Face*. Basingstoke: Macmillan.

Love, Heather. 2007. *Feeling Backward: Loss and the Politics of Queer History*. Cambridge, MA: Harvard University Press.

Lustig, T.J. 1994. *Henry James and the Ghostly*. Cambridge: CUP.

MacCormack, Patricia. 2009. 'Unnatural Alliances'. In *Deleuze and Queer Theory*, ed. Chrsanthi Nigianni and Merl Storr, 134–149. Edinburgh: Edinburgh University Press.

Marx, Karl. 1983. 'The Eighteenth Brumaire of Louis Bonaparte'. In *The Portable Karl Marx*, ed. Eugene Kamenka, 288. Harmondsworth: Penguin.

McCallum, E.L. 2014. 'The "Queer" Limits in the Modern Gothic'. In *The Cambridge Companion to the Modern Gothic*, ed. Jerrold E. Hogle, 71–86. Cambridge: Cambridge University Press.

Mellor, Leo. 2011. *Reading the Ruins: Modernism, Bombsites and British Culture*. Cambridge: Cambridge University Press.

Mighall, Robert. 2003. *A Geography of Victorian London: Mapping History's Nightmares*. Oxford: Oxford University Press.

Mishra, Vijay. 1994. *The Gothic Sublime*. New York: State University of New York Press.

Moers, Ellen. 1978. *Literary Women*. London: The Women's Press.

Morland, Iain, and Annabelle Wilcox. eds. 2005. *Queer Theory*. Basingstoke: Palgrave Macmillan.

Morris, David B. 1985. 'Gothic Sublimity'. *New Literary History* 16/2:299–319.

Morton, Donald. 1997. 'Birth of the Cyberqueer'. *PMML*, 110/3:369–381.

Najarian, James. 2002. *Victorian Keats: Manliness, Sexuality, and Desire*. Basingstoke: Palgrave Macmillan.

Nelson, Emmanuel S. 1992. *AIDS: The Literary Response*. New York: Twayne.

Palmer, Paulina. 1993. *Lesbian Gothic: Transgressive Fictions*. London: Cassell.

Palmer, Paulina. 1998. '*The Passion*: Storytelling, Fantasy, Desire'. In *Jeanette Winterson and the Politics of Reading*, ed. Helen Grice and Tim Woods, 112–130. Amsterdam: Rodopi.

Palmer, Paulina. 2008. '"She Began to Show Me the Words She Had Written, One by One": Lesbian Reading and Writing Practices in the Fiction of Sarah Waters'. *Women: A Cultural Review*, 19: 69–86.

Palmer, Paulina. 2009. 'Antonia White's *Frost in May*: Gothic Mansions, Ghosts and Particular Friendships'. In *Queering the Gothic*, ed. William Hughes and Andrew Smith, 105–122. Manchester: Manchester University Press.

Palmer, Paulina. 2012. *The Queer Uncanny: New Perspectives on the Gothic*. Cardiff: University of Wales Press.

Parkin-Gounelas, Ruth. 2001. *Literature and Psychoanalysis: Intertextual Readings*. Basingstoke: Palgrave.

Prosser, Jay. 1998. *Second Skins: The Body Narratives of Transsexuality*. New York: Columbia University press.

Punter, David. 1994. 'The Passions of Gothic'. In *Gothic Origins and Innovations*, ed. Allan Lloyd Smith and Victor Sage, 218–233. Amsterdam: Rodopi.

Pyrhonen, Heta. 2008. 'On Finding the Balance Between Earth and Sky: Jeanette Winterson, Charlotte Bronte and the Bluebeard Tale'. *Contemporary Women's Writing* 2/1:50–51.

Quist, Bella. 2014. 'Challenges for LGBT People in the Workplace and How to Overcome Them'. *The Guardian*, July 28, 2014 (Quist).

Reyes, Xavier Aldana. 2013. 'Who Ordered the Hamburger with AIDS?': Haematophilic Semiotics'. *Tru(e) Blood'*, Gothic Studies 15/1:55–65.

Reyes, Xavier Aldana. 2014. *Body Gothic: Corporeal Transgression in Contemporary Literature and Horror Film*. Cardiff: University of Wales Press.

Rich, Adrienne. 1977. *Of Woman Born: Motherhood as Experience and Institution*. London: Virago.

Rigby, Mair. 2009. '"Do You Share My Madness?" *Frankenstein's* Queer Gothic'. In *Queering the Gothic*, ed. William Hughes and Andrew Smith, 36–54. Manchester: Manchester University Press.

Rosario, Vernon A. 2007. 'The History of Aphallia and the Intersexual Challenge to Sex and Gender'. In *A Companion to Lesbian, Gay, Bisexual Transgender and Queer Studies*, ed. Molly Mc Gary and George E. Haggerty, 263–281. Oxford: Blackwell.

Rosenberg, Jordan. 2007. '"Serious Innovation": A Conversation with Judith Butler'. In *A Companion to Lesbian, Gay, Bisexual, Transgender and Queer Studies*, ed. George E. Haggerty and Molly McGarry, 381–387. Oxford: Blackwell.

Royle, Nicholas. 2003. *The Uncanny*. Manchester: Manchester University Press.

Royle, Nicholas. 2009. *In Memory of Jacques Derrida*. Edinburgh: Edinburgh University Press.

Salotto, Eleanor. 2006. *Gothic Returns in Collins, Dickens, Zola and Hitchcock*. Basingstoke: Palgrave Macmillan.

Savoy, Eric. 2004. 'Theory *a Tergo* in *The Turn of the Screw*'. In *Curiouser: On the Queerness of Children*, ed. Steven Bruhm and Natasha Hurley, 268. Minnesota: University of Minnesota Press.

Sears, John. 2011. *Stephen King's Gothic*. Cardiff: University of Wales Press.

Sedgwick, Eve Kosofsky. 1980. *The Coherence of Gothic Conventions*. London: Methuen.

Sedgwick, Eve Kosofsky. 1985. *Between Men: English Literature and Male Homosexual Desire*. New York: Columbia University Press.

Sedgwick, Eve Kosofsky. 1990. *Epistemology of the Closet*. New York: University of California Press.

Sedgwick, Eve Kosofsky. 1994. 'Queer and Now'. In *Tendencies*, ed. Sedgwick, 8. Durham: Duke University Press.

Showalter, Elaine. 1992. *Sexual Anarchy: Gender and Culture at the Fin de Siecle*. London: Virago.

Sinfield, Alan. 2004. *On Sexuality and Power*. New York: Columbia University Press.

Smith, Andrew. 2007. 'Hauntings'. In *The Routledge Companion to Gothic*, ed. Catherine Spooner and Emma McEvoy, 1147–54. London: Routledge.

Smith, Andrew. 2010. *The Ghost Story: 1840–1920: A Cultural History*. Manchester: Manchester University Press.

Smith, Andrew, and Diana Wallace. 2009. *The Female Gothic: New Directions*. Basingstoke: Palgrave.

Snitow, Ann, Christine Stansted, and Sharon Thompson. eds. 1984. *Desire the Politics of Sexuality*. London: Virago.

Spooner, Catherine. 2006. *Contemporary Gothic*. London: Reaktion Books.

Spooner, Catherine. 2013. 'Gothic Charm School, or, How the Vampire Learned to Sparkle'. In *Open Graves, Open Minds: Representations of the Vampires and the Undead from the Enlightenment to the Present Day*, ed. Sam George, Sam and Bill Hughes, 146–164. Manchester: Manchester University Press.

Spooner, Catherine and Roger McEvoy. eds. 2007. *The Routledge Companion to Gothic*. London: Routledge.

Stephanou, Aspasia. 2013. 'A "Ghastly Operation": Transfusing Blood, Science and the Supernatural in Vampire Texts'. *Gothic Studies* 15/2:53–67.

Stryker, Susan. 2006. '(De)Subjugated Knowledges: An Introduction to Transgender Studies'. In *The Transgender Studies Reader*, ed. Susan Stryker and Stephen Whittle, 1–18. New York: Routledge.

Taylor, Matthew. 2005. 'Schools Accused of Abandoning Thousands of Children to Classroom Bullies'. *The Guardian*, May 9, 2005, 20.

Thomas, Calvin (ed.). 2000. *Straight with a Twist: Queer Theory and the Subject of Heterosexuality*. Urbana and Chicago: University of Illinois Press.

Townshend, Dale. 2009. 'Love in a Convent: Or, Gothic and the Perverse Father of Queer Enjoyment'. In *Queering the Gothic*, ed. William Hughes and Andrew Smith, 11–35. Manchester: Manchester University Press.

Traub, Valerie. 2007. 'The Present Future of Lesbian Historiography'. In *The Blackwell Companion to Lesbian Gay, Bisexual, Transgender and Queer Studies*, ed. George Haggerty and Molly McGary, 124–126. New York: Blackwell.

Veeder, William. 2004. '"Carmilla": The Arts of Repression'. In *Gothic: Critical Concepts in Literary and Cultural Studies*, ed. Fred Botting and Dale Townshend, vol. 3, 117–134. London: Routledge.

Vicinus, Martha. 1989. 'They Wonder to Which sex I Belong: The Historical Roots of the Modern Lesbian Identity'. In *Homosexuality, Which Homosexuality?*, ed. Dennis Altman and Carole Vance, 172. London: GMP.

Vidler, Anthony. 1999. *The Architectural Uncanny: Essays in the Modern Unhomely*. Columbia, MA: MIT Press.

Warner, Michael (ed.). 1993. *Fear of a Queer Planet: Queer Politics and Social Theory*. Minnesota: University of Minnesota Press.

Waters, Sarah. 2002. 'Hot Waters'. *The Guardian*: G.2, Thursday, September 26, 2002, p. 9. http://wwww.guardian.co.uk/books/2002/sept 26/ arts feature.

Weeks, Jeffrey. 1999. 'Discourse, Desire and Sexual Deviance: Some Problems in a History of Homosexuality'. In *Culture, Society and Sexuality: A Reader*, ed. Richard Parker and Peter Aggleton, 125–149. Routledge: London.

Weeks, Jeffrey. 2007. *The World We Have Won: The Remaking of Erotic and Intimate Life*. London: Routledge.
Wenzel, Helene Vivienne. 1981. 'Introduction to Luce Irigaray's "And the One Doesn't Stir without the Other"'. *Signs: Journal of Women in Culture and Society* 7/1:60–67.
Weston, Kath. 1993. *Families We Choose: Lesbians, Gays, Kinship*. New York: Columbia University Press.
Whitford, Margaret. 1991. *Luce Irigaray: Philosophy in the Feminine*. London: Routledge.
Whitford, Margaret. ed. 1991. *The Irigaray Reader*. Oxford: Blackwell.
Wigley, Mark. 1995. *The Architecture of Deconstruction: Derrida's Haunt*. Cambridge, MA: MIT Press.
Williamson, Milly. 2014. 'Let Them All In: The Evolution of the Sympathetic Vampire'. In *Screening the Undead: Vampires and Zombies in Film and Television*, ed. Leon Hunt, Sharon Lockyer and Milly Williamson, 71–91. New York: I.B. Taurus.
Williams, Linda. 1984. 'When the Woman Looks'. In *Re-Visions: Essays in Feminist Film Criticism*, ed. Mary Ann Doan, Patricia Mellencamp and Linda Williams, 83–97. Frederick, MD: University Publications of America.
Winter, Kathleen. 2010. *Annabel*. New York: Black Cat Press.
Winterson, Jeanette. 2012. *The Daylight Gate*. London: Arrow Books.
Wisker, Gina, 'Devouring Desires: Lesbian Gothic Horror', in William Hughes and Andrew Smith (eds), *Queering the Gothic* (Manchester: Manchester University Press, 2009), pp. 123-141.
Wisker, Gina. 2009. 'Devouring Desires: Lesbian Gothic Horror', in *Queering the Gothic*, eds. William Hughes and Andrew Smith, pp. 123–141. Manchester: Manchester University Press.
Wolff, Cynthia Griffin. 1993. 'The Radcliffean Gothic Model: A Form for Feminine Sexuality'. In *The Female Gothic*, ed. Juliann Fleenor, 210. Montreal: Eden Press.
Wolfreys, Julian. 2002. *Victorian Hauntings: Spectrality, Gothic, the Uncanny and Literature*. Basingstoke: Palgrave.
Wood. 1992. 'Cat and Dog: Lewis Teague's Stephen Kings's Movies'. In *Gender, Language and Myth: Essays on Popular Culture*, ed. Glenwood Irons, 3013–3017. Toronto: University of Toronto Press.
Young, Elizabeth. 2008. *Black Frankenstein: The Making of an American Metaphor*. New York: New York University Press.
Zimmerman, Bonnie. 1984. 'Daughters of Darkness: The Lesbian Vampire on Film'. In *Planks of Reason: Essays on the Horror Film*, ed. Barry Keith Grant, 253–263. Inc. Methchen, NJ: Scarecrow Press.
Zimmerman, Bonnie. 1992. *The Safe Sea of Women: Lesbian Fiction 1969–1989*. London: Only Women Press.

INDEX

A
Abraham, Nicolas, 29, 48, 133–134
Ackroyd, Peter, 5, 6, 113–121, 138, 145, 146, 178
Across the Acheron (Wittig), 113
Affinity (Waters), 6, 14, 26, 33, 34, 36–40, 58, 154, 176–177
Ahmed, Sara, 14, 66
AIDS, 6, 12, 18
  comparison with bubonic plague, 87, 89, 91, 92, 94, 104, 175
  crisis, 12, 71, 87, 88, 91, 94
  narrative, 87, 88, 177
AIDS: The Literary Response (Nelson), 88
A la Recherche du Temps Perdu (Proust), 94
Alder, Emily, 151
Alderson, David, 155, 156
Alfred Lord Tennyson, 118
American Gothic, 42
Animal transformation, 84
  See also Shape-shifting
Annabel (Winter), 5, 6, 13, 129–137, 146, 152, 177, 179
An Oracle (White), 26

The Apparitional Lesbian (Castle), 23
The Architectural Uncanny (Vidler), 100
At Risk (Hoffman), 88
At The Mountains of Madness (Lovecraft), 100
Azzarello, Robert, 84

B
Bakhtin, Mikhail, 139
Baldwin, James, 142
Bataille, George, 18
Beckford, William, 18
The Beetle (Marsh), 5, 86
Beloved (Morrison), 23
Beneath the Blonde (Duffy), 9, 153
Benjamin, Jessica, 70
Benshoff, Harry M., 113
Benstock, Shari, 152
Berman, Steve, 5, 6, 13, 16, 26–33, 36, 158, 176
Between Men: English Literature and Male Homosexual Desire (Sedgwick), 17
Between the Worlds (March), 153
Bhabha, Homi K., 141

Bierce, Ambrose, 142
Bildungsroman, 59, 132
Bisexuality, 1, 13
Black Frankenstein: The Making of an American Metaphor (Young), 142
The Blackwater Lightship (Toibin), 88
Bleak House (Dickens), 39–40, 58
Blood, 56, 71, 74–75, 81, 84, 88, 102
Body horror, 5, 57, 115, 124
Bornstein, Kate, 55
Botting, Fred, 2, 52, 69, 161
Bowen, Gary, 5, 72, 78–85, 104–105, 154, 177
Bowers, Maggie Ann, 127
Braddon, Mary, 74
Bram, Christopher, 115
Bray, Alan, 152
Brewer, William D., 9
The Bride of Frankenstein (Whales), 115
Brodsley, Laurel, 89, 92
Brome, Vincent, 6, 87–94, 104, 105, 177, 178
Bronfen, Elisabeth, 93
Bronte, Charlotte, 44, 125
Brothers Grimm, 124
Brown, Judith, 17
Brown, Marshall, 85
Brown, Rebecca, 41
Bruhm, Stephen, 13
Bubonic plague, 87, 89, 91, 92, 94, 178
  comparison with AIDS epidemic, 87, 89, 91, 92, 94, 104, 175
Buck, Rebecca, 41
Buse, Peter, 15
Butler, Judith, 7, 8, 15, 87, 99, 103, 158

C
Califia, Pat, 71
The Call of Cthulhu (Lovecraft), 113
Calvino, Italo, 125
Carmilla (Le Fanu), 68, 69, 75, 79, 81–82
Carroll, Rachel, 37
The Case Book of Victor Frankenstein (Ackroyd), 5, 114, 115, 120, 121, 138, 145, 178
Case, Sue Ellen, 71, 76, 104
The Castle of Udolpho (Radcliffe), 52
Castle, Terry, 10, 16, 23, 24
Cather, Willa, 50
Cereus Blooms At Night (Mootoo), 50
Christabel (Coleridge), 112
Chrystal Heart (Kingston), 6, 72, 73, 104, 105, 177
City of Night (Rechy), 152
Civil partnerships, 11–13, 18
  See also Marriage
Cixous, Helene, 38
Clausen, Jan, 77
Clermont (Roche), 52
Coe, Jonathan B., 87
Cohen, Jeffrey Jerome, 112, 114
Collins, Wilkie, 43
Coming out, 5, 13, 28, 43, 49, 59, 77, 83, 104, 177
Commodity fetishism, 23
Copjec, Jean, 47
Cosslett, Tess, 125
Could It Be Magic (Magrs), 72
Cox, Elizabeth, 24
Craft, Christopher, 68
Creed, Barbara, 71
Crimp, Douglas, 88
Crypt, 62, 142
Currier, Jameson, 25, 41
Cyborg, 73, 75–77, 94, 104, 105, 177

A Cyborg Manifesto (Haraway), 75
Cycle of salience model, 27, 58

D
Daffron, Eric, 86
Dark Matter (Paver), 6, 14, 154, 164, 166, 168, 171, 175
Darwin, Charles, 84, 128
Davies, David Stuart, 86
The Daylight Gate (Winterson), 1–4, 6, 114, 121, 123, 125–127, 145, 177–179
Day, William Patrick, 90, 155, 157, 158
Death, 16–18, 117–178, 154, 159
Defoe, Daniel, 89
De Lauretis, Teresa, 113
De Lynn, Jane, 152
Derrida, Jacques, 15, 32, 38, 42
The Descent of Man (Darwin), 84
Dewey, Joseph, 91
The Dialogic Imagination (Bakhtin), 139
Diary of a Vampire (Bowen), 5, 72, 78, 83, 105, 154, 177
The Diary of a Vampire (Bowen), 5, 72, 78, 83, 104, 105, 154, 177
Diary of the Plague Year (Defoe), 89
Dickens, Charles, 39–40, 58, 151
Dinshaw, Carolyn, 4
Dollimore, Jonathan, 18
Domestic violence, 5, 51, 52, 54
Don Juan in the Village (De Lynn), 152
Donoghue, Emma, 128
Doppelganger, 85–86, 90, 111, 112, 120, 134, 136
See also Doubling
Dora (Freud), 38
Double, The, *see* Doubling

Doubling, 85–105, 129, 135, 136, 146, 155, 157, 159, 175, 178
See also Uncanny double
Dracula (Stoker), 5, 17, 68, 69, 75, 84, 112, 121, 151
Dream Boy (Grimsley), 153
Dr. Haggard's Disease (McGrath), 9
Duffy, Stella, 9, 152
Du Maurier, Daphne, 47, 50
During, Lisabeth, 171
Dusk, 126
Dyer, Richard, 65, 71, 104

E
Edel, Leon, 51
Edelman, Lee, 80
Edwards, Justin, 139
Edwards, Nicky, 153, 156, 158, 159
Eliot, T.S., 156
Enthrallment, 90, 155, 158, 164
Entropy, 56, 151
The Epistemology of the Closet (Sedgwick), 17
Eribon, Didier, 152
Excess, 18, 47, 53, 83, 112, 116, 171
The Exorcist (Friedkiss), 113

F
Families We Choose (Weston), 43
Father of Frankenstein (Bram), 115
Fealy, Terri, 171
Female Gothic, 10–11, 47, 50
The Female Gothic: New Directions (Smith and Wallace), 11
Female invisibility, 35
Feminism, 33, 35–37, 48–49, 52, 54, 68–69, 76, 128, 130–136, 152
Ferro, Robert, 88
Fincher, Max, 18, 42, 80, 81, 112
Fingersmith (Waters), 36, 152

Flannery, Dennis, 50
Fletcher, John, 23
The Folding Star (Hollinghurst), 6, 154–155, 175–178
Folklore, 115, 139
Folk tales, 124, 145, 170
Forbidden room, The, 47–48, 71, 113
Forster, E.M., 145, 153
Foucault, Michel, 112, 162
Frankenstein (Shelley), 114, 115, 142, 145, 169
  cinematic and other adaptations, 115
Freccero, Carla, 16, 27, 32, 33, 58, 176
Freeman, Elizabeth, 18, 43, 46, 49
Freud, Sigmund, 3, 4, 15, 29, 38, 43, 51, 52, 85, 93, 97, 121, 124, 135, 157, 169
Frost in May (White), 9, 95–96
Furneaux, Holly, 39
Fuss, Diana, 8

G

Gallop, Jane, 38
Gaskell, Elizabeth, 24, 40, 151
Gentle Warriors (Mains), 88
Geographical locations, 6, 114, 146, 151–155, 175, 178
  cities, 151–153
  rural, 153–154, 159, 164
Georgivia, Margareta, 59
Ghost, 16, 18, 23, 26, 42–43, 45–46
  story, 5, 6, 13
  See also Spectral visitation
Ghost (Zucker), 15
Ghosts: Deconstruction, Psychoanalysis, History (Buse and Stott), 15
Ghosts of Winter (Buck), 41
The Gilda Stories (Gomez), 72
Goblin Market (Rossetti), 111
Gomez, Jewelle, 72
The Good Lady Ducayne (Braddon), 74

Gordon, Joan, 69
The Gothic Body (Hurley), 111
Gothic city, 90
Gothic monster, *see* Monster
Gray, Alasdair, 113, 151
Gregory, Dick, 142
The Grey Woman (Gaskell), 24
Griffin, Gabriele, 27
Grimes, Hilary, 34–35
Grimsley, Jim, 5, 42, 51–59, 151, 153–154, 176, 178
Grossberg, Benjamin Scott, 112
Grosz, Elisabeth, 84
Grotesque body, The, 8, 88, 111

H

Haefele-Thomas, Ardel, 166
Haggard, Rider, 166
Haggerty, George E., 9, 16, 20, 27, 86, 114, 116, 145, 169, 170
Halberstam, Judith, 6, 18, 66, 94, 112, 128, 138, 153
Halperin, David M., 54
Hans Christian Andersen, 124
Hanson, Ellis, 17, 71
Haraway, Donna J., 75, 76
Harris, Charlaine, 84
Hart, Hannah, 82
The Haunted Heart and Other Tales (Currier), 25, 41
Haunted Hearth's and Sapphic Shades: Lesbian Ghost Stories (Lundoff), 25
The Haunted Hotel: A Mystery of Modern Venice (Collins), 43
The Haunted House (Brown), 41
Haunted house narrative, 5, 40–44, 51, 58, 59
The Haunting of Hill House (Jackson), 10, 24, 45, 47, 86, 164
Hayes, Elizabeth T., 126
Hay, Simon, 24, 32

Herdman, John, 90
Herren, Greg, 65, 66
Heteronormativity, 2, 3, 14, 23, 25, 44, 66, 112, 171
Heterotopia, 161, 162, 179
Hirsch, David A. Hedrich, 138
Hoffman, Alice, 88
Hoffmann, E.T.A., 51, 52, 121
Hogg, James, 9
Hogle, Jerrold, 13
Hollinger, Veronica, 69
Hollinghurst, Alan, 6, 154–165, 175, 176, 178, 179
Holmes, Trevor, 85
Home, 2, 5, 13, 28, 31, 33, 40, 46, 51–53, 55–57, 59, 72, 79, 89, 92, 93, 95, 96, 98, 99, 121, 123, 127, 134, 136, 139, 141, 151, 153, 156
Homographesis (Edelman), 80
Homophobia, 7, 9, 80, 113, 137, 145, 152, 153
Homosexual
 identity, 80, 152
 legibility, 80–82, 104, 177
 panic, 112
Hop-Frog (Poe), 111
Hughes, William, 8
Hugo, Victor, 95
The Hunchback of Notre Dame (Hugo), 95
The Hunger (Scott), 72
Hurley, Kelly, 9, 111, 128
Hutcheon, Linda, 137, 140

I
Identity categories, 1, 7, 67, 72, 76, 156, 179
In Memoriam (Tennyson), 118
Intersex, 5, 6, 128–146, 152, 177
Intertextuality, 38–40, 47, 53, 73, 79, 81–83, 94, 114, 116, 121, 125–8
Interview with The Vampire (Jordan), 82
Interview with The Vampire (Rice), 82
Invisible Cities (Calvino), 125
Irigaray, Luce, 35, 48, 96
The Italian (Radcliffe), 8, 97
I, Vampire (Scott), 77

J
Jackson, Rosemary, 2, 56, 75
Jackson, Shelley, 115
Jackson, Shirley, 10, 24, 45, 86, 164
Jagose, Ann Marie, 76
James, Henry, 23, 24, 29, 41, 51, 86, 170
James, M. R., 40, 43, 164
Jane Eyre (Bronte), 17, 44, 47, 50, 125
Johnson, Colin R., 153
Just Queer Folks:Gender and Sexual in Rural America (Johnson), 153

K
Kahane, Claire, 10
Keats, John, 117–118, 145
Kenan, Randall, 113, 129, 137–140, 142–146, 178
King, Stephen, 43, 52, 113
Kingston, Meg, 6, 72–79, 104, 105, 122, 177
Kinkaid, James, 99
Kinship theory, 43
Kontou, Tatiana, 36
Kristeva, Julia, 111, 117, 131, 169

L
Lanark (Gray), 151
Lansbury, Coral, 24
Leavitt, David, 72
Le Fanu, Sheridan, 68, 69, 79, 81, 82

Lesbian, 17, 33–40, 43, 51, 68, 71–8, 104, 113, 122, 127, 152, 99–110
  feminism, 48–50, 70–3, 75–77
  fiction, 70
  sexual radical movement, 67, 70, 71, 103
Lesbian and gay liberation movements, 4, 7, 8, 12, 18, 23, 24, 59, 67, 70, 71
Lesbian Gothic: Transgressive Fictions (Palmer), 24
Let the Dead Bury Their Dead (Kenan), 129, 137, 139, 140, 146, 178
Lewis, Matthew, 8, 9, 86, 98–103, 105, 124, 157, 162, 178
Livia, Anna, 71, 73, 79
Lloyd Smith, Allan, 145
London, Jack, 168
Lord Byron, 116, 119–121
Love at First Bite (Dragoti), 72
Lovecraft, H. P., 100, 111, 113, 119
Love, Heather, 3, 178
Love in the Plague (Brome), 6, 87–89, 94, 104, 105, 177
Luna (Peters), 87, 129
Lundoff, Catherine, 25
Lustig, T.J., 51

M
Macbeth (Shakespeare), 124–126, 145
MacCormack, Patricia, 85
Magic, 1–3, 119, 123, 124, 126, 140
Magical animism, 2
Magical realism, 126–127
Magrs, Paul, 72
Maid (servant), 34, 37–40, 58, 177
Mains, Geoff, 88, 89
March, Caia, 153
Marriage, 11–13, 18
  See also Civil partnerships

Marsh, Richard, 5, 9, 86, 112
Martin Chuzzlewit (Dickens), 151
Mary Shelley's Frankenstein (Coppola), 115
Masculinity, 24–25, 54–55, 98, 101–103, 105, 112, 118, 132, 136, 171
Maurice (Forster), 145, 153
McCallum, E.L., 12
McGrath, Patrick, 9
Melville, Herman, 50
Merk, Mandy, 15
Metamorphosis, 66, 73, 79, 99, 124, 129
  See also Shape-shifting
Meyer, Stephanie, 78, 81
The Mezzotint (James), 40
Mighall, Robert, 90
Miller, Isabel, 145
Minnimax (Livia), 71
Mirror images, 87, 94, 159
Mishra, Vijay, 139
Moers, Ellen, 10
The Monk: A Romance (Lewis), 8, 9, 86, 157, 162
Monster, 5, 15, 17, 50, 54, 66, 69, 75, 83–85, 111–146, 178
  in film, 112
Monsterization, 5, 17, 113, 116, 119, 121, 145, 178
Mootoo, Shani, 50
Morland, Iain, 12
Morris, David B., 17
Morrison, Toni, 23
Moxton's Master (Bierce), 142
Mud, (Edwards), 153

N
Najarian, James, 118, 145
Near Dark (Bigelow), 74
Nelson, Emmanuel S., 88

Neo-Victorian fiction, 26, 34, 40, 58, 78, 104
Night Shadows (Herren and Redmann), 65
The Night Watch (Waters), 152
Number 13 (James), 43

O

O'Brien, Richard, 115
The Old Nurse's Story (Gaskell), 40, 151
On the Origin of Species (Darwin), 84
Oranges Are Not the Only Fruit (Winterson), 125
Out of the Deep (De La Mare), 41

P

The Page Turner (Leavitt), 72
Palmer, Paulina, 20, 21, 148
Panopticon, 112
Paranoid Gothic, 9
Parkin-Gounelas, Ruth, 40
The Passion (Winterson), 113, 119, 125
Patchwork Woman (Jackson), 115
Patience and Sarah (Miller), 145
Paver, Michelle, 6, 14, 16, 154, 155, 164–166, 168–171
Pendle Forest, 1, 3, 6, 122, 123, 146, 179
Perkins, Pam, 124
Peters, Julie Anne, 87, 129
Pet Sematary (King), 53
Phantom-text, 38
The Picture of Dorian Gray (Wilde), 12, 82
Pirandello, Luigi, 120
Poe, Edgar Allan, 56, 111
Polidori, John, 79, 81, 82, 116, 119–121
The Present Future of Queer Historiography (Traub), 33

The Private Memoirs and Confessions of a Justified Sinner (Hogg), 9
Prosser, Jay, 16, 94, 95, 99
Proust, Marcel, 94
Psychoanalytic theory, 9, 10, 28, 48, 49, 71, 120, 177
Punter, David, 13–14
Pyrhonen, Heta, 125

Q

Queer, 1–19, 23, 24, 26
  gothic, 3–7, 7–19, 34, 59, 65, 66, 85, 103–105, 128, 145, 146, 154, 155, 164, 175, 176, 177, 179
  history, 3, 4, 9, 16, 26, 27–40, 176–179
  theory, 7, 15, 16, 67, 69, 76, 103
Queer Dickens, Bleak House (Furneaux), 39
Queering the Gothic (Hughes and Smith), 8
The Queer Uncanny (Palmer), 50, 115, 153

R

Race and racism, 72–74, 99, 111, 114, 119, 138, 139, 141, 146
Radcliffe, Ann, 8–10, 97, 135
'Real, The', 2, 4, 126–128
Rebecca (Du Maurier), 47, 50
Rechy, John, 152
Redmann, J.M., 65–66
Reyes, Aldana, 57, 84, 124
Rhys, Jean, 50
Rice, Ann, 72, 82, 152, 162
Rich, Adrienne, 8, 52
Rigby, Mair, 114, 116, 119, 145
Roche, Maria, 52

The Rocky Horror Picture Show, 115
The Rocky Horror Show, 115
Rosario, Vernon A., 129
Rossetti, Christina, 111
Rowe, Michael, 66
Royle, Nicholas, 98, 99, 139

S
Saki, 102
Salotto, Eleanor, 49
The Sandman (Hoffmann), 51, 52, 93, 121
Schelling, Friedrich, 3, 42
Scott, Jodi, 71, 73, 77, 79, 177
Séance, 14, 28, 31, 33, 34, 36, 38, 40, 58, 177
Second Son (Ferro), 88
Secrets, 2, 3, 15–17, 29, 34, 36, 41–45, 47–51, 58, 80–83, 95, 100, 102, 116, 119, 132–135, 137, 151, 161, 177
  intergenerational, 49
Section, 12, 20, 28, 11, 71
Sedgwick, Eve Kosofsky, 7, 8, 15, 17, 56, 80, 83, 165, 169
Sexual identity, 99, 152
Sexuality, mobility of, 7, 17, 66, 72, 76, 177
The Shadow over Innsmouth (Lovecraft), 111, 119
Shape-shifting, 5, 66, 84, 85, 104, 105, 112, 119, 123, 128, 129, 146, 178
  See also Animal transformation; Metamorphosis
She (Haggard), 166
Shelley, Mary, 5, 54, 86, 111, 114–121, 138, 142, 145, 169

Shepherd, Lynn, 115
Sherman, Leona, 13–14
The Shining (King), 43, 52, 162
Short stories, 24, 26
Showalter, Elaine, 9, 86, 112
Sinfield, Alan, 8, 135
Six Characters in Search of Author (Pirandello), 120
Slaves, 23, 128–146, 178
Smith, Andrew, 8, 11, 15, 23, 29, 51
Social class, 33, 37–38, 41, 51–54, 121–24, 153, 165–166, 169–70
Something Leather (Gray), 113
Spectral double, 16, 26, 169
  See also Doubling
Spectrality, 14–16, 23–40, 45, 51, 53, 58, 59, 88, 124, 154–172, 175, 176, 179
Spectral visitation, 3, 4, 24, 41, 139
  See also Ghost, story
Spinsters, 35, 58, 177
Spiritualism, 6, 14, 26, 33, 35, 51, 58, 154, 177
Spooner, Catherine, 69, 78
Sredni Vashtar (Saki), 102
Steam punk, 73–74, 104, 177
Stephanou, Aspasia, 74
Stevenson, Robert Louis, 9, 12, 86, 111, 112, 138, 157
Stir Fry (Donoghue), 128
Stoker, Bram, 4, 17, 68, 69, 75, 84, 112, 121, 151, 152
The Stone Gods (Winterson), 75
Stott, Andrew, 15
The Strange Case of Dr Jekyll and Mr Hyde (Stevenson), 9
Stryker, Susan, 115, 130
Surplus value, 23
Swan, Susan, 5, 6, 13, 87, 94, 95–98, 101, 102, 103, 154, 178

The Swimming Pool Library (Hollinghurst), 155
Symonds, John Addington, 80, 118

T
Taboo, 2, 3, 30, 71, 81
Tessier, Suzan, 25
Thomas, Calvin, 11–12
Toibin, Colm, 88
Tondeur, Louise, 5, 42–47, 49–51, 58, 59, 122, 133, 154, 176, 177
Torok, Maria, 29, 48
Townshend, Dale, 86
Transgender, 5, 6, 9, 15, 19, 59, 65, 67, 85–87
Transitioning (gender), 17, 94, 103, 129, 136, 137
Transsexuality, 9, 16, 17, 55, 59, 85–105, 115, 129, 152, 153, 178
Transvestism, 9, 77, 86, 115
Traub, Valerie, 27, 33, 58, 177
A Treacherous Likeness (Shepherd), 115
True Blood (television series), 84
The Turn of the Screw (James), 24, 29, 31, 86, 170
Twilight (Meyer), 78, 81

U
Ulrichs, Karl Heinrich, 67–68
The Uncanny (Freud), 124
Uncanny double, 59, 65–105, 114, 164, 175
  See also Doubling
'Uncanny, The' (Freud), 43, 121
Unheimlich, 3, 43, 99

V
Vampire
  female, 68, 70, 71
  in film, 65–66
  lesbian, 10, 68, 71–73, 76, 79
  as a metaphor for homosexual identification, 80, 82, 104
  narrative, 5, 72, 74, 177
  sparkly, 78
  sympathetic, 59, 70, 72, 75, 83, 104, 177
The Vampire (Califia), 71
The Vampire Chronicles (Rice), 72
The Vampire's Portrait: Winters' Curse (Hart), 82
The Vampyre (Polidori), 79, 81, 121
Vathek (Beckford), 18
Veeder, William, 9, 68, 69
Vicinus, Martha, 27
Victorian Gothic, 5, 128
Victorian Keats: Manliness, Sexuality, and Desire (Najarian), 118
Vidler, Anthony, 100
Vintage: A Ghost Story (Berman), 5, 6, 13, 26, 27, 58, 176
Voyeurism, 154, 158, 175

W
Wallace, Diana, 11
Walpole, Horace, 9, 17, 124
Warner, Michael, 7
The Wasteland (Eliot), 156
The Water's Edge (Tondeur), 5, 42–44, 50, 51, 58, 133, 154, 176, 177
Waters, Sarah, 6, 14, 26, 27, 33–40, 58, 152, 154, 176–177
Weeks, Jeffrey, 152
Weston, Kath, 43
Whale, James, 155
What a Carve Up (Coe), 87
When the Woman Looks (Williams), 76
White, Antonia, 9, 95

White, Edmund, 26
The Wide Sargasso Sea (Rhys), 50
Wigley, Mark, 52
Wilde, Oscar, 12, 82
Wilderness, 132, 136, 137, 139, 144, 145, 166, 179
  See also Geographical locations
Williams, Linda, 76
Winter Birds (Grimsley), 42, 51, 54, 58, 59, 151, 154, 176, 178
Winter, Kathleen, 5, 6, 13, 113, 129–137
Winterson, Jeannette, 1–4, 6, 75, 113, 114, 119, 121–127, 145, 177, 178–179
Wisker, Gina, 68–69
Witchcraft, 2–4, 114, 115, 125, 127
Witch trials, 1, 145
Wittig, Monique, 113
The Wives of Bath (Swan), 6, 13, 87, 94, 95, 154, 178
Wolff, Cynthia Griffin, 135
Wolfreys, Julian, 28, 38, 165
Wood, Robin, 113
Wuthering Heights (Bronte), 164

Y
Young, Elizabeth, 142

Z
Zimmerman, Bonnie, 10, 153

The manufacturer's authorised representative in the EU is Springer Nature Customer Service Centre GmbH, Europaplatz 3, 69115 Heidelberg, Germany. If you have any concerns regarding our products, please contact ProductSafety@springernature.com

Printed and bound by CPI Group (UK) Ltd, Croydon, CR0 4YY

23/03/2026

02076668-0002